Christ in All Things

The Canterbury Studies in Spiritual Theology series:

Law and Revelation: Richard Hooker and His Writings
Edited by Raymond Chapman

Heaven in Ordinary: George Herbert and His Writings
Edited by Philip Sheldrake

Before the King's Majesty: Lancelot Andrews and His Writings
Edited by Raymond Chapman

Christ Alive and At Large:
The Unpublished Writings of C. F. D. Moule
Edited and introduced by Robert Morgan and Patrick Moule

Happiness and Holiness: Selected Writings by Thomas Traherne
Edited by Denise Inge

The Sacramental Life: A Gregory Dix Reader
Edited and introduced by Simon Jones

To Build God's Kingdom: F. D. Maurice and His Writings
Edited and introduced by Jeremy Morris

Firmly I Believe: An Oxford Movement Reader
Edited by Raymond Chapman

The Truth-Seeking Heart: An Austin Farrer Reader
Edited by Ann Loades and Robert MacSwain

God Truly Worshipped: Thomas Cranmer and His Writings
Edited by Jonathan Dean

A Heart Strangely Warmed:
John and Charles Wesley and Their Writings
Edited by Jonathan Dean

Charles Gore: Prophet and Pastor: Charles Gore and His Writings
Edited by Peter Waddell

Christ in All Things: William Temple and His Writings
Edited by Stephen Spencer

Canterbury Studies in Spiritual
Theology

Christ in All Things

William Temple and His Writings

Edited and Introduced by

Stephen Spencer

CANTERBURY
PRESS
Norwich

© In this compilation Stephen Spencer 2015

First published in 2015 by the Canterbury Press Norwich
Editorial office
3rd Floor, Invicta House,
108–114 Golden Lane,
London EC1Y 0TG, UK

Canterbury Press is an imprint of Hymns Ancient & Modern Ltd
(a registered charity)
13A Hellesdon Park Road, Norwich,
Norfolk NR6 5DR, UK

www.canterburypress.co.uk

All rights reserved. No part of this publication may be reproduced,
stored in a retrieval system, or transmitted,
in any form or by any means, electronic, mechanical,
photocopying or otherwise, without the prior permission of
the publisher, Canterbury Press.

The Author has asserted his right under the Copyright, Designs and
Patents Act 1988
to be identified as the Author of this Work

British Library Cataloguing in Publication data

A catalogue record for this book is available
from the British Library

978 1 84825 728 3

Typeset by Manila Typesetting Company
Printed and bound in Great Britain by
Lightning Source

Contents

Preface		ix
Introduction: William Temple's Life and Publications		xi
1	**The Case for Christian Belief: *The Faith and Modern Thought* of 1910**	1
	i The Grounds of Our Belief in God	2
	ii The Person of Christ	7
	iii The Spirit of Christ and the Church	12
2	**From Philosophy to Theology: *Mens Creatrix* of 1917**	19
	i Philosophy and Theology Working Together	21
	ii Knowledge and Personality: The Society of Intellects	24
	iii The Word Incarnate	27
3	**Teaching the Faithful: Westminster Sermons, 1919–20**	37
	i The Eternal God	38
	ii The Comforter	43
	iii The Ascension	47
4	**Theological Investigations: *Christus Veritas* of 1924**	53
	i How Can God Forgive Us?	55
	ii How Can God Be in Eternity and in Time?	62
	iii Exploring the Love of the Trinity	66
5	**Political Thought: Writings and Lectures, 1917–28**	71
	i Liberty: Individual and Political	71
	ii The Church and Labour	80
	iii The Power State and the Welfare State	83

6	Reasonable Evangelism: The Oxford Mission of 1931	92
	i A Call to Prayer	94
	ii A Call to Holy Communion	99
	iii A Call to Serve Church and World	103

7	Philosophical Theology: *Nature, Man and God* of 1934	112
	i How Revelation Occurs	116
	ii The Relationship of History with Eternity	122
	iii The Sacramental Universe	130

8	Seeking Christian Unity: Addresses and Sermons	138
	i Reunion and the Place of the Episcopate	142
	ii A Call for Christian Unity	154
	iii Christmas Broadcast to Germany	160
	iv Unity in the British Isles	162

9	Meditating on Scripture: *Readings in St John's Gospel*, 1939–40	165
	i The Prologue: John 1.1–14	167
	ii The Woman at the Well: John 4.5–26	175
	iii The Prayer of the Son to the Father: John 17.1–5	183

10	Guiding a Nation at War: Addresses and Letters	189
	i The Spirit and Aims of Britain in the War	193
	ii The Real Meaning of the War	198
	iii Nazi Massacres of the Jews	203
	iv Some Letters about the War	204

11	Looking Forward to a New Society: Addresses and Writings	211
	i Christian Social Principles	217
	ii Practical Social Objectives	226
	iii Industry, Trade, Finance and Land	232
	iv True Education	241

Postscript: Some Personal Letters in Wartime   248

Bibliography   256
Index of Names and Subjects   261

For Stephen Platten,
with gratitude

Preface

There has been a need for some time for key chapters and passages in William Temple's extensive publications to be made accessible within one volume. One or two of his books have remained in print or been reprinted in recent years, such as *Readings in St John's Gospel*, *Christian Faith and Life* and *Christianity and Social Order*. But the majority have disappeared from view. After his death A. E. Baker published an anthology, *William Temple and His Message*, which collected together sets of statements on a range of topics. It provided some classic Temple 'gems' of insight, but there was a random quality to the selection, with little sense of the overall shape and development of Temple's thought. Most of the extracts were very short, so that there was little to demonstrate Temple's great gift of building a case logically and methodically over the course of a chapter. This volume seeks to rectify that: to present a series of longer extracts and chapters that show his style to full advantage, and to provide an overview of the main fields of his thought, from the philosophical theology, through the biblical exposition, to the ecumenical and social thought. Temple was a systematic thinker and this volume seeks to demonstrate that quality from the complete range of his publications.

It is important to add that there are some limitations to what is printed here. Not every topic he wrote about can be included, and some of his most famous statements are not within these pages. In particular his frequently quoted saying, that the Church is the only society on earth that exists for the benefit of those who are not its members, does not appear here! A number of readers, myself included, have trawled through his writings looking for where it might appear in print, but without success. A related thought was expressed in the final address of his Oxford Mission of 1931, which is printed on p. 107, but unfortunately that is as close as we get. Other famous sayings are also missing, such as his apocryphal 'Personally, I have always looked on cricket as organized loafing.' However, there are many other gems to be found within these pages.

It has been a privilege to have been given the opportunity to produce this volume. My earlier book of 2001, *William Temple: A Calling to Prophecy*, provides an account of his life as a whole and an introduction to the main contours of his thought. It provides initial orientation but there always comes a point where the reader should move from the secondary literature to the primary sources, in this case the writings of Temple himself. This volume provides an opportunity to do that (also drawing on, revising and refining some of the introductory commentary of that volume, including an updated bibliography). I would like to thank Canterbury Press, and in particular Natalie Watson, for commissioning this volume and making it now possible for there to be access to the writings of this remarkable theologian and church leader. Thanks are also due to the staff at Lambeth Palace Library who have enabled me to revisit the William Temple Papers and incorporate some of his unpublished writings into this volume.

Introduction:
William Temple's Life and Publications

William Temple died on 26 October 1944, which means that 2014 is the seventieth anniversary of his death. Why publish a series of extracts from his writings to mark this anniversary? There are at least two reasons. The first is the way he combined involvement in some of the great issues of the twentieth century with a firm and profound Christian faith. He was deeply committed to extending education across society, to housing and welfare reform, to reforming the industrial and financial sectors and to the search for ecumenical unity. Yet at the same time he upheld the historic faith of the New Testament and the ancient creeds and was persuasive in arguing for their truth. He is therefore someone *of* our time and also someone *not* of our time, which means engagement with his writings is a challenging and fruitful experience.

The second reason is very well described by R. H. Tawney, the acclaimed historian and close colleague of Temple:

> He combined the mind of a philosopher with an inexhaustible fund of energy and practical wisdom. What strikes a reader of his books, especially his volumes of printed addresses, is their extraordinary combination of penetrating thought with terseness of expression. Surprisingly often, he says profound things; but he says them without an effort, and does not dwell upon them. There is no fumbling or diffuseness. Every sentence contains a distinct statement. Every statement fits into its place in the argument, and never oversteps it. The result is a pregnant brevity, which conveys the impression, in his case just, of immense reserves of will-power and conviction. (Tawney 1945, p. 44)

Nevertheless, in our own time Temple's style can sometimes be off-putting. He tends to capitalize the first letter of key concepts; he only very occasionally uses inclusive language; there can sometimes be a sense of Edwardian triumphalism about the West and its civilization, even in some of his later writings; in his philosophical writings there can also be a too-easy assumption of the existent reality of the metaphysical concepts that he is describing. It can therefore be quite easy to open one of his volumes at random and read a paragraph that suggests he has little to say to our own time. Yet if we persist, turning the pages backwards or forwards, we will begin to see why Tawney wrote of him in the way that he did.

The other challenge with Temple's writings is that he published a huge amount, some 34 books as well as countless articles for journals, newspapers and shared volumes. Many of his books were collections of sermons and addresses, which means there is repetition in many places. This requires the reader to sift and select the best examples of his characteristic statements. In some places, furthermore, he develops the points he is making, expressing them more clearly or provocatively than before, which means that later examples must be selected over earlier examples.

But when such sifting and selection is undertaken there is, as Tawney suggests, a rich seam to mine. Furthermore, the broad sweep of his publications reveals an unmistakeable unity to his writings, almost as if they all provide a series of windows on to a ready-formed and balanced world view. Every sentence, as Tawney hints, has its place within an ongoing argument, one that began when he was a young philosophy lecturer at Oxford and continued to the end of his life as Archbishop of Canterbury. For this reason it is possible to compile a series of extracts, as this volume does, and for those extracts to cohere to a high degree, building up a portrait of a thinker who covered an impressively broad range of subjects with clarity and thoughtfulness.

What was that argument? It can be summed up by two quotations, one from his first book and the other from his last book published in his lifetime:

> But if it is true that [Christ] is the Incarnation of the divine Word, of the principle by which God rules the whole of existence and through which He made the world, then it is made quite clear that I can never for an instant be outside His influence. It is the governing fact of all facts, and never for a moment can we be away from the divine purpose which is manifest in Christ. (*The Faith and Modern Thought*, 1910, p. 148)

This fact of all facts should therefore condition everything that we do:

> Our need is a new integration of life: Religion, Art, Science, Politics, Education, Industry, Commerce, Finance – all these need to be brought into a unity as agents of a single purpose. That purpose can

hardly be found in human aspirations; it must be the divine purpose. That divine purpose is presented to us in the Bible under the name of the Kingdom (Sovereignty) of God, or as the summing-up of all things in Christ, or as the coming-down out of heaven of the holy city, the New Jerusalem.

In all those descriptions two thoughts are prominent: the priority of God and the universality of scope. Nothing is to be omitted; 'all things' are to be summed up in Christ, but it is in Christ that they are thus gathered into one. (Preface, *The Church Looks Forward*, 1944).

Temple devoted his life to serving this purpose, of finding Christ in all things, past, present and future. It therefore aptly provides the title of this volume.

Who was William Temple? The story begins in 1881 when William was born in the Bishop's Palace at Exeter. His father, Frederick Temple, was the Bishop of Exeter and would go on to be Bishop of London and Archbishop of Canterbury from 1897 to 1902. (This would be the only time a son would follow his father in that position.) His father was a very accomplished self-made man, coming from humble origins in Cornwall and working his way to the top. William was close to his father but also in awe of him. He assisted his father as a pageboy when in Westminster Abbey Frederick crowned Edward VII as king.

William, then, had a very privileged upbringing, growing up in bishops' palaces, attending Rugby School and then winning a scholarship to Balliol College, Oxford, where he studied Greek and Latin literature and philosophy. What is important, though, is that he chose to put the benefits of these privileges at the service of others, first through teaching philosophy within the university and then through ordination as a deacon and priest.

As a teacher he quickly developed an extraordinary fluency with words. He had the gift of being able to communicate what he had learned with a calm and infectious enthusiasm. Even as a young lecturer he was being invited to speak around the country, and his first book, *The Faith and Modern Thought* of 1910 (with extracts in Chapter 1), shows the Temple style, described above by Tawney, already almost fully formed. At this time he also developed a large waistline, having a lifelong passion for strawberry jam and strawberry ices. He sometimes told the story of how he sent his white surplice to the laundry and when it came back cleaned and pressed it had a label attached saying 'bell tent'. He had what seemed an everlasting good humour and a distinctive high-pitched laugh. His manner was relaxed, friendly and simple, wholly unpretentious, never rattled, never confrontational.

In 1905, while still at Oxford, he joined the Worker's Educational Association, which brought together working people with university teachers in co-operative education. He later said this work, and especially his contact with Albert Mansbridge, the founder of the WEA, was one of the most formative experiences of his life: 'As a personal matter... he invented *me*' (Iremonger 1948, p. 77). He maintained his involvement with the WEA for many years, being elected its president continuously between 1908 and 1924.

He offered himself for ordination and was surprised when Francis Paget, the Bishop of Oxford, turned him down because of his doubts over the virgin birth and the bodily resurrection of Christ. At this stage Temple was something of a theological liberal, though would later revise his beliefs in a more orthodox direction. Two years later Randall Davidson, the Archbishop of Canterbury, decided that Temple *was* ready for ordination and ordained him in Canterbury. Paget had been overruled.

Temple then became the headmaster of Repton School, following in the footsteps of his father who had been a distinguished headmaster of Rugby. But this role did not really suit him (he was no disciplinarian) and four years later he moved to be Rector of St James' Church, Piccadilly. Here he continued to work on philosophy, and in 1917 published a weighty volume, *Mens Creatrix* (Creative Mind) (see Chapter 2). This and later books drew on his philosophical studies of Plato as well as German and British Idealist philosophy, his love of literature, especially Robert Browning's poetry, and biblical theology, especially the Fourth Gospel. He would later publish a companion volume, *Christus Veritas* (Christ the Truth), in 1924. This is more theological in approach (see Chapter 4).

In 1916 Temple married Francis Anson, who also shared a commitment to social reform and to publishing. They did not have children and Temple was frequently away from home, but surviving letters show the couple enjoying a supportive and loving partnership throughout their married life.

Temple became involved in church reform and after three years left St James' to work for the Life and Liberty movement, which campaigned to get Parliament to give the Church of England greater powers of self-government. The Enabling Act of 1919 was its outcome, an act which created the Church Assembly and set-up parochial church councils with electoral roles. Davidson then moved him to become a canon of Westminster Abbey, where his preaching and teaching ministry gained national prominence. Some of his sermons were published in the volume

INTRODUCTION

Fellowship with God (see Chapter 3). The journalist Harold Begbie has provided a portrait of Temple at this point in his life:

> Picture to yourself the youngest-looking middle-aged man you ever encountered, of a full countenance, and a body inclined to heaviness, with as much hair on his head as when he was twenty (in a condition a little untidy, like a boy's of fourteen), spectacles in front of bright and extremely steady eyes, a meeting of the brows at the centre in a line of concentration. (Begbie 1920)

In 1921, at the age of 40, he was called north to become Bishop of Manchester, then the most populous diocese outside London. Here he combined pastoral duties around the diocese with writing and speaking up and down the country. He would spend part of each summer at weeklong missions in Blackpool, sometimes on the beach, and would expound the New Testament, including Revelation, to the holidaymakers. Invariably by the end of the week the audience would be too big for the venue. He travelled up and down his large diocese, from Manchester in the south to the edge of the Lake District in the north, and quickly decided that with a population of 3.5 million and over 600 parishes it was too large for one diocesan bishop. It needed dividing, and after negotiations and fundraising the new Diocese of Blackburn was created in 1926.

As Temple travelled through the northern industrial towns he saw the acute social and economic hardships faced by the majority of the population. Those who worked in the mills faced hard regimes, and those who were unemployed could not rely on social security because there was none. Nor was there a national health service, nor education beyond the age of 11 except for a few. The scourges of want, disease, ignorance, squalor and idleness stalked the land. As Temple himself wrote a few years earlier:

> We see on the one side a considerable number of people enjoying a great many of the good things of life with singularly little regard to the needs of others, and we see on the other side a vast amount of real want and destitution, and also a great amount of vice which is largely due to poverty. That is a state of affairs with which the Christian cannot rest content. (*The Kingdom of God*, 1912, p. 74)

Temple did not rest content. He was determined to galvanize opinion within the churches to build up pressure for change. So he convened and chaired the Conference on Politics, Economics and Citizenship

(COPEC), which met in Birmingham in 1924 with 1,400 delegates from different churches. Adrian Hastings, an acclaimed historian of this period, says of COPEC that its

> immediate consequences were small. Its importance lay within a longer process of adult education whereby the leadership, clerical and lay, of the Church was being weaned from high Tory attitudes to an acceptance of the Christian case for massive social reform and the development of a welfare state. In this it and its like were almost over-successful. (Hastings 1987, p. 179)

Importantly, Temple himself coined the term 'welfare state' in some lectures of 1928. He contrasted the 'power state' of the pre-war Prussian nation, in which the state coerced its citizens for its own ends, with a 'welfare state', which is formed to serve the welfare of all its people and which is needed now (see Chapter 5).

In 1929 Temple became Archbishop of York. This was an ideal post for him because, without a large urban diocese to run, he had more time for preaching and lecturing at national level. This he did with renewed gusto, giving university mission addresses in Cambridge, Dublin and Oxford, the last of which became one of his most popular books, *Christian Faith and Life* of 1931 (see Chapter 6). He was also invited to give the prestigious Gifford Lectures on natural theology in Glasgow, which were then published as *Nature, Man and God* in 1934. These were his most extensive and mature essays in philosophical theology (see Chapter 8). Through all of this his main concerns remained the same: to communicate a vision of the whole of life, religious, personal, economic, political, with Christ at the centre as the one who makes sense of the whole and illuminates it with his truth. He also became more and more involved with the ecumenical movement, becoming one of its leaders as plans were drawn up for the forming of a world council of churches. He provided careful mapping of how the Church of England should relate to this movement, and he took a lead in encouraging its growth nationally and internationally (see Chapter 7).

But the 1930s were a time of gathering storms, with the rise of the Nazis in Germany and the Fascists in Italy calling into question the optimistic view of life that Temple cherished. To his credit he began to revise the tone and content of his speaking, recognizing that the world as it now stands does not make sense but is in need of redemption. In one of his best known books, *Readings in St John's Gospel* (1939–40), he now compared the world to a dark night in which only one light was visible, like a single but powerful ray from a lighthouse on a headland. For Temple that ray of light was Christ, shining through the darkness of the world, 'cleaving it but neither dispelling it nor quenched by it' (see Chapter 9).

When war with Germany was declared in October 1939, after Hitler's invasion of Poland, Temple rose to the occasion. In a BBC radio broadcast to the nation he avoided the kind of jingoism that many churchmen had preached at the start of the First World War and, as became clear afterwards, he perfectly captured the mood of many in the country. The public mind, he said,

> is completely void of excitement. There is a deep determination, accompanied by no sort of exhilaration, but by a profound sadness. Men are taking up a hateful duty; the very fact that they hate it throws into greater relief their conviction that it is a duty. It is a duty first to Poland; but that is rather the focus than the real essence of our obligation . . . for our purpose is to check aggression, and to bring to an end the perpetual insecurity and menace which hang over Europe, spoiling the life of millions, as a result of the Nazi tyranny in Germany. ('The Spirit and Aims of Britain in the War', in Chapter 10)

This broadcast turned Temple into a national leader. There was now little doubt that after the retirement of Cosmo Gordon Lang, the Archbishop of Canterbury, Temple would replace him. This duly happened in April 1942. Temple and his wife moved into Lambeth Palace in London, living on the ground floor because the rest of the house had been badly bombed (Lang had preferred to live at the Athenaeum Club). He was seen catching the bus across Westminster Bridge and many ordinary people now knew they had a champion in the Archbishop. He fulfilled his duties while putting up with flying bombs by day and air raids by night, and his continual travelling took place on crowded buses and trains in the blackout.

The social and economic needs of the population were very much in his mind, and he was asking what kind of society Britain should become once the fighting was over. In 1942 he published a slim Penguin Special, *Christianity and Social Order*, which quickly became a bestseller, with 142,000 copies eventually being sold (see Chapter 11). With radical clarity but also a lightness of touch, he set out the fundamental Christian principles that should govern the way a society organizes its life, and drew out some of the practical implications of these principles. In writing the book, he received advice from William Beveridge and John

Maynard Keynes, among others, and its popularity and influence has resulted in Temple being described as one of the architects of the post-war welfare state created by Clement Attlee's Labour Government.

Then, in 1942 and early 1943, in the Albert Hall in London, he made some widely publicized remarks on the banking system, suggesting that the Government should put curbs on profits and should place restrictions on the issuing of credit by banks. The remarks were heavily criticized by financiers in the City of London, but they again showed Temple challenging the current order in favour of a new and fairer post-war world.

In 1942, when it became clear how badly the Jewish peoples of Eastern Europe were being treated by the Nazis, in public meetings and in the House of Lords Temple called for immediate action to provide help and asylum for those Jews able to escape from Hitler's domains (see Chapter 10). He had already been a co-founder of the Council for Christians and Jews in 1942 and had built up good relations with Jewish leaders. When he died, the Jewish community in Britain paid a special heartfelt tribute to him for these and other efforts.

In 1944 he gave crucial backing to R. A. Butler's Education Act, which for the first time set up a national system that would include both state and church schools, and raised the school leaving age to 15. The act led to the surrender of some church schools to the state in some parts of the country, because the churches could not afford their upkeep, and was controversial. Temple backed the act because he saw raising the school-leaving age to be more important for the whole population than the Church retaining control of some of its schools (see Chapter 11).

He continued to be a keen ecumenist, involved not only internationally but at home: he shared a platform with Cardinal Hinsley, the leader of the Roman Catholic Church in England and Wales, and helped with the creation of the British Council of Churches. He preached at the inauguration of the Council (see Chapter 7). If he had survived the war it is extremely likely that he would have been the first president of the World Council of Churches.

But he did not survive the war. After a prolonged attack of gout (from which he suffered all his life but which was now exacerbated by overwork), he died of a heart attack on 26 October 1944 (see Postscript). This was barely two and a half years after becoming Archbishop of Canterbury. He was not to see Allied victory in the war, nor was he to assist with the social and economic reconstruction of the country in the post-war years. It was a huge loss, especially as the Church of England was then given an archbishop (in Geoffrey Fisher) who seemed more interested in reforming canon law than providing a vision for society as a whole.

How should Temple be assessed? In terms of his impact on politics, Frank Field has written that Temple

> was as important as anyone in convincing the electorate both that it was safe to vote for radical change and that radical change was what the poor and the working class should demand. To the middle class he sold the idea of a continuing sacrifice [their taxes would pay for the welfare state], while for the working class and the poor he helped to convince them that their position of deference in British politics was coming to a close. Although William died in October 1944, his lasting influence was to be seen almost a year later as the ballot papers were strewn across the counting tables. Clement Attlee emerged with a record parliamentary majority, in no small measure thanks to the life of political campaigning by Frederick Temple's son William. (Field 2010, p. 35)

Field adds a personal comment: 'Those of us who are war-time babies, or who were born since, owe him a debt for helping to make our lives so different from the lives of those who grew up in the inter-war years. Temple raised people's hopes and encouraged them not to settle for another round of the 1930s (Field 2010, p. 60; for a historian's perspective that in general supports this view of the influence of Temple and his colleagues, see Grimley 2004).

David Jenkins, the ex-Bishop of Durham, has drawn attention to the spiritual dimension of this political impact:

> As a teenager I attended the Albert Hall meeting which Temple addressed, along with others including Sir Stafford Cripps, and what I drew from this, as well as what I read of his utterances and writings, was a clear understanding that we should be deeply Christian and deeply concerned with current affairs. Christianity was neither a purely private religion nor a merely spiritual religion. This was so because of the nature and purposes of the God to whom Christianity was a response. Temple was, surely, a powerful devout man, and the demands which he put before one were clearly religious, devotional and godly. But godliness required concern for the affairs of society because men and women were so socially shaped, and often socially distorted, and because the transcendent God was committed

to worldly particularities for the furthering of his purposes and the sharing of his love. (Jenkins 1981, pp. 321–2)

George Bell, Temple's contemporary as Bishop of Chichester, summed him up in a different but striking way. Temple, he wrote, 'had all the vividness and swiftness of a flame ... he communicated warmth and light to all who saw or heard him' (Bell 1946, p. 47). But George Herbert's comment on people like Temple can be added to this: 'Ministers of good things are like torches, a light to others, waste and destruction to themselves.'

I

The Case for Christian Belief:
The Faith and Modern Thought of 1910

While a lecturer at the Queen's College, Oxford, and in the year that he was made a deacon by Randall Davidson, the Archbishop of Canterbury, Temple was invited to deliver a set of lectures to the Student Christian Movement in London. His audience were students and other young people wrestling with the challenges to faith posed by scientific discoveries and the rise of scepticism in many parts of society. The lectures were very well attended and there was a demand that they should be published. This took place in 1910 with the title The Faith and Modern Thought. *It became a bestselling volume of apologetics, being reprinted several times, and established Temple as an up-and-coming luminary in the Church.*

Many of Temple's characteristic themes and approaches from later publications are already apparent in these lectures. In particular they display his fondness for arguing towards a conclusion from two directions at once, in particular from scientific and philosophical insights to the probability of God's existence and the likelihood of the truth of Christianity, and from religious experience to the same conclusions, the one line of argument supporting and validating the other.

This style of reasoned argumentation, carefully building a case, clearly and logically, shows Temple's philosophical training. But it is presented with a brevity and lightness of touch that leads the reader on, and is supplemented by some memorable images, such as way-marking stones in the Lake District, to illustrate and support his argument. There is a freshness about these lectures.

As already mentioned, the modern reader needs to be prepared that Temple comes from an era of non-inclusive language, and that he has a habit of capitalizing the first letter of key concepts in his argument. But, on the other hand, he begins his argument in a seemingly postmodern way, not with logical reasoning on its own but from within the reality of religious experience, in particular the experience of dependence upon God. In this first book, then, Temple provides us with an example of faith seeking understanding.

i The Grounds of Our Belief in God

Lecture I, 'The Grounds of Our Belief in God', pp. 4–8

Now the first evidence to the religious man of the existence of God is his own religious experience. No one who has had even a moment of such experience can afterwards quite ignore it; it will perpetually challenge his attention. He may, of course, find great difficulty in combining the fact which he seemed then to reach with all the other established facts of science and everyday life. It remains there as a problem; and as evidence it always has this peculiar perplexity about it, that it is incommunicable. If another man says, 'I have not the faintest idea what you mean when you talk about communion with God,' how can we explain it to him? And if he then goes on and says, 'Moreover, how are we to be sure that this experience of yours was not due to self-hypnotism? May it not very well be the case, that you had this experience, whatever it may have been, because you expected to have it, and your imagination worked at the command of your expectation, or else because you were in the company of a large number of other people who were liable to this peculiar disorder, as it may be, of the mental faculties?' How is one to answer that? Suppose he still goes on and says, 'Besides, there is no evidence apart from your experience that this Being, with whom you have met, exists at all. It is possible to explain all you tell us simply by referring it to morbid psychology and pathology. There is no fact there for you to apprehend.' And what shall the religious man say? When these two considerations are both before us, the incommunicability of the experience itself, and the apparent absence of any independent ground for believing that the 'fact' which we reached in that experience exists at all, don't we feel as if the whole foundation of our religious life were exceedingly precarious? Most of us, I think, have been disturbed by that charge of self-hypnotism. How can we disprove it? Don't we feel very much as the old Psalmist felt when he was kept away from the Temple services? – 'Like as the hart desireth the water brooks so longeth my soul after Thee O God. My soul is athirst for God, yea, even for the living God; when shall I come to appear before the presence of

God? My tears have been my meat day and night; while they say daily unto me, Where is now thy God?'

It is to meet that state of mind, if we can, that these lectures have been arranged. For there are some who, though they have been in touch with what is spiritual, have felt compelled by motives which we must respect, by reverence for truth, to believe that it was all illusion; while others have never come in touch with what is spiritual at all, because the intellectual barrier has always stood in the way and prevented them from yielding themselves to the influences. That means that religious experience appeals for external support. It is not enough for it in the mind of a scientific man that it happened to him, that the man should have had such and such feelings, such and such momentary convictions; if that is all that is to be said, morbid psychology is the science to which the study of this experience belongs. We want some evidence, apart from the religious experience altogether, that the God whom we reach in that experience is really existent. And this makes a peculiar feature of the whole of theology, or of the science of religion. All the other sciences at least assume the existence of their subject matter. The physicist is not called upon to prove that mechanical forces exist. The geometrician is not called upon to prove there is such a thing as space. He is allowed to assume it and no one quarrels with him. But when the theologian begins to try to develop a theory of the world on the basis of this experience, he is at once challenged with the question: How do you know that this experience is really a valid guide to fact? And that question must first be answered, because it is undoubtedly true that some people have very little or even none at all of this specifically religious experience.

But may I say immediately that by religious experience I do not mean an ecstasy or an extraordinary thing that happens to a few people here and there, but simply that impulse, which comes upon most people at some time, to throw oneself back upon a Power greater than oneself, and the sense, the perfectly sure sense, that that Power has received one and is supporting one. Numbers of people have felt something of that sort. It is a sense of self-abandonment and yet of safety; and that seems to demand, as I have said, further support from outside; and that support must be of a rigidly scientific character: nothing else will do.

Temple then discusses a number of attempts to provide such support, such as the argument from causation, that there must be a first cause. He does not find this convincing and instead looks for a principle that will explain not just individual experiences or events but 'the whole series together' (p. 15).

Pages 16–24

Now there is in our own experience already one principle which does answer the question, 'Why?' in such a way as to raise no further questions; that is, the principle of Purpose. Let us take a very simple illustration. Across many of the hills in Cumberland the way from one village to another is marked by white stones placed at short intervals. We may easily imagine a simple-minded person asking how they came there, or what natural law could account for their lying in that position; and the physical antecedents of the fact – the geological history of the stones and the physiological structure of the men who moved them – give no answer. As soon, however, as we hear that men placed them so, to guide wayfarers in the mist or in the night, our minds are satisfied. And speaking generally, the moment we agree with anyone that a thing is good it never occurs to us to ask why it should exist. There is no problem of the existence of good. Purpose is a principle which we have already gauged in our own experience and which, where it is applicable, gives a final answer to the question Why; and there is no other principle known, at any rate to me, that does give a final answer to the question, Why. We have already seen that the principle of Causation in the ordinary sense does not. It can only state facts of history, and you may always say, Why this history? The only principle then that will satisfy the scientific demand for complete intellectual satisfaction is the principle of Purpose; science requires, therefore, that: there should be a real Purpose in the world. (NB – This is not the argument from Design, which does not deal with the world as a whole, but rests on the adaptation of one part to another part.) Grant that, and the whole of our experience, as it seems to me, immediately begins to become coherent. Of course the problem of Evil remains: why was the Purpose this which we see and not another? That for the moment we shall leave, but we shall come back to it in the subsequent lectures. But surely it is scientific, when you already have a principle capable of explaining the fact, at least to investigate and see what can be done with that principle. It is not as though we had to invent the term 'Purpose' to explain the fact of the world, as the old scientists invented Caloric to explain the fact of heat. Purpose exists in our everyday experience. It supplies an answer to our question. It is then scientific to accept that answer provisionally as a hypothesis.

I believe that the effort to understand this Purpose is not so hopeless as it looks at first. Scientific principle requires us at least to take seriously the hypothesis of a Purpose in the world, and, therefore, a real Will behind the world. That hypothesis will not be justified until we have seen it through, until we see how it does as a matter of fact cover all the facts and particularly the fact of Evil. And let me say here that to declare the problem of Evil insoluble is Atheism or Agnosticism. The problem of Evil must be soluble. The Revelation of God in Christ exists to be the solution. Whether or not we shall be able to grasp that solution in a single course of lectures – or in our whole life-time – is of course another question. Yet I think we may get clearer about it than perhaps we have been before.

But now, leaving the further development of this thought of the Purpose that is in the world, let us go back to our starting point, which was religious experience. These two seem now to support each other. For what is the leading characteristic of the religious experience? Surely it is this: that in it the man is in contact with a Being who appears to know him through and through, who is intimate with him as no human being is, and yet whose knowledge is not felt to be intrusive or in any sense a vexation. We might feel that it was an intrusion if some even of our friends had the faculty of knowing all our inmost thoughts, however much we tried to keep them to ourselves; we should probably resent it; and people do resent that claim when it is made. Nobody ever dreams of resenting the thought that God knows him through and through. He may tremble at the thought, but he does not resent it. Now what Being is there who could conceivably know me in this way, a Being other than myself, who yet has an absolute knowledge of everything that goes on in my innermost nature? Only one possible Being, surely: the Being who made me. He might know; no one else, as far as I can see, could know. If there is a Being who made us, He might have such knowledge.

It seems, then, that the two sides of the argument are beginning to support each other. It appears from the investigation of science, from investigation of the method of scientific procedure itself, that there must be a Will in which the whole world is rooted and grounded; and that we and all other things proceed therefrom; because only so is there even a hope of attaining the intellectual satisfaction for which science is a quest. And here is an experience, very common among men, which claims to be a direct contact or communion with a Being, who, if He exist at all, must be the Maker at least of the man who has the experience; and if we already believe, on quite other grounds, that there is such a Being existing, it is surely the very height of presumption to say that the man who believes that he is in communion with that Being is deceived, simply on the ground that we perhaps have not had a similar experience. If it can be shown that God exists, then there can be no objection in principle to the thought of His revealing Himself directly to the individual. The difficulty about the religious experience was not any doubt in the man's mind as to whether he had it or not: he knew he had it; he knew that this extraordinary event had taken place in his life; but the difficulty was that so many other people had not had it, and at first there was no evidence for the existence of the Being whom he then perceived; he remembered how under various influences people may perceive things which have no real existence; and he wondered whether he himself was the victim of such a pathological condition. But when he has found that the most rigid investigation of experience that can be made leads to the hypothesis of a creative Will which is the root of all existence, then he says, 'Now I have proved that what I then perceived does really exist. Other people may be blind to it: that does not affect my vision; I have seen it.' And so it seems to me the demand of Reason and the religious experience support one another; either without the other would be precarious. The demand of Reason by itself would set up an ideal to be reached, which yet nobody had reached. It would say that there must be somewhere the Creative Will; but would still admit that no one has in any way ever perceived it. And on the other side the religious experience is precarious in the way that we have shown; but the two together support each other; the intellect demands the existence of such a Being, and if so, then agnosticism (if by that we mean anything more than the reverent confession of our own intellectual failure to understand completely the Object of our religious worship) is not scientific; it is precisely a refusal to apply the scientific method itself beyond a certain point, and that a point at which there is no reason in heaven or earth to stop. The way in which it arises, I think, is simply that people become so much occupied with the consideration of what they know, that they entirely forget the perfectly astounding fact that they know it. It is by considering the fact of knowledge itself and what is involved in knowledge, namely, this astounding demand of the intellect that experience shall be made to appear coherent and so forth – it is by considering these facts that we are led on to the further principle, which lies outside the field of natural science no doubt, but is yet reached by the application of the strictly scientific method.

And then, if all that is true, it will follow that the course of the wise man will be to study with all his power the character of that Will and Purpose which governs the world; he will wish in every way he can to increase his knowledge of this subject, for upon that everything else depends: and recognising, moreover, that this Power is almighty, since all proceeds from it, it will be his wisdom, unless indeed the Power shall turn out to be definitely evil, to ally himself with it as far as he may, and to cultivate the faculty of communion with it – a faculty that can be either cultivated or stunted. And then, too, as he comes to understand the character of that Purpose, he will try to apply it in his own life, not only from the strictly religious motive, but also from the strictly scientific motive, for he will want to verify his hypothesis: he will say, 'The hypothesis is that God exists, and has such and such a character: let me live in the light of that hypothesis and see what happens; let me make experiment with it in the one place I can, in my own life. Possibly, as the old theologians used to say, I must believe in order that I may understand. I cannot believe unless I understand a little; but I shall not understand much, unless I am willing at first to take a certain amount on trust and make experiment with it: and that experiment must be made in myself, because my will is the only will that I can bring, or begin to bring, into harmony with the divine Will. It is only in my own person that I can try to discover what alliance with the divine Will means.' And so the scientific and the religious impulses will combine, and will lead a man to submit himself and all his powers to the God in whom his reason has led him to believe.

ii The Person of Christ

These paragraphs present a portrait of the Christ whom Temple followed throughout his adult life. They work towards a memorably simple description of the heart of Christ's life and teaching, summed up in the phrase 'love, and the capacity to grow in love'. There is also a concise description of the way the sign of Holy Communion points to the heart of the gospel. Finally, Temple provides an introduction and elucidation of his favourite Gospel, the Fourth, drawing out the way it provides an integration of the historical Christ of the Synoptic Gospels with the doctrinal insights of Paul, and the way it highlights the immanence of God in Christ. Temple would return to exposition of this Gospel at many points later in life.

Lecture IV, 'The Person of Christ', pp. 94–103

What is that secret [of Christ's ministry]? In any dramatic story one finds the significance by looking for the conflict. The first task for any critic of tragedy is to find what are the opposing parties in the tragic conflict. What are here the opposing forces? Christ on the one side; what on the other? Of course, we are at first inclined to say, Sin; and that is right, if we mean enough by the word 'sin'. But it does not mean that the Lord's enemies were of the criminal classes. The background of darkness against which the Light of the world stands out in its splendour is not sin as we ordinarily conceive it; it is dead religion. The great opposing force against which Christ, in the days of His flesh, could effect little was the established and self-satisfied religion of the time; and once at least He expressed His judgment that the deadness of that religion was something beyond the reach of the divine forgiveness. What was it that had happened? He had healed a man possessed of a devil, and those who watched asserted that He did this in the power of the devil. He replies, That is to suppose that the devil divides his house against itself, which seems improbable: but it is also to say of a plainly good thing that it is a bad thing. And he adds, Say what you like about Me; 'Whoso speaketh a Word against the Son of Man, it shall be forgiven him'; but if when the very spirit of goodness is at work before you, you call it evil because it happens not to fit into your scheme, then there really is no hope; 'Whosoever speaketh against the Holy Spirit, it shall not be forgiven him, neither in this world, neither in the world to come' (Matt. 12.22–32). They were not peculiarly wicked people; they were the upholders of a conventional righteousness: but they were contented. That is always in the Gospels the one hopeless condition. The Pharisee praying in the temple was no doubt a very much better man than the publican. That is, in fact, the point of the parable; he really was a good man according to the standards of the time; but he was contented; he was going to stay where he was and never get any better. He was content with thanking God that he was not as other men are. And the other man, who no doubt stood much lower in the moral scale at the moment, but knew his imperfections and his need of forgiveness and of growth, is justified rather than the Pharisee (Luke 18.9–14).

So it is too in perhaps the most extraordinary of all the stories of the Gospels, when there was brought to the Lord a woman taken in adultery that He might pronounce judgment; having first shamed into silence the accusers, He says to the woman, 'Neither do I condemn thee; go and sin no more.' It is possible to say, 'Neither do I condemn thee'; because it is also possible to say, with effect, 'Go and sin no more' (John 8.1–11). The one thing demanded is always the power to grow. Growth and progress in the spiritual life is the one thing Christ is always demanding; and however low the moral state of any individual may be, provided that capacity for growth is not lost, there is always hope, hope even of ultimate perfection. But however high the moral state may be, if perfection is not yet reached and the power of growth is gone, then the imperfection is permanent and salvation is impossible.

But it is not enough to learn that our Lord's one demand is for the power to grow and that the one deadly foe we have to meet is spiritual stagnation. What is it in which He requires that people shall grow? There is one ceremony and one ceremony only which He has commanded His disciples perpetually to celebrate. Let us go back behind all the theology, and all the meanings which have quite rightly gathered round that ceremony, to its first institution; let us think what it must have looked like to the people who were there, before they began to meditate upon it, and before they could find what it could do for them in their own lives. In a time of quite intense emotional stress – the last time that the Lord was to sup with His friends – He took bread and said that it was His body; and He gave thanks for it, He broke it, and He gave it to them and said – 'Do this in remembrance of me' (1 Cor. 11.23–25). He took the bread of which He said it was His Body – 'This is My Body: as I treat this bread, so I treat My Body' – and He gave it to them; and said, 'Do that if you want to show you remember Me.' Do what? The sign, no doubt. But, far more important, what it signifies. The demand is nothing less than this, that men should take their whole human life, and break it, and give it for the good of others. The quality in which we are to grow is service to the point of absolute devotion and complete sacrifice.

Love, and the capacity to grow in love, is the whole secret. And He in His own life realises His own ideal. If one takes all these precepts and sets over against them the life itself from its relatively happy opening, when the people flock to Him in Galilee, to the dark conclusion in the Garden, before Pilate, and on the Cross, all through we feel that this quality of absolute selflessness is manifest in perfect completeness. It would never occur to anyone to say of Christ before Pilate that He was a great man; it would never occur to anyone to say that. He was noble-minded; all these expressions, which have about them some suggestion of dominance and the imposition of a man's own will upon others, are inappropriate. He rises superior to all about Him, not because He imposes His will upon them, but because He does not impose His will at all, because He has apparently no will of His own except to do what His Mission requires.

And so, both in His teaching and in His life, He is the climax of human ethics. For there is no morality beyond absolute devotion to the public good. That is the climax of morality; you cannot go further. He taught it and He practised it. And He is the perfection also of human religion, for not only does He combine together all the strands that can be woven together in the religious life, but also His will is in perfect dependence upon the will of God. In His experience prayer was always answered; and it is His promise that whatsoever we ask in His name, in His spirit, will be answered, for it will be the will of God. There is the fact; there at least are just a few, a very few, of the leading features of that great fact.

How are we to understand it? We will not attempt today either to grasp more fully than before a theological system or (still less) to formulate a new one. Let us rather go back to a document which we were careful last time not to consider, the Fourth Gospel. Now there is a great dispute about the question who wrote the Fourth Gospel. I cannot help thinking that it does not very much matter. The writer had either been present at the scenes which he records, as I believe, or else He was absolutely steeped in the record of that Life. In either case He is finding in that story the manifestation of the divine Christ with whom he is in daily communion. It is perfectly clear, for instance, that the style of the discourses belongs to the writer and not to our Lord. If the Lord spoke as He speaks in the Synoptic Gospels, then He did not speak as He speaks in the Gospel of St John. It is quite clear also, as the writer says himself, that he selects episodes specially adapted to bring out the lessons which He Wishes to teach (John 20.30–31). Here then we have a writer who is not merely recording what he remembers, or has heard, of the Lord's life, but is exhibiting the identity between the historic Christ and the spiritual Christ of religious communion. And thus the Gospel fulfils what would otherwise be a great need in the New Testament. In the Synoptists we have the outward facts recorded; in St Paul's Epistles we have the theory of those facts gradually evolved by one who perhaps had never seen the Lord, who stood at a little distance, who looked at the great Fact and tried to estimate its value and meaning. But so the Lord had become rather remote. The risen, glorified Christ of St Paul's Epistles, if taken alone and apart from the Gospel narrative, would not have the intimacy of human appeal which we need. In St John we have one who writes with the whole wealth of Pauline meditation at his disposal, and who then reveals the absolute identity of that human figure in Palestine with the divine Spirit known in the communion of the worshipper.

And this makes the Gospel surely not less valuable, but more so. It is the inspired comment on the old story, the comment of one who can fitly be represented as saying,

> To me that story, that life and death
> Of which I wrote, it was, to me, it is,
> Is here and now; I apprehend nought else.
> (Browning, *A Death in the Desert*. The best commentary on St John's Gospel)

How does he set about the great task? He begins with a conception almost universally accepted at the time, just as it is almost universally accepted now, although its name is now generally different – the conception of the divine Word or Logos. Everyone at any rate understood what was meant by the prologue of St John's Gospel; it was common property. The theory had been elaborated by the Stoics and had been combined with Jewish speculation by Philo. Everyone would understand it: and it would serve not only to bring the Gospel into relation with the modes of thought habitual to the people for whom it is written, but it would also serve to bring out the full significance of that life, or at any rate more of the significance than previous attempts had been able to do. It was of no use to say to a Gentile community that the Messiah was come; they had not been brought up to expect any Messiah to come; it would be an announcement wholly without interest for them. But to say that the indwelling principle of the world, which governs everything, has been made manifest in a single Life is to say something whose importance is beyond all parallel. They believed, as we believe, that the world is a single system governed by a single principle; and there is nothing which matters so much as to know the character of that principle. St John says that this principle, the Logos, by whom all things were made, and without whom was not anything made which was made, became flesh in Christ. We are to see there the character of the principle or spirit which made the world and holds it in being – nothing less than that; and he constructs his narrative in such a way as to bring out this character.

Pages 107–8

There are some quite definite points that emerge in the Gospel to which I would like to call attention. It is pre-eminently the Gospel of Divine Immanence. It begins with the conception of the immanence in the world of a principle, the Logos, or Word; it is the manifestation of the indwelling God. But all through the Incarnate Word refers to 'Him that sent Me' as someone above and beyond Himself. And that is a step that we must take. We found in the first lecture that we cannot in the last resort understand the world at all, except by regarding it as the expression of a purpose, which must be rooted in a Will. To speak about an immanent purpose is very good sense; but to speak about a purpose behind which there is no Will is nonsense; and to speak about an immanent Will is nonsense. It is the purpose, the meaning and thought of God, that is immanent, not God Himself. He is not limited to the world that He has made; He is beyond it, the source and ground of it all, but not it. Just as you may say that in Shakespeare's work his thoughts and feelings are immanent; you find them there in the book; but you don't find Shakespeare, the living, thinking, acting man, in the book. You have to infer the kind of being that he was from what he wrote; he himself is not there; his thoughts are there. And so we must follow St John very carefully; for, in our interest in insisting upon the divine immanence, we are in danger of forgetting that God is a Spirit who makes the world, upon whose will it depends, but who is not the sum total of its natural laws.

iii   The Spirit of Christ and the Church

This extract also introduces many of Temple's characteristic themes: the freedom yet determinism of religious experience; the way science seems to undermine faith but in fact supports it at a deeper level; the way political history seems to do the same; and the centrality of the doctrine of the incarnation to his whole outlook, that Christ is in all things and provides the key to unlocking the meaning of the universe in which we live. All of this leads Temple to emphasize the guiding role of the Holy Spirit in the believer's life, a role that naturally leads the believer into membership of the Church, which is the body of Christ growing across the world.

Lecture VI, 'The Spirit, the Church and the Life Eternal', pp. 149–64

God cannot be omnipotent except by the revelation of His Love. By His power He could control our actions, but not our wills. If He is to be Lord of all that exists, He must be Lord of our wills. But the will is not amenable to force; it can only be governed through what seems to it good; God can only rule our wills through a complete and intelligible manifestation of His Love. The secret and hidden and undetected operation of the Power of God can never reach its own goal. If that goal is to be reached, the divine Principle itself must appear before us in all the splendour of its glory.

And so we reach a clue to the great paradox which we found in all religious experience. We found that in all religious experience we are at once vividly conscious of our own responsibility before God, and also of the fact that all our lives are in His hands; that He guides and shapes our destiny from beginning to end; that He is omnipotent yet we are free; and that remains an unintelligible paradox, until we remember that the change in man's will that is accomplished when love is won from his heart by the love of another is at once his own act and the act of the other. When St Paul said, 'I live, yet not I but Christ liveth in me' (Galatians 2.20), he did not mean that his will was suppressed and checked; he did not mean that either without his will, or against his will, he preached the Gospel under some strange compulsion; he meant that his life was wholly governed by Christ, because, seeing the nature of Christ and the beauty of His character, he had accepted that character freely as his own. He was absolutely governed by Christ; but it did not follow that he was not free; rather it followed that for the first time he was perfectly free, for he had freely yielded himself to the love of God and in that yielding of himself had for the first time found his own satisfaction and peace.

So it is in all our experience of God; we are not driven on by some external force as a mechanical body is set in motion by an external force; but love is won from our hearts by the love of God. We cannot resist giving it, when we see the love of God; but what makes it impossible for us to resist is just our human nature; nothing else. We are free precisely in our inability to refuse our love. It is the expression of our own nature; it is not something imposed upon us from without; it is the natural expression of what we are.

And so with the greatest difficulty, as it sometimes seems, in the commencement of the religious life, people find that they cannot approach God without His help, and then they wish to pray for His help and find that they cannot even pray without that help. From the beginning to the end our lives are in His hands absolutely. But we are in His hand as the child is guided by the love of the father, not as a physical object is moved by an external force. And the motion of our wills which is wholly due to Him is none the less the free motion of our own will: it is the answer of our hearts to His love. The true conclusion to draw from the discovery of our impotence is not a fatalistic quietism and spiritual indolence, but a complete selflessness and surrender to God. This religious sense of the individual's helplessness has not in history led to inactivity, but to an energy that the isolated individual could not command.

Now in this conception of a governing divine Spirit which is in all the world, treated and interpreted as it is in the Christian theology, I believe we have the clue to the chief of our modern difficulties; for these difficulties, if I understand the matter aright, do not arise from any new way of thinking of specifically religious things. It is a change, not in our theology, but in our total habit of mind, to which we have to adapt ourselves; and this change is due to two main causes. The first is of course, the development of natural science. A hundred and fifty years ago people supposed that God had made the world and had imposed certain laws upon it and then left it to go more or less its own way according to those laws, interfering now and then by way of a miracle; and still we have in popular language certain events, usually, I am afraid, calamities, which are classified as the Act of God – a relic of that old way of thinking. Then gradually the development of science produced its effect upon the public mind, and men began to believe that everything can be explained by natural law. And very often religious people are distressed at this for it seems to have curtailed the sphere of the divine activity. But it was they who had curtailed it in the first instance by allowing that it was only in miracle that we could see the hand of God. What has really happened to us is that instead of seeing the divine activity here and there or now and then, we have again an opportunity of seeing it, as we should always have seen it, everywhere and always. There is nothing which God does not do. 'Through Him all things were made and apart from Him hath not one thing happened.'

The growth of science, then, is one main factor in the situation; the other is the growth of democracy. As long as nations were governed by kings, it seemed natural to extend the analogy to the universe; men thought of God as King of the Universe; and I believe you will find that in all ages popular theology rests upon such political analogy. Then in the eighteenth century, when it was thought to be necessary to respectability that man should believe in the constitutional necessity of a monarch, but contrary to political prudence that he should be allowed to do anything, you have in theology the extraordinary phenomenon of Deism, which insisted strongly that God exists, but regarded it as fanaticism to suppose that He ever does anything. And now, in our time, we have a conception of Government as a power not acting upon the subjects from without, but through them from within; a conception which maintains that the only power before which the individual should bend his will is the collective will of the whole community; and parallel with that you have a great insistence on the doctrine, always in the Church from the outset, of divine immanence; and when any preacher finds a way of expressing the divine immanence so that people can understand it, they crowd to him as to a new revelation. We must, I think, in our day, begin with this conception of the indwelling divine power, because it is at this point that we, like St John, can find a starting-point common to ourselves and those to whom we speak; but we must not end with it; and we must not be content to leave it uncharacterised. We must not end with it, because as we said before, what is immanent in the world is the divine purpose, not the divine Will: an immanent Will is nonsense. And we must not leave it uncharacterised; we must ask how it operates, and to what goal it is leading us. The answer for the Christian is the life and death of Christ. 'The Word was made flesh and we beheld His glory.' There is all the difference in the world between the divine principle of progress as mediated by nature or by tribal worship or by secular civilisation and that same divine principle mediated through its own perfect manifestation in Jesus Christ. When we have seen it manifest in Christ we can take it as the clue to our experience and see that in every department of life the Spirit which was in Him is operative. But if we had begun with biology and human history we should never have reached any conception of the governing divine principle as one whose only characteristic is love, whose glory is moral not spectacular, and whose pre-eminence is through sacrifice and not through power. It is only through Christ that we can come to the Spirit as the whole power of God operating in its fullness upon our spirits. It is indeed in all the world. The Word is the agent of Creation; it is in all the world, and we can never be altogether outside its influence; but it will not have its full effect on our wills until we understand and appreciate it and yield ourselves to it; that is to say until it has been fully manifest in the terms of our own life. So the Spirit proceeds, not only from the Father, but from the Father and the Son. We may look back upon the previous history of the world before Christ and see how the same Spirit, which was in Him, was guiding the ages up to Him, as it has guided the Church ever since. But in the fullness of its power it does not exist in the world till after the Incarnation and Crucifixion. 'There was not yet Spirit, because Jesus was not glorified' (John 7.39).

The Spirit, therefore, which governs the world, must be mediated for us through Christ; we must never for a moment suppose that we can find that same spirit anywhere else without His help. When we have found it in Him we may see its operation elsewhere. We cannot first find it elsewhere, and then discover that it was manifest in Him. For in all the rest of our experience there is no evidence that the character of the Spirit is the character of Christ; but if Christ is a fact, then, as we have often said before, the governing Power of the world must be something capable of expressing itself in that fact; it must be adequate to its own greatest achievement.

And so the Spirit is to be taken, not only as the guiding power of the world, but as the guiding power of the world as seen in Christ. Only so can it have its full effect upon our hearts and wills. No doubt the Spirit is present in all men – it 'lighteth every man'; and it is no doubt more fully present in some who are not Christians than in some who are. But its full manifestation is in Christ alone; others have the Divine Spirit in their degree, but He alone is altogether God. And though this or that man may reach great moral heights without any conscious relation to Christ, only the Love made manifest in the Cross is sufficient to take away the sin of the world.

And yet another condition is necessary; the Spirit must be mediated through Christ, and it must be operative in the Church. The whole reason why this sort of discussion is necessary is that our religious experience always appeals for logical support; it is always anxious to defend itself against the charge of self-hypnotism; it wishes to know that the God revealed to it is not the object of a dream, but is the real and living God; that is to say, our religious experience knows itself to be precarious as evidence, and it appeals to philosophy for support; and a philosophical argument always fails to carry complete conviction to anyone who is alone in believing in it. I may think out some long train of reasoning which seems to me perfectly cogent; but if when I tell others they reject it, though I cannot see the flaw, I cannot help wondering whether there is not some flaw which they detect, though it escapes my notice. And so even when we have corroborated the evidence of our religious experience by philosophical reasoning, we are still in a precarious position; we still need further support because we cannot be perfectly sure that our own reasoning is without flaw. We need, therefore, if our faith is to be absolutely secure that all men, nothing less, should come to believe what we believe. As long as there is one man who, after thinking the problem over, still doubts, there will be a haunting doubt in our own faith; and, as a partial realisation of that universal support by all humanity, we collect together in the Church to support our own faith, because there we find other people who, either through the same reasoning, or from different reasoning, or else simply on the basis of their own religious experience, have reached the same conclusions as ourselves; and it strengthens our own belief in those conclusions to meet with others who have reached them. If the conclusions are untrue, the charge of mutual hypnotism can be made; but if the conclusions are true, nothing in the world can be more rational than that we should take every possible step to secure that our belief in them is vital.

But there is more than this involved, for our belief does not end in intellectual assent; it must become a living faith, the impulse to a life singularly alien from our natural impulses. If this further step is to be taken, we need again the support of others – the support this time not so much of their intellects as of their wills, and above all of their affection. We need to consort with people all pledged to the realisation of the same ideal that we may catch their fire.

And then further we know quite well that any really living society is a far greater thing than the sum of the persons who compose it. England is not the name for the fact that a large number of us happen to inhabit a particular island; it is a spiritual entity with a life of its own, a life to which we all contribute in co-operation, but a life, none the less, greater than the mere sum of our own lives. Still more is it true that in the Church we have a great society professing an ideal which scarcely any, if any, of its members has ever realised, professing an ideal which probably not one of its members has ever fully grasped. Only in the whole Church is the whole truth known; only indeed when the whole Church is the same as the whole world will the whole truth be fully known; for each has his own contribution to make to the life which is to be lived under the impulse of the divine love; each individual is unique and different from all others; and as long as there is any who is withholding what he alone can give, that life remains imperfect.

But if all this is true, then it follows that in order to bring ourselves under the full operation of the Spirit we must be members of the Church. It would take us far away from the fundamental questions that are occupying us in these lectures, if I were to go into details as to the exact meaning of the word 'Church'; but at least it must mean this, a body with an intelligible form and definite organisation, to which we can consciously belong. It must not be a mere group of persons who happen to be congenial to one another; that would be the narrowest conceivable sort of sect. It must be a full life, collecting together all the types of spiritual experience which can flow from the love of God; and in our full membership in such a body, in devoting ourselves absolutely to its service, we shall be bringing our contribution to the whole life of the

CHRIST IN ALL THINGS

body of Christ. That body of Christ is something which is steadily being built up. You will remember how, particularly in the later Epistles, St Paul perpetually speaks about the building up of the Body of Christ, and the goal of it all is that we shall 'come to one perfect Man', which will be the 'measure of the stature of the fullness (or the completion) of Christ' (Ephesians 4.13). He does not mean, of course, that each of us is to become perfect in that sense, that each of us is to attain to the measure of the stature of Christ. Of course not. He means that the whole human race is to become so knit together through the purpose of God that it will be a single whole, with one life expressed through all its members; so closely knit together that it can be called 'one perfect Man': and that will be the 'measure of the stature of the fullness of Christ'; that will be the manifestation of the full glory of the Spirit of Christ: for if we limit the work of Christ to what He accomplished when He was upon earth, then that life becomes an isolated event and the rest of the world becomes an insoluble enigma. But if we say in that life there was manifest a principle which becomes increasingly manifest in the life of the whole world until at last the whole human race will exhibit the same character, then we see how the glory of Christ is not yet completely revealed and will only be known altogether when the whole world is showing it forth. He is the Head of the Body, and from Him 'the whole body fitly joined together and compacted by that which every joint supplieth, according to the effectual working in the measure of every part, maketh increase of the body unto the building of it in love'. And from this point of view, may I suggest that we get a new impulse to the work of foreign missions? For we see that even our own faith can never be complete, and our lives never be under the full influence of the Holy Spirit, until the whole world is Christian. Only then will the Holy Spirit be active in the plenitude of His power.

2

From Philosophy to Theology: *Mens Creatrix* of 1917

Mens Creatrix, *a philosophical study of 'creative mind', was a heady brew of philosophy, theology, poetry and political thought. It had been planned in 1908 when Temple had been lecturing in philosophy at Queen's College, and was written in odd moments at Oxford, Repton and in London. More than half of it, he admitted, was dictated in spare half-hours at St James', Piccadilly. Temple modestly described its 370 pages as 'a stimulus, if it may be so, to some real philosopher to do more adequately what I am only able to sketch out'. Nevertheless the book is a serious contribution to philosophical enquiry. It tries, ambitiously, to show how the kinds of questions raised by philosophy, especially the philosophies of knowledge, art and ethics, can be answered by religion, which is described as the culmination of science, art and morality, and in particular by the incarnation of Christ. The Prologue, printed below, describes all of this in a colourful way.*

But Temple was quite clear, as in The Faith and Modern Thought, *that reasoned argument alone would not prove the case he was trying to make: 'Yet even at the last the security is of Faith and not of Knowledge; it is not won by intellectual grasp but by personal loyalty; and its test is not in logic only, but in life' (p. 4). The living of the Christian way, in other words, was the only sure route to knowing the truth of Christianity, another seemingly postmodern sentiment.*

The argument of Mens Creatrix *was based on the idealist philosophy Temple had learnt at Oxford, from Edward Caird and, behind him, T. H. Green. It sought to show how the natural sciences, art (including drama and poetry) and morality, were activities that could be seen as exhibiting different facets of 'Mind', an all-encompassing reality that showed there was an underlying unity behind these different activities. For Temple its reality had evolved through an organic and unfolding process of evolution and, within that, of human history.*

The earliest and most primitive forms of life were not sentient, they were not thinking beings. Only towards the end of the evolutionary process, when humanity came into being, did Mind emerge. It was responsible for the achievements of human culture, not least the cultures of Greece, Rome and Palestine (as Thomas Arnold had argued). Temple believed that Mind was the goal towards which evolution had been moving: it was also the thing that had been drawing evolution to this goal. The full disclosure of Mind would therefore provide the key to reality, though philosophy itself was unable to find this disclosure.

At this point in the argument Temple had prepared the ground for his presentation of Christ as the incarnation of Mind:

> *The whole process of that revelation which has been going on through nature, through history and through prophets, comes to complete fulfilment in the Incarnation . . . Only in the life of Christ is this manifestation given. What we see in Him is what we should see in the history of the universe if we could apprehend that history in its completeness. (pp. 317–18)*

And for Temple the Fourth Gospel, as we have already seen, comes closest to expressing this mystery when it declares, 'The Word was made flesh and we beheld His glory.'

Mens Creatrix has been criticized by the philosopher Dorothy Emmet, who commented that in spite of its clarity of style and exposition it

> *is a curiously disjointed book. It bears the marks of having been dictated in odd half-hours . . . It passes quickly from one large topic to another: from idealist logic to discussions of art, tragedy, ethics, international and social politics, and Christian theology, without the ground gained at each stage being established sufficiently firmly to bear much searching criticism. (Iremonger 1948, p. 523)*

Even more seriously, the discussion of evil, which occupies the longest chapter in the book, may not be as convincing as it needed to be. The existence of evil in the world was obviously a problem for Temple's argument. How could the evolution of the world be the purposeful unfolding of Mind when there was clearly so much that was so terribly wrong, not least the carnage taking place on the fields of Flanders and France when the book was being published. Temple recognized the problem of evil and grappled with it. He argued that the existence of evil served a greater purpose. With human suffering, for example, there was often a positive good that could come out it:

> *Pain, coupled with fortitude in its endurance, especially when this is inspired by love, and meeting the full sympathy which at first lightens it and at last destroys it by removal of its grounds, is sometimes the condition of what is best in human life. (p. 278)*

He admitted, though, that this could not be seen with all cases of human suffering in the world. J. W. Rogerson, in a sympathetic discussion of Temple's philosophical thought, asks what of the suffering of the concentration camps, a suffering arising out of an evil that was so appalling it could never be justified by any future outcome? Temple writes:

> *All we can claim is that we have found a principle on which, where we can trace its operation, suffering becomes a necessary element in the full goodness of the world; that in some cases this principle can actually be traced; that in others its action must be assumed if we are to maintain the rationality of the world. (p. 281)*

Nevertheless, despite these limitations, Mens Creatrix is an impressive attempt to see how the truth revealed in Christ could provide a way of interpreting and understanding the underlying meaning and truth of the world in which we live. There is much to be learnt from the way Temple seeks to do this, and there are important discussions of key concepts along the way, including his reflection on the nature of political liberty (see Chapter 5), and his extended exposition of the doctrine of the incarnation (see Section iii).

i   Philosophy and Theology Working Together

Prologue, pp. 1–4

> 'In the beginning was the Word . . . and the Word was made flesh.'
> St John

The Argument of this book is as follows. It traces the outline of the Sciences of Knowledge, Art, Morality, and Religion, as the author understands these, not pausing to discuss what is disputable but merely affirming the position which is adopted. The four philosophical sciences are found to present four converging lines which do not in fact meet. Man's search for an all-inclusive system of Truth is thus encouraged and yet baffled.

Then the view-point changes. The Christian hypothesis is accepted and its central 'fact' – the Incarnation – is found to supply just what was needed, the point in which these converging lines meet and find their unity.

Book I, entitled 'Man's Search', is philosophical in method; Book II, entitled 'God's Act', is theological. It will make my subsequent procedure more intelligible if I state what I conceive to be the difference between these two.

Philosophy is the attempt to reach an understanding of experience. It may be called the science of the sciences. It takes the results of all departmental studies and tries to exhibit them as forming one single system, just as these separate sciences themselves try to exhibit the facts which they study as united in coherent systems. Philosophy has no presuppositions or assumptions, except the validity of reason (or, to put it otherwise, the rationality of the universe). Philosophy assumes the competence of reason – not necessarily your reason or mine, but reason when free from all distraction of impulse – to grasp the world as a whole. It begins with experience, and may include within that all which we can mean by 'religious experience'; it may even give to this the chief place among the various forms of experience; but it begins with human experience and tries to make sense of that. If it reaches a belief in God at all, its God is the conclusion of an inferential process; His Nature is conceived in whatever way the form of philosophy in question finds necessary in order to make Him the solution of its perplexities. He may be a Person, or an Impersonal Absolute, or Union of all Opposites – whichever will meet the facts from which the philosophy set out.

But religion is not a discovery of man at all. It is indeed an attitude of man's heart and mind and will; but it is an attitude towards a God, or something put in the place of a God, who (or which) is supposed to exist independently of our attitude. In particular, Christianity is either sheer illusion, or else it is the self-revelation of God. The religious man believes in God quite independently of philosophic reasons for doing so; he believes in God because he has a conviction that God has taken hold of him. Consequently, in theology, which is the science of religion, God is not the conclusion but the starting-point. Religion does not argue to a First Cause or a Master-Designer or any other such conclusion; it breaks in upon our habitual experience – 'Thus saith the Lord.' It does not say that as nature, in the form of human nature, possesses conscience, therefore the Infinite Ground of nature must be moral; it says that God has issued orders, and man's duty is therefore to obey. If the religion is one of fear, it may be something far inferior to naked ethics; but if it is of love then it is far superior. Anyhow, it starts with God, whose Being and Nature are its primary certainties; it goes on to show, so far as it can, that God, as He has revealed Himself, is indeed the solution of our problems. In the language of the old-fashioned Euclid, philosophy attempts a problem – to construct a conception of God equal to the universe; theology attempts a theorem – to show that our God is equal to the universe.

Now, it is abundantly clear that a perfect theology and a perfect philosophy would coincide. There can only be one Truth. And it is one of the great glories of Christianity that it has fully recognised this. It insists that the Life of Christ is an act of God; Christ did not emerge out of the circumstances of His time; He is not just the supreme achievement of man in his search for God; He is God Himself, 'who for us men and for our salvation came down from heaven'. And yet He is also, in perfect manifestation, the Eternal Wisdom of God, which was in the beginning with God, and apart from which there hath never a thing happened. He is that which philosophers would have found if they could have collected the whole universe of facts and reasoned with perfect cogency concerning them.

But while theology and philosophy are ideally identical in result, though not in process, it is equally plain that they are not at all identical in their present stage of development. Philosophy working inwards from the circumference, and theology working outwards from the centre, have not yet met, at least in such a way as to present a single system whose combination of comprehensiveness and coherence would supply a guarantee of its truth. The Christian who is also in any degree a philosopher will not claim that by reason he can irrefragably establish his faith; indeed, it is possible that his search may lead him to nothing but perplexity, from which he saves himself only by falling back upon his unreasoned convictions, which come to him from the authority of the saints or from his own specifically religious experience. In the same way his theology may fail to give a satisfying account of empirical facts – of this war, for example, and all its horrors; but he still believes that by loyalty to his central conviction he will find his way through the maze at last. We live by faith and not by sight. But the aim of this book is to indicate a real unity between faith and knowledge as something to which we can even now in part attain.

We shall watch the Creative Mind [*Mens Creatrix*] of Man as it builds its Palace of Knowledge, its Palace of Art, its Palace of Civilisation, its Palace of Spiritual Life. And we shall find that each edifice is incomplete in a manner that threatens its security. Then we shall see that the Creative Mind of God, in whose image Man was made, has offered the Revelation of Itself to be the foundation of all that the Human Mind can wish to build. Here is the security we seek; here, and nowhere else. 'Other foundations can no man lay than that which is laid, which is Jesus Christ.'

Yet even at the last the security is of Faith and not of Knowledge; it is not won by intellectual grasp but by personal loyalty; and its test is not in logic only, but in life.

ii Knowledge and Personality: The Society of Intellects

An important stage in Temple's argument is the move from the observations of philosophy to the doctrines of Christianity. The extract below is part of this move, still at this point using abstract philosophical language. It brings together some of his leading themes, such as the link between value and meaning, and the central place of a mind (or 'Mind') to the meaning of this universe. It introduces the key concept of 'personality' in his metaphysics, which gives human community an essential role in the full apprehension of reality, something that will undergird his social thinking (see Chapter 5).

Chapter VIII, 'Knowledge and Personality: The Society of Intellects', pp. 82–6

Actual knowledge is not only the work of Mind but of this mind and that mind. Every mind is a separate focus of the universe; according to its capacity it apprehends the World about it, and according to its instinct for totality (or will to know) it tries to increase its range and hold together in a united system all that it can experience. We conceived at the end of the last chapter a mind whose range was that of the whole universe. Such a mind would be in possession of all truth.

And yet it would focus it in its own way. For its apprehension must always be coloured by the history preceding and conditioning it. No amount of development of my mind can make irrelevant the circumstances of my birth and early training, the ease or difficulty with which various departments of knowledge have been, or hereafter shall be, mastered. If not the knowledge itself, yet its preciousness is vitally affected by the mode of its attainment. And here as elsewhere there are values of great excellence, which are yet not compatible with one another, and must be realised, if at all, in different subjects.

We have introduced the category of Value; and that carries us on at once to a new stage of the enquiry. We now need to make a distinction, somewhat parallel to that drawn by Locke between Primary and Secondary Qualities. Without entering on the controversy between Realism and Idealism, we can see that there are certain propositions which are true (if at all) for all minds, and some which are only true for certain minds; or perhaps it is more accurate to say that certain aspects of reality are only actualised in the experience of certain minds.

Thus the qualities which can be mathematically estimated are identical for all intelligences; but there are other qualities, equally real, which vary from one person to another. The colour of a red and green object has a totally different aesthetic value for a man with normal sight from that which it has for a colour-blind man; the very words 'red' and 'green' have different meanings for the two men. But the statements of optical science as regards 'wave-lengths' in the ethereal undulations and so forth have the same meaning for all minds which attach any meaning to them at all.

It is to be noticed that the variable element is always to some degree adjectival; it is a product of the qualities which are mathematically determinable and therefore constant in the sense of identical for all intelligences. But these 'secondary' qualities, to use Locke's term, are perfectly real, whether they are in the object or in the percipient, or are produced by the meeting together of these two; these qualities are real, but certain persons can never apprehend them.

We have considered the most elementary case; but it is clear that there is a peculiar excellence in the easy grace of a character richly endowed by nature and developed by favourable conditions; there is another excellence in the grit and force of a character richly endowed by nature and developed through a persistent struggle with unfavourable conditions; and there is yet another excellence in the steady worth of a character not richly endowed which is content to fulfill conscientiously the tasks for which it is fitted. These three types cannot be realised in the same person. Again each of these three types will be appreciative of different excellences and so bring to its completion a different function of Reality. In countless ways it appears that only through the diversity of personalities is the whole of Reality apprehended or its whole Truth known. For it seems impossible to deny that when a beautiful object is appreciated, it gains in quality itself.

Whether or not a thing can fitly be called beautiful if no one can see it, I do not know; but I am quite clear that, if no one can see it, it does not matter whether it is beautiful or not. Its value begins when it is appreciated. Good must mean good for somebody; apart from consciousness, value is non-existent.

And yet it seems impossible to say that the value is in the appreciating mind. It exists for it, and only so; but it is in the object. So the object when appreciated becomes something which it was not until then. But if so, and if there are various Values which cannot be all realised for the same consciousness, then the variety of intelligences is necessary for the full actualisation of the value of the world. The complete truth, therefore, if we include Value, is only grasped by the whole society of intelligences, and can never be fully grasped by one alone.

This phase of the subject cannot be ignored. For the value-judgment – even within the realm of Art – is still a judgment, an act of the intellect. It is possible to conceive a state of things where every one made the same value-judgments, but only if many of these are accepted from others on trust; and there is a clear difference between the judgment 'This is beautiful', where it is a real analysis of experience, and 'This is beautiful' where it is a repetition of the verdict of an expert: in the former case it means, 'This gives me aesthetic pleasure', while in the latter it means, at best, 'This would give aesthetic pleasure to any one of sufficiently trained susceptibilities', and in this case the value is itself still potential and not actual.

But our value-judgments depend upon our characters – not just our moral character, but upon the whole psychic quality of our nature. This looks as if we were reduced to utter chaos, for it is clear that no one man can dictate what values another ought to find. But inasmuch as there is a particular character which every individual, as this member of the society of spirits, ought to make his own, so, by consequence, there are certain values which he ought to appreciate and thereby actualise.

So when we consider our experience as it is handled by knowledge, we find a world which is known and appreciated by the whole society of finite intelligences. The whole grasp of their collective experience cannot be held in one centre of consciousness however 'Absolute' or 'Infinite', because some of the elements are intrinsically incompatible. There cannot be one Mind which includes all of this. The Absolute Being (so far) appears precisely as the society of intelligences.

But why should we bring in the Absolute Being at this point at all? We are bound to do so because the impulse of Self-Transcendence, of which the Will to Know is one manifestation, is always an impulse to the Whole; it reveals itself alike in the sacrifice of love or loyalty and in the search of science; it is the determination to get beyond one's mere particularity (though we can never leave it behind), and apprehend the whole and our place in it and dependence on it; 'Love is the mainspring of logic.' And this effort towards the Whole is stultified, and therefore all science is in principle stultified (for science is a phase of this effort), unless there is a Whole.

But this Whole or Absolute appears at this stage only as the physical world and the perfected – or rather the mutually self-perfecting – society of spirits. And this is a real Whole. From the standpoint of the Will to Know we can demand no more. The intellect working only upon the principles of its own procedure will never lead to the Transcendent God of Religion, for its claims can be satisfied with less, and the further step is a leap in the dark such as Science may not take.

Let us, however, not underestimate what is implied in the Will to Know. The conception of the Universe coming to focus in a multitude of intelligences, and realising its own value in their manifold appreciation of it, is not a notion which degrades our spiritual life; nor is it alien from the life of religion; for this Society of Spirits is the Communion of Saints, and the agency that builds it up is the Holy Church, which is that Communion as so far realised and active, and its spirit of self-transcendence and self-sacrifice (which are two names for one thing) is the Holy Spirit.

For the Society of Intelligences in which the truth and value of the world is grasped must be independent of the chances of Time. If the value realised by the heroes and artists of antiquity is simply perished, and other similar values come into being and again pass out of it almost daily, and if this flux is all that can be said to be at all, then our Society and the world of values make up no Whole at all, and again the effort towards the Whole is stultified. Somehow that Whole must be Supra-temporal, and hold within itself all the values realised in all the ages.

iii The Word Incarnate

The climax of the argument in Mens Creatrix *is where Christ is introduced as the one who sums up and expresses this 'Whole', which is the incarnation of Mind. The chapter, though, does not base its argument within philosophy but, vividly, within historical theology and especially the history of Israel. A contrast is drawn between the kind of messiah expected by the Jews and the actual messiahship of Christ himself, who does not bring salvation through force and coercion but through seeking to win the hearts and affection of the people. This leads into one of Temple's finest expositions of his life, death and resurrection and the way these events express both something new, the in-breaking of God's revelation, and something already immanent within world history, its fundamental meaning. The incarnation expresses both the immanence and transcendence of God. Drawing heavily on the Fourth Gospel, Temple gives an account of the victory and glory of the cross and then of the resurrection and the role of the Spirit in making all this real in our own lives. The chapter ends with a ringing description of the victory achieved by Christ on the cross over the darkness and power of evil.*

Chapter XXIII, 'The Word Incarnate', pp. 311–23

There had been in the religion of Israel two forms of anticipation of a Divine Deliverer. The earlier of these had represented Him as accomplishing His purpose by the ordinary methods of an earthly monarch. His purpose would indeed be perfect righteousness, but His means would not be different from those which other kings employed. In a certain sense the deification of the Caesars may be said to represent a similar outlook among other nations. These, indeed, had not anticipated any heaven-sent king; but the impulse to hail as divine the Caesars who had established peace throughout the world and had given to mankind the undoubted benefits of Roman law, was akin to the earlier form of the Messianic hope. At a later time among the Jews an anticipation had arisen that the Messiah would do His work by Divine authority manifestly displayed. He would give the sign from heaven which would convince the most obstinate; in other words, He would inaugurate the Kingdom by miracle. This view of the matter holds the field with many variations in the apocalyptic writers of the second and first centuries before Christ. The Jews' demand for a sign comes quite straight from it, and the Greeks' desire for wisdom is not essentially alien from it. For their hope was to receive a proof which would entirely convince the intellect.

Mingled with both of these anticipations there is a certain strain of selfishness, for each of them requires that the claim of the Kingdom shall make itself good through the process of rendering it worth while for men to accept it. And so lying behind both of them there is in reality the suggestion that the Messiah shall bribe men to accept Him. There was, however, a profound truth in both the anticipations. The Messianic work was to be the culmination of all that kings and kingdoms strive to be; it was also to be a manifestation of the Divine power and wisdom in their fullness; but in the form which the Jews had given to their hope, it was defective because it failed to operate through the free will of men. The Kingdom of God must be the Kingdom of the Almighty, the All-Ruler; but the Almighty only rules over all if He controls not only our conduct but also our hearts and wills. These can neither be bought nor coerced. A man's action may be determined by force through his fear of penalty; his heart and will can only be controlled by the manifestation of love. There is as a mere matter of fact nothing else which is effective to change the motives and inclinations. Consequently the political Messiah and the apocalyptic Messiah were alike inadequate to the task which they were to accomplish.

At the beginning of His Ministry our Lord faced and rejected all these suggestions. The power with which, as Messiah, He was endowed could not be used merely to satisfy His own or other people's creature comforts. In the service of His Kingdom, He would indeed feed the hungry and heal the sick, but this was not to be the basis of His work; it was the mere automatic action of love possessing power when confronted with human need. Those whom He healed were to say nothing about it; and when His works of healing created popular excitement, He immediately withdrew and would not continue his proclamation of the coming Kingdom in that atmosphere. So again when He thought of the kingdoms of the earth and the glory of them, He would not claim them as He might upon their own terms, the terms of the Prince of this world. To do that would be merely to repeat the rule of Caesar Augustus on a higher moral level. Not so should the Kingdom of God come in. Nor will he give to Himself or to others the sign from Heaven which shall establish His authority for ever. What could be further from discipleship than one who was convinced that Christ is the revelation of God, while wishing all the time that He were not? In rejecting the three temptations He has resolved that He will not cajole, He will not coerce, and He will not demonstrate. He will use none of the means by which men's conduct may be controlled otherwise than through the free devotion of their hearts and wills. But He will live in the spirit of Holy Love and in that spirit die. By the Resurrection, God set His seal upon this life as that of His own Son, and so while the Greeks seek wisdom and the Jews a sign, the disciple of Christ proclaims 'a Messiah on a Cross, to Jews a scandal and to Gentiles an absurdity, but to the very people who are called both Jews and Greeks a Messiah who is power and God's wisdom' (1 Cor. 1.23-24).

The Kingdom was to be based upon the free response of the human heart to the love expressed in love's own act of sacrifice. But it was to be a real Kingdom, which has laws that are the fulfilment or completion of all other laws. Other legislation aims at maintaining the life of a community or fellowship against the impulses and passions that would lead men to destroy the community or make its life impossible. The laws of this Kingdom are for those who have come to understand what fellowship is and to value it for its own sake. They are the laws which regulate the relations of men who are already in fellowship with one another. This is the whole significance of the Sermon on the Mount; it is the climax or 'fulfilment' of the Mosaic law and all other legislative systems. Its method is different because the objects at which those systems aim are steps to be secured before it is set in operation. In fact its laws merely work out the principles involved in the belief that man's true nature is found in his membership of the Kingdom where Christ is King.

But as the Kingdom is a real one and the anticipation of the earlier prophets is fulfilled, so is the manifestation of Divine power and wisdom also real and the anticipation of the apocalyptists is fulfilled. For when once the love of God is declared there is found in that love the one power which can convince the heart and will, a power stronger than even irresistible force. The Lion of the tribe of Judah is no Lion but 'a Lamb standing, as it had been slain' (which is to say living with the marks of sacrificial death upon Him) (Rev. 5.5, 6). This faith can only maintain itself if it is accepted in all its completeness. If we begin by saying that God is Love and then make up our image of love and our own suppositions with regard to its action, we may very easily produce a conception of God which the whole of the universe at every step repudiates, and which is morally enervating to ourselves. Everything depends upon what we really think good for man. The parent who supposes that enjoyment is the end of life will show love for his child by leniency and indulgence, and when God's government of the universe seems to be the very opposite of lenience and indulgence both the man and his children will be likely to say that God is no loving Father. But if what is good for man is to be made like Christ, to be used and used up in the service of God and men; and if love aims rather at the formation of a character which has in itself the secrets of joy and peace because it is rooted in love, discipline will at once appear to be as essential an activity of love as any indulgence can ever be. Men have so long spoken of Christ as one who was most obviously meek and gentle, that other elements in His nature have been obscured; but certainly the fierceness of His anger against hardness and self-complacency are quite as conspicuous features of the Gospel portrait as His gentleness towards those whom the world called sinners. He is in many respects a terrible figure – an austere and lonely figure. Only once did one of His disciples venture to offer Him advice; then the answer was – 'Get thee behind me, Satan.' Many men were afraid of Him; even those who came to arrest Him went backward and fell to the ground when He came out from the garden enclosure and stood defenceless before them. It was only children who were entirely free from fear or wonder in His presence; and perhaps this fact is connected with His requirement that we should become as little children if we are to enter His Kingdom.

Those who were still innocent, or who knew themselves to be sinners, found from Him the readiest and tenderest welcome; but those who were full of self-concern, who had a pride to maintain and appearances to keep up, did not find in Him unmixed gentleness. On the contrary there are no denunciations so terrible as those which He launched at the self-satisfied good folk. They are all the more terrible because of their complete freedom from personal bitterness. He stood among men ready to save, but for that precise reason always pronouncing judgment; for He offered life, and those who rejected the offer were thereby involved in condemnation. So He spoke of Himself as a stone whom the builders rejected, a stone on which whosoever should fall would be broken: but on whomsoever it should fall it would scatter him as dust. This picture of Him as inevitably pronouncing judgment is one great characteristic of the Fourth Gospel. St John sees Him standing among men unchanged Himself while they react to His influence in the most diverse ways. Gradually the followers and rejectors are sifted out from one another and stand in two opposing groups. His presence in the world constitutes the world's judgment. It supposes itself to pronounce judgment on Him; but therein it is in fact itself subjected to judgment. 'Now is the judgment of this world' are words spoken in close connection with the sentence of death which He knows that the world is about to pronounce upon Him.

All of this is in the strictest harmony with the Figure set before us by the Synoptists, when we have learned to read their story rightly and without the sentimentalism which we have allowed to colour our interpretation. But it also fits peculiarly with the governing thought of St John's Gospel, which pervades and interprets the whole. The Lord is here set forth not merely as the promised Messiah, but as the manifestation once for all of the eternal principle which governs the universe. The Logos was a familiar enough conception at that time; it stood for that over-ruling and unifying principle which the mind must inevitably presuppose when it starts upon its work of explaining the world in which we live. With this sense it had been used by heathen philosophers, and by theologians in Alexandria it had been connected with the Word of the Lord in the Old Testament. St John begins his Gospel with commonplaces; yet these commonplaces are full of the most far-reaching implications; for they involve that it is of the very nature of God that He should reveal Himself. The Logos, thought or speech, is the means by which a mind reveals itself to another. To say then that this eternally exists in relation to God and is itself Divine is to affirm of God that He is in His own nature self-revealing. The whole process of that revelation which has been going on through nature, through history and through prophets, comes to complete fulfilment in the Incarnation.

We are thus given the union of two points of view: which as a matter of fact it is very hard to hold together, but on the combination of which all real understanding of the revelation of Christ depends. Upon the one side this revelation is an altogether new fact; it does not rise out of the previous history of the world, though the previous history of the world had been so guided as to prepare for it. It is an invasion from without. And yet what thus breaks in is itself the power which had always been in control. It was not an alien principle coming into the world but precisely He by whom the world was made and apart from whom, as St John with emphasis declares, there has not even one thing happened. We cannot therefore think of the world as something which, even for a moment, moves independently of God, and which God intervenes to correct or adjust; but neither on the other hand can we think of the world-process in anything less than its entirety as supplying an exposition of the Divine purpose in Christ. Only in the life of Christ is this manifestation given. What we see in Him is what we should see in the history of the universe if we could apprehend that history in its completeness. (Note: And even then it is to be remembered that we have not the World-History without the Incarnation as one expression of the Divine Will and the Life of the Incarnate as another; for that Life is a part of History, though it reveals the principle of the whole, and it is through its occurrence in the midst of History that History is fashioned into an exposition of the principle there revealed. We have here a series which is part of another series and is yet perfectly representative of it. (Cf. the Supplementary Essay in Royce's *The World and the Individual*.) But here the series which is contained (the Life, Death, Resurrection of Christ) only becomes representative of the series which contains it (the entire history of the world) in virtue of the influence which by occurring within the latter it is able to exercise upon it. Therefore, though Transcendence and Immanence are fused into one, the Transcendent aspect is always dominant.) What have been called immanence and transcendence are here perfectly combined, and this without the smallest sacrifice of one to the other. They are not merely held together; they are fused into each other. Our faith is fixed upon One 'Who for us men and for our salvation came down from Heaven', and who yet had been always in the world, the Creator of all things and the Light that lighteneth every man.

This complete fusion of the transcendent with the immanent is made most of all manifest by St John's habitual use of the term 'glory'. St Paul had used language suggesting that our Lord had left the glory of Heaven when He came on earth, returning to it after His Resurrection; and this language of course expresses one truth about the matter, for the humiliation and the sacrifice were voluntarily undertaken. Yet St John takes us deeper with his insistence that the humiliation and the sacrifice are themselves the culmination of the glory. 'The Word was made flesh and we beheld His glory.' The word 'glory' is used with increasing frequency as the Passion approaches. The threefold expression – 'The hour is come that the Son of Man should be glorified'; 'Now is the Son of Man glorified'; 'The hour is come, glorify thy Son' – all have direct reference to the Passion and its fruit.

In the High-priestly prayer, in which the Son dedicates Himself to the final sacrifice, His prayer is that He may now be glorified with the eternal glory which he had with the Father before the world was. When the sacrifice is made perfect, the manifestation of the glory is made complete. And what is thus manifested is something eternal and not momentary. The Passion and the Resurrection are two sides of one truth. It was necessary that they should be set forth successively. If we think of a triumph won by sacrifice either the cost will dim the brightness of the triumph or the triumph will irradiate the darkness of sacrifice. He must pass through the uttermost defeat, and the sense that even God has deserted Him, if out of the very depths of defeat He is to bring victory, and the light from the darkest of all possible gloom. But this is His glory – the completeness of the sacrifice and the completeness of the triumph which by that sacrifice He wins. Therein His work is in one sense accomplished; the prefect revelation has been given, and through it the power of God in its plenitude is at work among men.

But if the victory is won, its fruit is still to be gathered. The realisation, in actual effect and upon the plane of history, of all that is involved in God's self-revelation is the work of the Spirit. God's power and love had indeed been guiding and controlling human history before Christ came; the eternal word was operative from the beginning and without Him hath not one thing happened. But one department remained in which this power could never reach its fullness while it remained to a great extent unknown. The free spirit of man, his heart and will, can only fully respond to an influence which it understands; and so, though God was guiding men in all the ages before the Incarnation, that guidance took a new form from the time of the Incarnation onwards. It is this new power of God (which is after all the old power mediated through its complete revelation) which St John calls the 'Spirit'. It could not come before the Incarnation simply because it is the operation of God through the revelation of Himself in intelligible form. 'There was not yet Spirit because Jesus was not yet glorified.' The Holy Spirit is the Word of God with the new power or influence which the Word acquired by becoming incarnate. (Note: This is not all that is to be said, but it is true as far as it goes.) So it may truly be said that it was in order to make possible the coming of the Spirit that Christ was born. It is not to the historic figure living at men's side that we are to cling, but to the same Divine Being present within our souls: 'It is expedient for you that I go away: for if I go not away, the Comforter will not come unto you; but if I depart, I will send him unto you.'

But while it is true that it was only to make possible the advent of the Spirit that Christ was born, it is equally important that it is only through His Birth and Life and Death and Resurrection that the Spirit could be sent. The new power is precisely that which is won through giving men a real understanding of and insight into the Divine love. To know that love is to be one of the elect who are sanctified by the Holy Spirit. St John after his manner represents this new power that should come upon those who had received the full revelation, by means of two contrasted episodes in the life of one of the Apostles. Before the Crucifixion the Lord declared that to the place where He was now going His disciples could not yet follow Him, for He was going to that innermost presence of God which is the absolute self-sacrifice of love, and there they could not follow. 'Whither I go, thou canst not follow me now; but thou shalt follow afterwards.' When the sacrifice had been completed, and the Lord had given His charge to this same Apostle, He looks forward to St Peter's death, contrasting his submission then with his earlier impulsiveness: 'When thou wast young, thou girdedst thyself, and walkedst whither thou wouldest: but when thou shalt be old, thou shalt stretch forth thy hands, and another shall gird thee, and carry thee whither thou wouldest not. Now this He spake signifying by what manner of death He should glorify God. And when He had spoken this He saith unto him, Follow me.' The following to that uttermost sacrifice, in which love is made perfect and which is therefore the presence of God, is now enjoined upon that Apostle for whom it was earlier impossible; for the revelation has been given and therein the power.

This episode recalls us to the fact already glanced at, that Christ in His earthly life is the greatest of all heroes. In the manner of His own life, and in His appeal to His followers, this is the supreme characteristic. He is one who is ready to face anything; and calls upon His followers to be ready to face anything, for the sake of the cause with which He is entrusted, and for the service of the Kingdom which He came to found. His life is a life of love; but His love shows itself not so much in giving comfort as in calling others to a love like His own, and, if that be involved, to sufferings like His own. His love is very terrible to all that is soft or self-indulgent or even self-regarding in our nature. He offers us Love, the greatest of all gifts. If we reject it, we reject the very principle of life and commit ourselves to death and destruction. Therefore though the purpose of His coming is our salvation, its result is always judgment. By the Judgment which crushes and breaks up the hard crust of self we are made at last if not at first responsive to love's appeal, so that the very pain which self-will causes becomes, when the judgment is fallen, the means of winning us from self and moulding us in the likeness of the Love which we had despised.

The Cross and Resurrection of Christ are the conquest not only of death, but of sin which brought Him to death. The powers of evil never achieved anything so great as when they secured the condemnation of the Lord of glory. Never was darkness so deep as that darkness of despair out of which the Divine Sufferer cried, 'My God, my God, why hast thou forsaken me?' This was no failure of right, due to the fact that its supporters were themselves tainted with evil or lacking in wisdom. When our attempts to serve God fail, We naturally suppose that we ourselves must be failing in some way or other to follow His will. But on the day of the Crucifixion the very cause of God, served with undeviating loyalty to the very method of God, was failing. God was rejected, and successfully rejected, in His own world. Evil was triumphant. So for the time at least it seemed to the Lord Himself; the God who had sent Him was failing Him: 'My God, my God, why hast thou forsaken me?' And this deep anguish, beyond what any of us can ever know, stands before us for evermore as something that has place in the very life and experience of God. For He who cried thus to His Father is He who also said, 'He that hath seen me hath seen the Father.' The evil that is in the world, and in our own heart, could bring this agony of despair upon the omnipotent and eternal God.

It is out of that uttermost gloom that the light breaks. The light does not merely shine upon the gloom and so dispel it; it is the gloom itself transformed into light. For that same crucifixion of the Lord which was, and for ever is, the utmost effort of evil, is itself the means by which God conquers evil and unites us to Himself in the redeeming love there manifested. Judas and Caiaphas and Pilate had set themselves in their several ways to oppose and to crush the purpose of Christ, and yet despite themselves they became its ministers. They sent Christ to the Cross; by the Cross He completed His atoning work; from the Cross He reigns over mankind. God in Christ has not merely defeated evil, but has made it the occasion of His own supremest glory. Never was conquest so complete; never was triumph so stupendous. The completeness of the victory is due to the completeness of the evil over which it was won. It is the very darkness which enshrouds the Cross that makes so glorious the light proceeding from it. Had there been no despair, no sense of desolation and defeat, but merely the onward march of irresistible power to the achievement of its end, evil might have been beaten, but not bound in captivity to love for ever. God in Christ endured defeat, and out of the very stuff of defeat He wrought His victory and His achievement. Language must be tortured to make it express what we see here. It is not only the enemy that was conquered; defeat itself was defeated, captivity was led captive, and its shame converted into the splendour of triumph.

Rooted upon this Divine achievement, the believer awaits whatever comes. His Master has conquered death and sin. He sees Him as His disciple saw Him (Rev. 1), clothed in the garments of a glorified High Priest; He has the snow-white hair of eternity; and the flaming eyes of omniscience, from which no secret can be hid; His feet of burnished brass affirm the immovableness of His authority, and the voice as the sound of many waters His right to command; He holds in His hand the seven stars, for He is the sustainer of the universe and the constellations move at His bidding; the tongue-like sword proceeds from His mouth, for every word He speaks is judgment; His countenance as the sun shining in His strength proclaims the Majesty of Him who dwells in the light that no man may approach unto. He is the Lord of Life and Death; He is Guide of all human history; and nothing can be done but under His supremacy.

3

Teaching the Faithful: Westminster Sermons, 1919–20

In 1919 Temple completed his campaigning work for the Life and Liberty movement. The Enabling Act, providing self-government for the Church of England, would soon become law. He now needed a job and was offered a canonry at Westminster Abbey. This would allow him to continue to have a role and voice in the national church and this attracted him. He wrote to his wife that Westminster would give

> what I think I most need after these three years of rushing about – and that is the opportunity and even duty to 'worship the Lord in the beauty of holiness'. I want (need) to renew depth in religious life, and the peace which goes with it, if I am to have anything to interpret to the world at all ... Anyhow, I hope and believe this will [also] give us more time together in some degree of peace ... But there is a lot to pray about, and I had better begin. (Iremonger 1948, p. 265)

While at Westminster his main work became the preaching duties of a canon, and the results are seen in a volume of published sermons, Fellowship with God *(1920). Through many of the sermons Temple urges that the fundamental fact about human life is that God, in his love, has entered into fellowship with humanity through the incarnation, so that human life may, in answering love, enter into fellowship with him. The social dimension of this relationship, implicit in the word fellowship, was all-important for Temple and provides a connection with his developing views on society and the state. But he argues that this response is not to take place through the practical life alone, but 'in the perfect blend' of the practical life with the devotional life (p. vi). Up to now he had neglected the devotional life in his campaigning work for Life and Liberty. At Westminster, he intended to give more time to this. And it seems to have happened because these sermons show him articulating some of the deepest spiritual insights to be found in any of his publications, alongside other statements that are very much of his time and not ours.*

i The Eternal God

Sermon V, pp. 57–70

Westminster Abbey, August 31st, 1919.

> 'Lord, thou hast been our dwelling place in all generations. Before the mountains were brought forth, or ever thou hadst formed the earth and the World, even from everlasting to everlasting, thou art God.' Psalm 90.1, 2

> 'Our fellowship is with the Father.' 1 John 1.3

The heart of religion is communion with the eternal. We rise above the tumult and conflict, above even the moral effort, of our normal life to the realm of eternal truth where the ideal is always realised, and perfection alone is actual. Our Lord taught us to pray that God's will may be done on earth as it is in heaven. In our best worship we ascend in heart and mind to the heaven where that Will is always done. We cannot permanently live there. Duty calls us back to the world of moral striving; our faults of character stand out in the clear light of the Divine Presence, and we sink from adoration to penitence even as Isaiah exclaimed, 'Woe is me, for I am a man of unclean lips', so soon as his eyes had seen the Lord of Hosts and his ears heard the song of the attendant seraphim. But though we cannot dwell permanently on the heights of adoration, all our spiritual health depends upon our rising to them from time to time, and it is good for us to fix in our minds by deliberate meditation the various aspects of our vision in those sacred moments.

Among these, and perhaps chief among them, is the eternity, the changeless perfection, of God. The world in which we live is always changing; it derives its whole meaning from the changes that take place in it. The development of natural science has shewn us that this is true of the animal and physical world, as well as of human history. In the first impetus of this idea men began to speak of the evolution of God and to insist that He, too, derives His significance and value from the changes that pass over Him. No doubt the course of history, natural and human deeply concerns the Creator. No doubt His purpose in Creation is progressively realised, and to that extent there is a progress from glory to glory which may be ascribed to God Himself. But if we take this development to be the last word, we make nonsense of the universe, and we deny the intimations that come through worship at its best and truest. When we lift our souls to God in adoration we do not have to ascertain afresh each time what degree of perfection He has now attained. He is always the same; our understanding of His glory may develop, but He Himself is unchanging. What we find Him to be, that Abraham also found when He communed with God and said, 'Shall not the Judge of all the earth do right?' What we find Him to be, that will unborn generations still find when science has revolutionised a dozen more times the external ordering of life, or when (God grant it may be so) the Spirit of Christ has transformed men's souls so that war and greed and bitterness are known no longer. Men change; if they cease to change they are dead. But God does not change; His very Life is eternal changelessness.

The expression of this truth to the mind and thought of men was rather the task of Greek philosophers than of Hebrew prophets. But the whole religion of ancient Israel is based upon it. The Name by which God reveals Himself to Moses – 'I am that I am'– expresses it, while also signifying His manifold revelation of Himself to His people. But apart from utterances so explicit we find from the beginning of the Bible to the end that this changelessness of God is everywhere implied. The covenant made with Noah is 'an everlasting covenant between God and every living creature of all flesh that is upon the earth'. The generations come and go, but God is unalterably the same. We have the same implication in the Second Commandment. But it is, as we should expect, by the Prophets and Psalmists that the spiritual value of the truth of God's eternity is most strongly emphasised. 'Thus saith the high and lofty One that inhabiteth eternity, whose name is Holy' are words introducing one of the noblest oracles of the Second Isaiah. But we find no nobler expression of it than in the 90th Psalm: 'Before the mountains were brought forth, or ever thou hadst formed the earth and the World, even from everlasting to everlasting, thou art God.' Or we may quote the words which are cited by the author of the Epistle to the Hebrews from the 102nd Psalm: 'Thou, Lord, in the beginning hast laid the foundation of the earth; and the heavens are the works of thy hands. They shall perish, but thou continuest, and they all shall wax old as doth a garment; and as a mantle shalt thou roll them up, as a garment, and they shall be changed: but thou art the same, and thy years shall not fail.'

In this contrast between our life, which 'creeps in its petty pace from day to day', and the Eternal God, in whose sight a thousand years are but as yesterday, we have the root fact of religion. It is the source of humility; for what is the greatest of man's achievements in presence of that immutable perfection? It is the source of assurance; for what is the worst of perils in presence of that unalterable glory? All that is mine disappears as I contemplate God's everlasting power and divinity. For 'all flesh is grass and all the goodliness thereof is as the flower of the field; the grass withereth, the flower fadeth'. What is not mine but God's, the cause of His righteousness, the beauty of His truth, the depth of His love – these things become more glorious in that same contemplation; for though 'the grass withereth and the flower fadeth', yet 'the word of our God shall stand for ever'. Men perish, but God endures.

As God led His people to the ever deeper knowledge of His unchanging Nature, this was among the first truths that He impressed upon them, even as it is among the first that we learn through our experience in worship. But along with it and closely interwoven with it was the truth of His holiness. He is unchanging because He is already and always perfect. The littleness of transitory man before the eternal God is emphasised by the meanness of selfish and greedy man before the God of purer eyes than to behold iniquity, in whose sight the very heavens are not clean.

In Jewish worship this was expressed by the awful seclusion of the Holy of Holies. That space where no image might be set up, was veiled from the eyes of men and only entered once a year on the Day of Atonement by the High Priest alone, who first passed through a solemn purification. So unapproachable was the Holy God. And here once more we find an ineradicable element of our own experience in worship. It is certainly a mistake to try to create a sense of sin in those who have as yet no realisation of God, but it is certainly an inevitable result of any realisation of God that a sense of sin takes possession of the soul. The first result of the vision of God must always be to throw us on our knees in shame for our own unworthiness. We cannot know God and still be self-complacent.

Men perish, but God endures: God is holy, but men are sinful. In those two contrasts spiritual religion has its birth. It was the supreme function of the revelation to ancient Israel to press those contrasts to the very uttermost. There are other truths beside these, some plainly taught and some obscurely intimated or felt after. But these two contrasts between God and men are the central thought of the Old Testament Scriptures, and they could not be more sharply set. 'From everlasting to everlasting Thou art God . . . we bring our years to an end as a tale that is told.' 'What is man, that he should be clean? And he which is born of a woman that he should be righteous? Behold, He putteth no trust in His holy ones; yea, the heavens are not clean in His sight. How much less one that is abominable and corrupt, a man that drinketh iniquity like water?' God reveals Himself to man; God has even entered the field of history and taken action for the deliverance of His people. There are bonds of gratitude from man to God, and a yearning love of God to man. But fellowship, communion of heart and will and nature? No; that is for ever impossible. 'God is in heaven and thou upon earth.' There is no fellowship of the perishing with the eternal, of the base with the holy. There is no fellowship of man with God.

'Our fellowship is with the Father.' St John makes his declaration with the whole doctrine of the Old Testament behind him. He has not come to this great conviction by any easy way such as many a Greek might have trod, for whom there was no vast gulf between human and divine to be bridged. God for the Christian evangelists and prophets is the infinitely exalted God of Moses and Isaiah and Ezekiel; man is the poor transient sinful being who consumes away in God's displeasure. The gulf is there, and by man it cannot be bridged. But the bridge has been built. 'Our fellowship is with the Father.' We are called to be 'partakers of the Divine Nature'. But we miss the revolutionary power of this declaration if we think of this fellowship as easy and natural, whether from God's side or from ours. From our side it is not easy or natural; it is impossible. From God's side it is natural indeed but not easy; it is accomplished through the Cross.

A great deal of modern religious thought prides itself upon its sure grasp of the doctrine of the Father's love. It deprecates all language of anxious approach or prostrate submission; the loving Father will not desire such an attitude in His children. But the truth of the Father's love becomes a dangerous error if it is forgotten who and what the heavenly Father is; it quickly degenerates into the 'good fellow' of Fitzgerald's 'Omar': 'He's a good fellow and 'twill all be Well.' Our fellowship is with 'the high and lofty One that inhabiteth eternity, whose name is Holy'. Our fellowship with Him may be intimate, but it cannot be familiar; it may be affectionate, but it cannot be casual. The fear of God of which the Old Testament Scriptures are full, the sense of littleness and worthlessness before God, never ceases. Any fear which consists in dread of punishment is cast out by perfect love; but not the sense of our insignificance and meanness. Therefore also, even when all terror is banished by love, our freedom before God is a conscious boldness. 'Having, therefore, brethren, boldness to enter into the holy place.' 'If our heart condemn us not we have boldness towards God.' Some moderns talk as though there were no need of boldness in approaching the

Most High God. Probably their language is misleading; but if not, we are driven to the conclusion that they have very imperfectly understood 'Him with whom we have to do'.

God is Love; that is the supreme Christian mystery. But it is only a supreme mystery because God is first known as eternal, holy, and almighty. He who is already known as eternal, holy, and almighty is also known to us as Love. This is the good news which apostles proclaim and which Christ died and rose again to vindicate. 'Let us therefore draw near with boldness unto the throne of grace, that we may receive mercy and may find grace to help us in time of need.'

How shall we rightly approach the eternal God so as to find the repose and strength that are in His eternity? Chiefly by dwelling in thought upon His unvarying holiness. To those who do not also know His love, this is crushing as well as uplifting. But we know that the holy God has sought us in our sin and suffered all our sin could do to draw us out of that sin to Himself. To us, therefore, the holiness of God is uplifting only. Let us come to Him to gaze and to enjoy. Our tendency is always to bombard Him with petitions. We scarcely speak to Him in language of our own except to ask for something. We will not let our very worship lift us above the chances and changes of this fleeting world to the realm of eternal holiness. We think of our desires, our needs, our anxieties, or of the evils that beset the world and the problems that perplex our minds. That is right in its place. But let us take care to give much of our time in prayer to fixing our thoughts on God as He is in Himself. In the public services of the Church, do not fear wandering thoughts, provided that they wander upwards. The reader may be praying for Parliament or for the whole state of Christ's church militant here on earth. It is well to join in the actual petitions; but we need not check our minds at such times if they soar towards the contemplation of God Himself while Parliament and Church pass out of our thoughts. It is the other movement of thought that must be checked, the movement away from God and petition to the daily concerns of secular life or the satisfaction of personal desires.

Above all, at the Holy Communion let us not only seek blessings, but rise on the wings of worship to the throne of the eternal God. It is a thousand pities that our reformers put the Prayer of Humble Access where they did. No doubt it expresses the humiliation which must follow on the vision of God to which we are summoned in the *Sanctus*; but it cuts short the moment of exultation and brings us to the Act of Consecration in the mood of suppliants rather than in exultant adoration of our Holy Father, the Almighty and Everlasting God. But there the great words are; let us take care to mean them with profound intention and revel in their praise. Let us rise again to the sublimity of the *Gloria in Excelsis*. Most of our thanksgivings are for mercies bestowed on us; but here is a thanksgiving with no thought of ourselves at all: 'We give thanks to thee for thy great glory.'

'Our fellowship is with the Father'; from communion with the eternal God we draw the strength to change this temporal world. The man who will do most to move the world is not he who concentrates all his attention upon the needs of the world, and dedicates all his energy to reforming labours. The man who will do most to move the world is he who truly dwells with God; for through him there will operate in the world the resources of omnipotence. He will not be weary nor stumble, for he has sources of perpetual refreshment and his feet are set firm upon the rock.

'Lord, Thou hast been our dwelling place in all generations'; 'we who are fatigued by the changes and chances of this fleeting world may repose upon Thy eternal changelessness.'

ii The Comforter

Sermon VII, pp. 81–92

Westminster Abbey, May 2nd, 1920.

> 'It is expedient for you that I go away: for if I go not away, the Comforter will not come unto you; but if I go, I will send him unto you.' John 16.7

'It is expedient for you that I go away.' How could that be true? What blessing can be conceived that is for a moment comparable to the companionship of the incarnate Son of God, the companionship of Jesus? That He should prepare His disciples for His departure, if indeed He must depart, would be natural and intelligible. But how can it be good for them that He should go?

What is the aim of every true educator? It is not to give to his pupils such stimulus and support as will make them dependent upon him at every turn; rather it is to help them in the development of their own capacities in such a way that they may learn to be independent of him. They will always be his debtors; but they will owe him most just in the degree that he avoids imposing his own personality upon them, and allows them to absorb what they can, guiding, steadying, restraining, quickening, but never imposing. The greatness of Socrates as a teacher may be gauged by the fact that at least three totally divergent schools of philosophy claimed him as their founder and chief inspiration. The greatest teachers do not implant in their pupils a body of beliefs or a fixed habit of mind; they evoke a spirit which is identical in all so far as it is of loyalty and devotion, but is different in each so far as it expresses itself in activities or methods.

The process of evoking this spirit is always the same. Educational theories vary from age to age; the curriculum of schools may be indefinitely altered; but the fundamental educational process remains always unaffected. It is the development of the less mature mind through intercourse with the more mature mind and with the deposit of other minds in the form of social traditions and conventions. When a boy goes to school he finds himself at once entangled in a net-work of such traditions; some of them he can at once see to be good; some are good, though at first he does not see their value; some are empty forms; some, probably, are more or less bad. All these traditions are the work, usually the unconscious work of other minds like his own as they passed through the school. In them he is in contact indirectly with those other minds. In the older boys, and still more in the masters, he meets directly with minds more mature than his own. And there may be someone personality who pervades the whole place, some great figure, either of past or present, whose influence seems to dominate all other influences, both strengthening some and moderating others. By sharing that life and holding intercourse, direct or indirect, with all the minds that constitute it, the boy is educated. He receives and assimilates according to his own capacities, and grows to the fulfilment of his own destiny. This ideal may be missed in a great variety of ways, but it remains the normal course of education.

Our spiritual growth follows the same principles. We live among people who have certain standards of life and conduct; these are the product or deposit of countless souls in the generations gone by. By those standards our lives are shaped; by those standards to a very great extent our consciences are formed. But we are brought up also in the Church which is the school of Christ; there, too, we find traditional beliefs and requirements which represent, in a sort of summary, the experience of Christ's pupils. We meet with souls who have developed far towards perfect discipleship, and by our intercourse with them are led to further stages of our own development. Above all, this school of Christ is dominated by the Person of Christ Himself; all things are referred to Him as the supreme arbiter; and even when corruption sets in, as it is likely to do from time to time in any society composed of human beings, it is by the standard of Christ's teaching and by His living power that reformation is achieved.

The Spirit which pervades the Church is the Divine Spirit, God the Holy Ghost. There we shall chiefly find Him, because He works in His greatest power on them who know the full revelation of God in Christ. But the Divine Word which was uttered in the Life and Death and Resurrection of Jesus is not something alien from all the world besides. 'All things were made by Him, and apart from Him was not anything made.' The Light of the world shone forth in Him in all its splendour; but it did not then shine for the first or only time; it has always shone in all men's hearts; it is 'The Light that lighteneth every man'. So the Church is not something alien from the world, but is or should be, the concentrated expression of what the world is striving to be, can be, and, by the Church's work within it, shall be. So it is with each individual; the Comforter, whom Christ sends to us from the Father to strengthen us for His service, is not merely some person or power outside us and distinct from us, but is the perfection of that same zeal and energy for righteousness which in some measure is already in our souls. For God made man in His own image; and the element within us whereby we are akin to God is also that which is most truly and fundamentally ourselves.

Education proceeds, we said, by the intercourse of the less mature mind with the more mature; it is limited by the learner's capacity to assimilate; this capacity depends mainly on the sympathy and community of interest which bind together teacher and pupil. We can only become what we already potentially are. The acorn may never become a tree at all; circumstances determine that; but if it does become a tree, it is bound to become an oak, and no manipulation of environment can train it to be an elm. So we can only respond to the fuller development of our own nature; we cannot imitate with any advantage a manner of life that is different from that which expresses our own nature. Like answers to like.

Now it was inevitable that the manifestation of God in the flesh should take place at a particular time and in a particular place. And though our Lord took no part in purely temporary or local movements, yet the setting of His life was that of Palestine in the first century of our era. So long as He was present with His disciples in bodily form, He was subject to all the limitations of time and space. Those limitations would have become an ever-increasing barrier to the diffusion of His influence. It was expedient that He should go away, in order that the Spirit, perfectly manifested once for all in Him, should energise in perfect freedom from all limitations both upon and within the hearts of all men through the entire world.

The Greek word translated Comforter means rather Advocate. The Holy Spirit is one whom we can call to our aid in difficulty or trouble. And even the English word Comforter has changed its meaning and through association with what we now call comfort has come to suggest soothing qualities of consolation. Musicians have accepted and encouraged this interpretation by setting the phrases where this word occurs to soft and soothing music. But when the Authorised Version of the Bible was made, the word Comforter meant chiefly Encourager and Strengthener; it means one who sustains our strength and courage by being Himself brave and strong beside us.

Jesus Christ is God incarnate; therefore His Spirit is the Spirit of God. Because the Spirit of Christ is the Spirit of God, that Spirit meets the need of every man made in the image of God. Each has his own life to live, his own part of the pattern to fill in. No other man can be to any man the perfect teacher. But God designs the pattern, and His help is just what each man needs. Each can find in Him the satisfaction of his own deepest desire, the fulfilment of his own highest hope; and what he finds is the perfect completion of just his own life and being. The kinship of what is deepest in our souls with the Spirit in the world and in the Church, who is the Spirit of Jesus, is what gives us the ground of our endless hope; for that kinship persists through all our sins and through all our futilities . . .

Deep in every one of us is that spark of the divine fire, which is scarcely ever – perhaps Never – extinguished in this earthly life. Through all our sins and all our frivolities it still burns on. Even if we have spent our days in selfish pleasures and our years in worldly ambitions, the deepest springs of our life are undefiled; our truest self is still to God's great service dedicate. For the deepest and truest self in every one of us, as many a mystic has learnt, is God the Holy Ghost Himself within us, helping the infirmities of our prayers with groanings that cannot be uttered, and always making for us the perfect intercession which is according to the will of God. God within us is answering to God without us and above us, to God as He issues His law from heaven, to God as He teaches His children through the human lips of Jesus. Like answers to like; deep answers to deep; God makes answer to Himself.

How then shall we seek the aid of the Comforter? Let me answer the question with another. Do you often pray to God the Holy Ghost? And if you do, what thought have you of Him to whom you pray? We pray to the Almighty Father, to whom we and all things owe our being. We pray to God our suffering Saviour, by whose passion we are redeemed. So far our thoughts are definite; when we turn to the Holy Spirit they are often vague. But our prayers will be enriched and made more potent if we add to them prayers to the Holy Spirit with an understanding of what we do.

Let us then pray to the Mighty Spirit who guides the processes of natural creation, the courses of the stars, the procession of the seasons, the development of species; who strives ceaselessly in human history to express in and through men that love which is the nature of God who made them; who works especially in the Church, the school of Christ's disciples, inspiring, correcting, reforming, supplying; who was given without measure to Jesus of Nazareth, so that in Him we see what the Spirit would make of us: and as we pray let us remember that this Mighty Spirit dwells within ourselves, soul of our souls, our own truest self, always, despite our chattering and our sinning, 'to God's great service dedicate'. So when we say, 'Come, Holy Ghost, our souls inspire', we are not only calling One to enter us from without; we are calling One forth from within our inmost hearts, that our words may be His utterance and our deeds His actions. Cease not to pray to God in Heaven; cease not to pray to God in Christ; but pray also to the God within your breast, the 'Almighty ever-present Deity', to the voice which urges you to right and warns you of wrong, and impresses the austere, imperious claims of beauty or of truth. Pray so, and God within your soul shall answer; you will find His power there ready to issue forth in words divine which your lips will speak, in godlike actions done through you. You shall learn what St Paul meant when he said, 'I live; yet not I, but Christ liveth in me.' For through all your weakness and meanness there will break the irresistible power of Almighty God – the Holy Ghost, the Comfortor.

iii The Ascension

Sermon IX, 'The Exalted Christ and the Coming of the Spirit', pp. 106–17

Westminster Abbey, May 16th, 1920.

> 'They therefore, when they were come together asked him, Saying, Lord, dost thou at this time restore the kingdom to Israel? And he said unto them, It is not for you to know times or seasons, which the Father hath set within his own authority. But ye shall receive power,

the Holy Ghost coming upon you: and ye shall be my witnesses.' Acts 1. 6–8

'Dost thou at this time restore the kingdom to Israel?' What a tedious and tiresome question! The Lord had lived before men and among His disciples the very Life of God; He had spoken as never man spake; He had died and had given them at the Last Supper the interpretation of His death as the perfect sacrifice whereby the new covenant between God and Man was inaugurated; He had broken the bonds of death and visibly appeared again among His friends; and what they want to know is whether their petty principality on the eastern shore of the Mediterranean is to recover its political independence – How tedious! How exasperatingly unperceptive!

Yet we are bound to remember what that political independence meant for the devout Israelite; it meant freedom to exhibit before the world the blessings that come to a nation which freely orders its life according to the law of God. Israel was Church as much as nation, and its spiritual inheritance was of supreme dignity: 'Whose is the adoption, and the glory, and the covenants, and the giving of the law, and the service of God, and the promises; whose are the patriarchs, and of whom is the Messiah as concerning the flesh, who is over all, God blessed for ever.' The subjection of this people to the yoke of a foreign empire seemed to prohibit the free expression of a national obedience to God. Israel alone could show any such thing to the World and Israel was prevented. Would the risen Christ create the opportunity?

He does not rebuke the question; He does not give a negative answer. He sets it aside as irrelevant. The course of human history is in the hands of the Father. The time when the kingdoms of this world shall be the kingdom of our God and of His Christ will surely come; but when it will come is no concern of men. The disciples receive no satisfaction for their curiosity; but instead they receive a promise and a charge. They receive the promise of power through the coming of the Holy Spirit; they receive the charge to bear witness to Christ.

The Ascension of Christ is His liberation from all restrictions of time and space. It does not represent His removal from the earth, but His constant presence everywhere on earth.

During His earthly ministry He could only be in one place at a time. If He was in Jerusalem He was not in Capernaum; if He was in Capernaum He was not in Jerusalem. But now He is united with God, He is present wherever God is present; and that is everywhere. Because He is in Heaven, He is everywhere on earth; because He is ascended, He is here now. In the Person of the Holy Spirit He dwells in His Church, and issues forth from the deepest depths of the souls of His disciples, to bear witness to His sovereignty.

The Ascended Christ is the source of the Holy Spirit as we know Him. Christ has departed from the physical companionship of men; but He has not left us comfortless; He has sent the comforter, the Spirit of Truth and Love. We have considered how we may seek the aid of the Comforter; we have reminded ourselves that He is the Spirit perfectly manifested in Christ and that only for the doing of Christ's work can we enjoy His help. Today we dwell on the truth that only as a result of the perfection of Christ's union with the Father could the Holy Spirit, as we know Him, come into the world. So St John says quite plainly – at a point in the middle of our Lord's ministry, 'There was not yet Spirit, because Jesus was not yet glorified.'

Yet we say of the Holy Spirit that He spake by the prophets, and no one limits this in his mind to the order of prophets in the early Christian Church. Assuredly the work of the Holy Spirit in the world did not begin after the Ascension of our Lord. But it is true and vitally important that only then, and only in the Christian Church, is the power of the Spirit to be found in all its fullness. For what, after all, is that power? It is not chiefly revealed in the laws of Nature by which the universe is maintained in one stupendous system; nor chiefly in the reactions whereby, under the general order of the world, self-seeking procures its own downfall. In such eternal ordinances we do indeed see the work of the Holy Ghost; but it is only because we have a knowledge of Him altogether transcending those spheres that we are able in the ordering of the world to trace the activity of no dead fate but of a living Person. The power of the Holy Spirit is revealed to us chiefly in the call of God to our souls; in the voice of conscience, pointing our duty; in the yearning for a fullness of life that is now beyond our reach; in the imperious claim that truth and beauty make upon the student and the artist; in the realisation of fellowship with the Eternal to which we have sometimes risen in prayer and meditation and worship and communion; in the strength beyond our own that has been given us in difficulty or trouble; in the growth and purification of character as we have persevered in duty and discipleship. To put it shortly, our experience of the Spirit is experience of a personal relationship.

All the various religions of mankind rest upon some apprehension of such a relationship. In the Old Testament writers we witness the steady deepening of just such an apprehension. The dealings of God with His people supplied the basis and background of the faith of Israel and its prophets. There is a clear consciousness of a relation between the whole nation and its God; and this differs vitally from the relation, at first sight similar, that existed between other nations and their supposed deities. For it was a moral, not a natural, relation. With other Semitic tribes this had not been so. Moab was as necessary to Chemosh as Chemosh was to Moab; his greatness consisted in the greatness of his people. But Jehovah was bound to Israel by moral ties alone; He chose Israel of His own free Will. The Lord and His people were linked together not by natural affinities but by the moral link of a covenant. His infinite exaltation left Him always far above the vicissitudes that might befall the Israelites. He could indeed win further glory by carrying them to greatness; but their failure and infidelity left His transcendence unimpaired.

On the background of that national faith, and out of it as from a goodly soil, sprang the faith of the prophets. With them at least the relationship with a personal God becomes an individual experience. No one can read the sixth chapter of Isaiah or the first of Jeremiah without a conviction that here we have a record of direct experience. Isaiah's realisation of the glory of God and his sudden sense of unworthiness in that Holy Presence – an unworthiness which is cancelled by the Divine purging and the Divine mission; Jeremiah's conviction of personal incompetence and Divinely-given strength – these are not fictions but realities. The same is true of Amos to whom the divine call came on the open hill-sides of Judea, and who repudiates the title of a prophet because it suggests something too deliberate and professional. It is true of the whole line from Elijah to Malachi, though there are many undulations.

In the Psalmists the individual relationship to God becomes deeper and more intimate, and to this day there are no phrases to express this central heart of personal religion more beautifully adequate than some passages from the Psalms.

Yet in all this record there is a curious incompleteness, and that in two especial ways. First we are struck and almost shocked by the alternations of far lower conceptions with the loftiest flights of inspiration. We who read, or ought to read, the Scriptures of the Old Testament with eyes illuminated by the splendour of God's perfect self-manifestation in Christ, are startled to find side by side with words that seem to express the religion of the Gospel other words that attribute to God the vindictive passions of an Oriental despot, and commands which we know cannot represent His will. In all inspired men the man remains as well as the inspiration.

The gold of divine truth is mingled with much human alloy. Sometimes in a single short Psalm we find tenderness and ferocity combined without any sense of incongruity, as in the 137th, which opens with the exquisitely beautiful lamentation of the exiles for the Sion they had left behind and ends with the hideous imprecation against Babylon: 'Happy shall he be that taketh and dasheth thy little ones against the rock.' We know that in such an utterance the writer is far from fellowship with the Divine Love.

Once more, with all the sense of dependence upon God and of fellowship with Him, there is a failure to enter into the reality of His Love. This is perhaps plainest in Ezekiel, who, for all his tenderness, will never dare to suggest that the Almighty and Eternal has any such concern for His people as the word love implies; it is not for their sake but for the glory of His own Name that He blesses them. And even prophets who never state the matter so sharply yet fail to maintain any steady realisation of His love as the constant motive of all God's activity. They hold intercourse with Him, but there is no completeness of fellowship; for He is as yet but partially known; and the word of prophecy always contains the note: 'Verily Thou art a God that hidest Thyself, O God of Israel, the Saviour.' To the end of the Old Testament, 'clouds and darkness are round about Him'.

Then the light breaks through. In Jesus Christ the glory of the Love of God appears in undimmed splendour. But it does so because it clothes itself in human flesh, acts through human will, utters itself through human thought and suffers with human feeling. Till then man's faith was an answer to a God still largely unknown. This could never be whole-hearted. Man can respond with all His soul only to what stirs His sympathy. Men knew that God was holy, and they worshipped; men knew that He was almighty, and they feared. But that is not an answer of the entire soul. What should make them love?

> See from His head, His hands, His feet,
> Sorrow and love flow mingling down;
> Did e'er such love and sorrow meet,
> Or thorns compose so rich a crown?

'He loved me; and gave Himself for me.' When I really believe that, my devotion becomes complete. Alas that we so seldom realise what we profess every day! When I really believe this, the Divine Spirit of Love within is released to carry my whole being into perfect devotion to the Love thus shown to me without; God rushes forth to blend with God, and my life becomes an atom in that all-embracing circle of Divine Love, which is the Blessed Trinity.

But my response can only be complete when the revelation of God's love is itself completely given in a form which we completely understand and which therefore calls forth a complete sympathy. That power of God upon and within the soul, which is the Holy Ghost, can only be complete when Jesus has been glorified through the completion of the obedience, which keeps Him without sin through all temptations, and leads to the perfect self-sacrifice and union with the Father. The experience of the Spirit which is allowed to us became possible through the Life, the Death, the Resurrection, the Ascension of Jesus our Lord.

'Having then a great high priest, who hath passed through the heavens, Jesus the Son of God, let us hold fast our confession. For we have not a high priest that cannot be touched with the feeling of our infirmities; but one that hath been in all points tempted like as we are, yet without sin. Let us therefore draw near with boldness unto the throne of grace, that we may receive mercy, and may find grace to help us in time of need.'

As we come into His presence we shall not ask to know of times or seasons. We shall not be dismayed by wars or rumours of wars, nor speculate on the arrival of a millennium of peace and goodwill, though we shall do our utmost to prepare the way for it. But we shall bear witness to our ascended Lord, through fellowship with whom the Holy Ghost is come upon us with a gift of power that we can utilise for His service if we will. We shall be His witnesses, declaring to men that only from Him comes the Spirit who gives men power to live as Sons of God. And we shall make our own communion with our Lord more constant, more intimate, more affectionate, so that His Spirit may work in us in ever greater power to the accomplishment of His loving purpose for the world.

4

Theological Investigations: *Christus Veritas* of 1924

Christus Veritas *(Christ the Truth) was Temple's second major volume of philosophical theology. It was written while he was Bishop of Manchester but, like* Mens Creatrix, *had its roots in his studies as a lecturer at Oxford. It began with the premiss that governed Temple's whole view of the world, that Christ and the Christian faith was 'the truth' for all people, and it restated this doctrine in some of the categories of the Idealist philosophy he had learnt at Oxford. Temple claimed the book was different from* Mens Creatrix, *which had been concerned with making a philosophical case for the underlying truths of Christianity. This second volume would be more theological in its interests, expounding the nature of religious experience, the relationship between history and eternity, the nature of God, worship, the atonement and the Trinity, and above all the significance and work of Christ.*

Temple stated that the book was an expansion of a note that appeared in Mens Creatrix. *This note (p. 318, printed above p. 32) argued that the incarnation of God in the life, death and resurrection of Jesus of Nazareth perfectly represents, and fashions, the entire course of world history, from the earliest beginnings at the start of evolution through to the final stages of human history. The incarnation influences the outcome of terrestrial history, in other words, and it provides the key to unlocking the meaning both of the world and of the peoples that live within it. And* Christus Veritas *is a 'sketch' of how this is so or, in his own words, 'an exposition of the Christian idea of God, life and the world, or, in other words, a Christo-centric metaphysics' (p. ix).*

How the incarnation represents and fashions terrestrial history is shown in the course of the book. The presupposition, an optimistic one, argued in Mens Creatrix, *is that value or, as Temple preferred to write, Value, is the ultimate reality in the world. The innate value of anything one cares to name, whether it be an object or a person or a situation or a group of things, provides the reason why it exists: 'Value is the element in real things which both causes them to be and makes them what they are, and is thus fitly called Substance' (p. 15).* He believed, in other words, that everything that existed expressed, to a greater or lesser extent, an element of absolute value. Biological evolution and human history, then, were viewed as part of one process, and this process would lead to the emergence of the supreme and absolute value which made sense of all values. The world was an integrated whole, made up of a hierarchy of being, with each level of being necessary for a higher level, until the absolutes were reached. So the goal of creation was the achievement of 'a commonwealth of values' – a human fellowship which realized in community the values of truth, beauty and goodness, inspired by absolute value.

He then argued that absolute value, which could also be described as Love, was bound to enter into the process of reality to bring about such a personal union with individuals, because that was its very nature. It would want to enter into the deepest possible fellowship with all those who had emerged from the evolutionary process. It would need to become incarnate as a human being to call and invite all people into a personal fellowship with itself.

In this way Temple prepared the ground for his presentation of Christ. Christ was not just a human being but was absolute value, or Love itself, expressing itself in human terms. And he was a love who would sacrifice himself in order to bring about the final glorious realization of ultimate value, a value that was the crowning goal of evolution. Christ's life, death and resurrection was, then, the key to understanding the purpose and meaning of reality and, within that, of the terrestrial world.

In an important passage in Christus Veritas *he summed up many of these claims:*

> Christian experience is witness, not to a Man uniquely inspired, but to God living a human life. Now this is exactly the culmination of that stratification which is the structure of Reality; far therefore from being incredible, it is to be expected, it is antecedently probable. Even had there been no evil in the world to be overcome, no sin to be abolished and forgiven, still the Incarnation would be the natural inauguration of the final stage of evolution. In this sense the Incarnation is perfectly intelligible; that is to say, we can see that its occurrence is all of a piece with the scheme of Reality as traced elsewhere. (p. 139)

Temple's Christology was therefore full-blooded: 'We may say, then, without any hesitation that Christ is not a man exalted to perfect *participation in the Divine Nature or Life; He is God, manifest under the conditions of humanity' (pp. 138–9). Taken as a whole the book was an ambitious and impressive attempt to interpret and represent the doctrine of the incarnation in modern terms.*

Whether it was a successful attempt depends on one's view of the argument about value. It suggested that all aspects of reality could be explained by the value they contained and that this value could be seen to be progressively realized through evolution and history. But, as with the argument in Mens Creatrix, *the fact and magnitude of evil in the world can undermine such optimism. Can the concept of value be understood as perfectly representing the world when so much of that world is needlessly cruel, harsh and wasteful? Temple himself had recently lived through one of the most destructive wars in history: was that also part of absolute value? (See above pp. 20–1.)*

Nevertheless, Christus Veritas *provides a striking affirmation of the incarnation of Christ by placing it within the order and structure of worldly reality. It also presents a number of finely crafted discussions of theological questions that show Temple expounding a range of doctrines beyond that of the incarnation. One of the most notable is his discussion of the atonement (see Section i), in which he criticizes an over-reliance on the analogy of the law court to explain what happened on the cross, preferring instead the idea of a personal restoration between God and the penitent. A second is his discussion of how an eternal God can comprehend the changes and chances of human history: Temple offers an answer through the use of a suggestive analogy of a dramatist and the unfolding drama of his play (see Section ii). A third is a more speculative and abstract discussion of the Trinity, in which he seeks to relate that doctrine to the problem of time and eternity. In that piece he also reflects on the love of God revealed in the Trinity and warns us not to reduce that love to a mere amiability, but to remember the awesome majesty of God requiring our 'abject self-abasement' (see Section iii).*

i How Can God Forgive Us?

Chapter XIV, 'The Atonement', pp. 255–65

What is the Christian doctrine of Forgiveness? We begin with the teaching of our Lord. This need not here be dealt with at length, for no one can read the Synoptic Gospels without noticing its prominence. Many of the miracles of healing are accompanied by declarations of forgiveness of sins; the claim to make such a declaration was one of the first occasions for accusation against our Lord by the religious leaders of the time. The Fourth Gospel does not anywhere use the words 'forgiveness' or 'forgive'; but, as we have received it, it contains the words spoken to the adulteress: 'Neither do I condemn thee; go and sin no more.' The classical expression of our Lord's teaching is of course the parable of the Prodigal Son. Its significance is luminously clear. The son is allowed to take his patrimony and go his own way; the father does not in any smallest degree curtail his liberty; when he is gone, the father longs for his return, and shows as soon as his son approaches that he has always been ready to restore him to the old relationship; but he does not send for him or fetch him; he waits until the son comes to himself and makes up his own mind to return as a penitent. Dr. [Hastings] Rashdall is perfectly right when he says that the plain teaching of the parable is that God freely forgives all who repent, and that the rest of the teaching of our Lord accords with this.

But what our Lord said must not be separated from what He did; and what He did supplies an answer to two problems that arise immediately in connection with the doctrine of free forgiveness conditioned only by repentance. The first of these is the question how forgiveness can be freely given without loss to the majesty of the moral law. The second is the question how, if repentance is the condition of forgiveness, that condition is in fact to be fulfilled. To those two questions the Cross gives the answer.

The great doctrine of the Atonement has suffered more, perhaps, than any fundamental doctrine of the Christian faith from the pendulum-swing of human thought as it sways from one reaction to another. Let us then make a few points clear at the outset. No doctrine can be Christian which starts from a conception of God as moved by any motive alien from holy love. If it is suggested by any doctrine of the Atonement that the wrath of God had quenched or even obscured His love before the atoning sacrifice was offered by Jesus Christ, that doctrine is less than Christian. The starting-point in the New Testament is never the wrath of God but always His love. 'God commendeth His own love toward us, in that, while we were yet sinners, Christ died for us' (Romans 5.8). 'God so loved the world that He gave His only-begotten Son' (St John 33.16).

(2) Forgiveness does not consist of remission of penalty. So long as we think of it in that way, we show that we have not reached the Christian

relationship to God. When a child who has done wrong says to his father, 'Please forgive me', he does not only mean, 'Don't punish me'; he also means, 'Please let us be to each other as if I had not done it.' If I have injured my friend and ask him to forgive me, I am not asking him to refrain from prosecuting me; I am asking him to let our friendship stand unbroken in spite of what I have done. To forgive is to restore to the old relationship. It is because men have pictured God's judgment of souls so much in the likeness of the courts of earthly justice that this has been so often obscured. The prisoner in the dock has never been in any close relationship with the judge on the bench. He is not occupied with anxious thoughts concerning the grief which his misconduct may have caused to that worthy fellow-citizen; his only concern with the judge is to know what the judge is going to inflict upon him. If we think so of our responsibility before God, we have not taken up our position as Christians at all. 'You did not receive a spirit of slavery to relapse into fear, but you received a spirit of adoption, in which we cry Abba, Father' (Romans 8.15). The slave has his orders and is punished if he disobeys; his only feeling when he has done wrong is fear. The son knows his father's love, and calls upon him by the name of endearment. So the forgiveness that Christ wins for us is not chiefly a remission of penalty; it is the restoration to the affectionate intimacy of sons with their Father. And it is for this that the Father longs.

(3) None the less, there is a real antagonism of God against the sinner so long as he continues in his sin. It is true, of course, that God loves the sinner while He hates the sin. But that is a shallow psychology which regards the sin as something merely separate from the sinner, which he can lay aside like a suit of clothes. My sin is the wrong direction of my will; and my will is just myself so far as I am active. If God hates the sin, what He hates is not an accretion attached to my real self; it is myself, as that self now exists. He knows I am capable of conversion, and desires not the death of the sinner but rather that he should be converted and live; in that most true sense, He loves me even while I sin; but it cannot be said too strongly that there is a wrath of God against me as sinning; God's Will is set one way and mine is set against it. There is a collision of wills; and God's Will is not passive in that collision. There is an antagonism of God against me – not indeed an ill-will towards me, for what He wills is my good – but most certainly a contrary will actively opposing me. And, therefore, though he longs to forgive, He cannot do so unless either my will is turned from its sinful direction into conformity with His, or else there is at work some power which is capable of

effecting that change in me. To forgive is to restore to the old intimacy; there can be no intimacy between God and me in so far as I set my will against His. Moreover, I am only one of His family. He cannot restore me to the freedom of the family if there is ill-will in me against the other members of it. (Note: A father might say to a son who had quarrelled with both the father and a brother, and after leaving the home in a rage was anxious to return – 'I am willing to have you back, but can you be friends with Jack?') Our tendency to draw illustrations from the law-courts makes us think of forgiveness concerning each of us singly; but that is false both to fact and to Christian principle. Consequently, so long as there is ill-will in me there is an antagonism on His side to be ended as well as on mine. It is of my making, but it exists in Him and not only in me. It is not anger, if by anger we mean the emotional reaction of an offended self-concern; it is anger, if by anger we mean the resolute and relentless opposition of a will set on righteousness against a will directed elsewhere. God must abolish all sinners; but He seeks to abolish sinners by winning them out of their sin into the loyalty and love of children in their Father's home.

(4) It is congruous with what has just been said that we should remind ourselves that our Lord came to save His people from their sins and not merely from the punishment of their sins. It is only through preoccupation with thoughts of punishment that people have come to invent doctrines of transferred penalty. Of course, it is true that if we are not sinners God will not treat us as if we were; and if by His suffering Christ has won us out of our sin, then by His suffering He has delivered us from the suffering that would have been the result of our continuance in sin. But it would be monstrous to speak of this as a transference of penalty. The Atonement is accomplished by the drawing of sinful souls into conformity with the divine Will.

We can now turn back to the two problems that arise out of our Lord's proclamation of God's free forgiveness on the sole condition of repentance. The first of these was the question, How can forgiveness be freely given without detriment to the majesty of the moral law? If, as soon as I repent, God welcomes me back to intimacy, does it not seem as though He had not greatly cared about my sin? This is the real root of all the theories of vicarious punishment which have so grievously offended the most sensitive Christian consciences. Those theories represent a wrong way of setting forth what is itself profoundly true. Free forgiveness is immoral if it is lightly given. It is a part of true love that the father should welcome home the returning prodigal; yet the prodigal knew something of what the father had suffered through his selfishness. But men do not universally understand what their selfishness means to the Father in Heaven. The promise of free forgiveness on condition of repentance to men so blind and callous as we are would be demoralising. It could only be safely given by One who was also to lay bare the heart of God and show what sin means to Him, and therefore how righteous as well as deep is the love from which the forgiveness flows.

For if the God who forgives suffers under the impact of sin in a fashion that requires Gethsemane and Calvary for its manifestation, it is impossible to say that He forgives through indifference. No one who hears the word which pronounces his pardon from the lips of the Crucified will be for a moment tempted to say, 'He does not mind.' Therefore the Cross, by showing what sin costs God, safeguards His righteousness while He forgives. On the Cross God set forth His Son 'to be a means of propitiation, through faith, by His life offered in sacrifice, to show Himself as righteous and as making righteous him that has faith in Jesus' (Romans 3.25, 26. I have paraphrased the word 'Blood'). St Paul regards the forbearance of God in the past as having imperilled His righteousness; but that righteousness is now fully vindicated by the Cross, which reveals the antagonism between God and sin. And this is what is required. There are two ways of expressing antagonism to sin; one is to inflict suffering on the sinner, the other is to endure suffering. Either repels the charge of moral indifference.

In choosing to show His righteousness by enduring pain and manifesting His endurance of it, God acted in the one way by which the other condition of perfectly righteous forgiveness can be fulfilled; that is, that the sinner be won from his sin to righteousness, from selfishness to love. Here experience can guide us. There is no doubt at all that the Cross of Christ has been His chief means of drawing men into fellowship with Himself. For St Paul union with Christ is something so complete and intimate that whatever may be said to have befallen Him has befallen the disciple also (Romans 6.1–11; 2 Corinthians 5.14; Colossians 3.1–3); and this makes it for ever impossible to describe his doctrine fairly as substitutionist. But it is on the moment of Death and Resurrection that this sense of union is concentrated. Whether or not our Lord actually spoke the words in St Matthew's Gospel at the distribution of the Cup at the Last Supper, experience shows that the shedding of Christ's blood was indeed 'for the remission of sins' in the sense that by His Passion they have been drawn to God and have received forgiveness.

All of this does not exactly amount to saying that the Death of Christ was a propitiatory sacrifice; but it does, as I think, prove that the Death of Christ fulfilled the aspirations previously expressed in such sacrifices, and I have no doubt at all that the Lord Himself intended to direct our thoughts to perceive this by the act which He performed at the Last Supper and the words by which He both marked this act as sacrificial and connected it with His Death, which took place on the following day.

We are at present dealing with the Atonement only in so far as it concerns the forgiveness of the sins of men. There is a wider range to be covered before we appreciate the full depth of that mystery. 'It was the good pleasure of the Father that in him should all the fullness dwell, and through him to reconcile all things unto himself, having made peace through the blood of his cross; through him, I say, whether things upon the earth or things in the heavens' (Colossians 1.19, 20). The fact that in human history the Atonement takes the form of the Passion is largely due to human sin. But human history is only an episode in the cosmic process, and the Divine Self-sacrifice, wherein is expressed the Love which is the inner heart of the Universe and its supreme Law, has a range of efficacy far beyond human history. What constitutes the problem is not only the sins of men, but also what St John calls the 'sin of the world' (cosmos). The words with which our Lord ended the discourse preparing His disciples for the Passion were, 'I have conquered the universe'... What is set before us in the Cross of Christ is not merely the reaction of the Divine Nature to human sin; it is the unveiling of a mystery of the Divine Life itself – the revelation of the cost whereby God wins victory over the evil which He had permitted, and thereby makes more glorious than otherwise was possible the goodness which triumphs. In so far as the term 'propitiation' represents something objectively accomplished in and by God Himself, apart from our forgiveness altogether (though that is involved) and even apart from our sins (except in so far as these are part of the cosmic evil) – to that extent it is the term which of all that are open to us carries us furthest into the mystery of the Atonement.

We may, then, summarise our Lord's teaching on forgiveness by saying that He did indeed proclaim God's free forgiveness of sin on condition of repentance; and He also did what alone could save that proclamation from imperilling belief in the divine righteousness, by showing in His Passion what men's sin means to God. By showing this He further secured that all who believe in Him should fulfil the condition. After all, others have taught that forgiveness follows repentance;

what no other could do was to secure that repentance should follow sin. But Christ has done this for all who believe that in Him we see the Father. Fear of punishment might deter me from sinful action, but it could not change my sinful desires; on the contrary, it would be more likely to intensify them by the action of that psychological law described by St Paul (Romans 7.7 to end) which we have lately learnt to call the Law of Reversed Effort. But to realise what my selfishness means to the Father who loves me with a love such as Christ reveals, fills me with horror of the selfishness and calls out an answering love. The non-Christian may say, 'Yes, God will forgive me if I can repent; but what can make me repent?' The Christian answers, 'By living in the fellowship of Jesus Christ, by prayer in His Spirit, by receiving His Life in His Sacrament, by practising His companionship, I can assure myself of true penitence for every sin into which I fall.'

Thus it is that we plead the sacrifice of Christ. His love, shown pre-eminently in His Death, has transforming power over all those who open their hearts to it. We mean to live in His fellowship; and we know that if we do so we shall be transformed into His likeness. It is because we can say first,

> Look, Father, look on His anointed Face,
> And only look on us as found in Him,

that we can go on to say,

> Lo, between our sins and their reward
> We set the Passion of Thy Son, our Lord.

We plead His Passion, not as a transferred penalty, but as an act of self-sacrifice which re-makes us in its own likeness. Its work on us is not yet perfect. We still misuse God's grace; our prayer is still languid and our faith dim. But Christ will perfect His work in us, and we ask our heavenly Father to regard us (as He Himself wills to regard us) not as the prodigals we are but as the true brethren of Christ that we are becoming.

There is one feature in our Lord's teaching about forgiveness which we have so far passed over. It is indeed misleading to say that Christ proclaims forgiveness upon the sole condition of repentance unless we remember how inclusive a term repentance is. For He does not anywhere state this condition of divine forgiveness, though He does suggest that it may be a condition of human forgiveness (Luke 17.3, 4; and even here the emphasis is not on the condition but on the duty to be ready to forgive repeatedly). The condition that He Himself lays down is that the sinner who would be forgiven must himself forgive any who have injured him. This is reiterated with an insistence which is unmistakable. The petition for forgiveness in the Lord's Prayer is the only one that has any condition attached to it – 'Forgive us our debts, as we also have forgiven our debtors' – and the only one on which a comment is added: 'For if ye forgive men their trespasses, your heavenly Father will also forgive you. But if ye forgive not men their trespasses, neither will your Father forgive your trespasses' (Matthew 6.12, 14, 15). This comment is reinforced by the parable of the unforgiving servant (Matthew 18.21–35).

We saw earlier that the purpose of forgiveness is to reconstitute the unity of the divine and the human. We now see how it accomplishes this. God's forgiveness of men and men's forgiveness of their brothers are bound up in each other; and it is not difficult to see how this comes to pass. God's forgiveness is restoration to intimate fellowship with God; but fellowship with God is fellowship with self-forgetful and self-giving Love, of which forgiveness is a necessary outcome. If we do not forgive, we are not in fellowship with God. The repentance, which is the condition of God's free forgiveness, is a turning away from our selfish outlook and the adoption of God's outlook, from which forgiveness necessarily proceeds. God's forgiveness of us and our forgiveness of our brothers are not related as cause and effect but rather as the obverse and reverse of one spiritual fact. They are in their own nature indissolubly united. It is not by an arbitrary decree that they are associated together; they are one thing. And here especially we have to remember that we are children before our Father. How can the Father take into affectionate intimacy with Himself two children who refuse to be on friendly terms with one another? He can only forgive us, as we forgive our brothers.

ii How Can God Be in Eternity and in Time?

Chapter XV, 'Love Divine: The Blessed Trinity', pp. 274–8

God [is] Creative Will, originating and sustaining all that is. As such, He has His being apart from all else, and in no way depends on the created universe for His existence. He is not merely the spiritual aspect of the universe, nor the sum of its values, nor even its totality, except in the sense that He is the ground of its totality which therefore falls within the scope of His will. This is what is represented in classical theology by the doctrine that the universe is not of the divine substance but proceeds from the divine will. If God ceased to be, the universe would immediately cease also; but if the universe ceased to be, God would still be God. His existence is independent of all else; He *is* absolutely.

This does not mean that creation is capricious, as represented in the words attributed to the Almighty by the youthful Shelley.

> From an eternity of idleness
> I, God, awoke; in seven days' toil made earth. (*Queen Mab*)

On the contrary, the Love which prompts creation is the very nature of God. Because He is Love, He is and must be self-communicating; in principle there is, and always was, the Word, eternally in close relation with God, eternally God (John 1.1). In this sense the universe is necessary to God. Being God He must create. But there is no reciprocal interdependence. The way in which God is necessary to the universe is utterly different from the way in which the universe is necessary to God; for in each case the ground of the necessity is in God. God is necessary to the universe in the sense that apart from God the universe would not exist: the universe is not necessary to God in that sense at all; it is necessary to God only in the sense that, being what He is, His nature leads to its creation.

It is this essential self-utterance of God which St John calls the Word, and the necessity of it, grounded in the moral character and being of God, is called the eternal generation of the Son. The reasons for attributing to the Word a distinctness sufficient to warrant such an expression will appear later. At present the point to notice is that what is rooted in the moral character of a spiritual being is that being's act; so that to say the generation of the Word is the act of the Father and to say that God is such that He must give Himself in love is to say one and the same thing. The love in which He gives Himself is known to Christians by the name of Holy Ghost. Father, Son, Holy Ghost – each name stands for the divine love in one of its necessary aspects.

But these are not only aspects. The Father is the ground or fountain of all being, and in Him all is implicit; to Him all is present. But 'present' is here a misleading term, used only because the limitations of human experience and language prevent the discovery of a better. 'Present' is distinguished from past and future; and when we say that to God the Father all is present, we inevitably suggest to our minds the thought of One who now comprehends the future. But that is precisely what is not intended. *Now* means *not then*; *then* means *not now*; but it is neither then nor now that God comprehends all time; it is eternally. This is something altogether beyond our apprehension, but our experience is not so utterly lacking in analogues that we can attach no meaning to the words. When we watch a play of which we know the plot already, we have an artificial imitation of an eternal comprehension; we see each episode and action in the light not only of its occasion, but of its consequences. Now imagine that the play is being acted by the children of the dramatist, and even composed by them as they act it, according to gifts of which he as their father is the source, and that he knows them well enough to be sure of the general course they will take – then his experience, as he watches, is something still nearer to the eternal comprehension. Christ taught us to think of God as Father, and we can conceive an ideal father who is a perfect artist in the living material of his children, so that, never infringing their freedom, he yet can guide them to a harmonious exercise of it. So we come still closer. It is true that all analogies fail; they ought to fail. If we had a conception of God which made His mode of being perfectly comprehensible to the finite mind, we should know for that reason alone that it was false. But we have in our experience indications of a superiority to Time which show us the intelligible possibility of an eternal comprehension, though such comprehension is itself for ever beyond our reach. (Coleridge says that the only safe form of the doctrine of Omnipresence is, not that God is present to all things, but that all things are present to God. This, perhaps, helps us further to see what is meant by an eternal comprehension.)

The difficulty of apprehending the divine comprehension of the world would be greater if it were an act of contemplation only. But it is not this. God, we have found, is Himself active in the process which He comprehends. That process is His own self-manifestation, wherein He Himself is active. Israel had learnt to trace His activity in the events of the nation's history; Christians have learnt supremely to find His positive act in the Birth, Life, Death, Resurrection, and Ascension of Jesus Christ, and the subsequent gift of spiritual power to His disciples. But in that supreme act of self-revelation we do not find One remote from all forms of trouble or exempt from disappointment. We see Him pleading, sometimes in vain; loaded with the weight of disappointment; amazed at the path marked out for Him; overwhelmed with despair. God, who eternally grasps the whole universe that He has created in all its extent of space and time, also acts at a particular part of space under the conditions of time, and so acting His struggle and effort are profoundly real – so real that in time and for a time they are sometimes genuinely frustrated; if any soul is ultimately lost, then God's purpose for that soul is finally frustrated.

Now we must use human language and human thoughts, because we have no other; and it is clear at once that while God, as we have been led to conceive Him, is certainly personal, He is as certainly not a Person. To attribute to *a* Person at once the eternal comprehension of the universe and the disappointment of Jesus Christ over Jerusalem or His cry of desolation on the Cross is to talk nonsense. It is one God; but it is two Persons – so far as human terms have any applicability at all. Here we find the ground for that degree of distinctness in the divine Word or self-manifestation of God in time, which makes it appropriate to speak of Him as begotten of the Father rather than as merely emanating from the Father.

Before all worlds, or eternally, He is begotten of the Father. Into this world He was born. It was no act of man that led to His birth. It was that active energy of Divine Love which is called the Holy Ghost. God's love, not man's will, caused His birth (John 1.13). Here already we find a divine activity within the process of time, which yet is other than the only-begotten Son. Disciples of the Incarnate Son, moreover, found within themselves a power which was so plainly that of the Incarnate Son that they called it the Spirit of Jesus; yet it is not personally identical with Jesus, for it points to Him and bears witness of Him. Moreover, it is a personal influence, more fitly called 'He' than 'It'. Here is a third activity of God; so we reach the Christian faith in three Persons who are one God.

In the period of preparation the distinction could not be drawn. It is a common but intellectually disastrous error to identify the Yahweh of the Old Testament with the First Person of the Christian Trinity. But, apart from all other modifications in men's thought of God to which the Incarnation led, the Yahweh of the Old Testament is the undifferentiated unity of the Godhead, and in as much as He is God self-revealed, He comes far nearer to corresponding with the Second Person in the Christian Trinity than with the First. But such discussions are very futile. It is only the full Christian revelation which brings the complete knowledge of God, so far as men can receive it. What is so revealed has, of course, always been true; it did not begin to be true at the beginning of our era. We can read back our fuller knowledge into the earlier religious history, but we must not identify the terms of our fuller (though still utterly inadequate) terminology with any particular terms of the less full and distinct apprehension possible to the ancients.

iii Exploring the Love of the Trinity

Chapter XV, 'Love Divine: The Blessed Trinity', pp. 278–85

The Holy Spirit, as made known to us in our experience, is the power whereby the created universe which the Father creates by the agency of the Son, His self-revealing Word – is brought into harmonious response to the love which originated it. The divine self-utterance is creative; within the thing so created the divine self-utterance speaks in Jesus Christ; the divine impetus which is in the created thing by virtue of its origin is thus released in full power to make the created thing correspond to the Creator's purpose. Love creates; Love by self-sacrifice reveals itself to the created thing; Love thereby calls out from the created thing the Love which belongs to it as Love's creature, so making it what Love created it to be.

This already lets us form some faint conception of the Divine Love itself. But there is first another question the answer to which will help us further. We said that what the Incarnation revealed had always been true. But this requires modification. The whole gist of our argument is that we must be thorough-going in our insistence that God grasps the whole universe in an eternal comprehension, and equally thorough-going in our insistence that He is at work in the process of time really doing particular things, really suffering particular things. It is sometimes said that the Incarnation and the experiences of Jesus Christ on earth cannot have made any difference to God. But this is only a half-truth. Eternally God is what He revealed Himself in Jesus Christ to be; therefore to say that He then became this would be false. But temporally God passed from creation to creation – from the creation of Light to the creation of worlds, of animals, of man; He passed from training Moses to training Isaiah; and continually He passes from experience to experience. This does not make Him different, but it does not leave Him unaffected. He is indignant at cruelty; He yearns over His wayward children; He rejoices in their love. If this is not so, the Bible is merely false and the Gospel story no picture of God. If He is thus affected by temporal occurrences, this must be true especially of the Incarnation.

God eternally is what we see in Christ; but temporally the Incarnation, the taking of Manhood into God, was a real enrichment of the Divine Life. God loved before; but love (at least as we know it) becomes fully real only in its activity, which is sacrifice. Temporally considered, we must say that the Love, which eternally God is in full perfection, attained its temporal climax when Christ died on the Cross; so that the Cross is, as Traherne called it, the 'Centre of Eternity' (*Meditations. First Century* 55). The act of sacrifice enters into the very fibre of love and makes the love deeper and stronger; for love at its fullness is not a disposition, it is rather 'the consciousness of survival in the act of self-surrender'. At that time God put forth His power; but also God therein fulfilled Himself. The Father is eternally perfect; the Son, sharing eternally the Father's perfection, temporally fulfils Himself in the historic process, which is the temporal expression of God's eternal being. Thus God is both absolute and relative, both transcendent and immanent: as transcendent He is the eternal One, unchangeable because all change falls within His perfect Being; as immanent, He passes from glory to glory, from love to greater love – not changing in nature but more perfectly actualising His nature, adapting His activity to changing conditions so as at all times to act in love and, so acting, to add to the love.

At an earlier point the doubt was raised whether the grounds for recognising a personal distinction in the Godhead between the Father and the Son did not apply also to the Incarnate Son, so that we must accept a Nestorian theory of a human Person subject to many limitations side by side with a divine Person, who takes the human Person somehow to Himself. If God the Son, the Word of God, is at once the sustainer of the universe and the Babe in the manger, does not this involve duality of Person in Him, on precisely the same grounds on which it was said that there must be more than One Person in the One God? No, not necessarily. The distinction within the Godhead we take to be fundamentally that between the eternal perfection and the progressive realisation which is its temporal aspect. But the Divine Word and Spirit we take to be essentially temporal and progressive energies, which are everlasting and are also eternal because, but only because, they are the (temporal) energies which both express and constitute the eternal perfection. (Note: . . . I am not aware of any former attempt to relate the Doctrine of the Trinity to the problem of Time and Eternity as I have done. I therefore submit the suggestion with some diffidence, and with perfect readiness to withdraw it if it be found incompatible with the intellectual and spiritual positions which it seeks to harmonise and safeguard.) Between the experience of the Son subject to human limitations in Jesus of Nazareth and the Son as progressively ordering the world according to the Eternal Purpose of the Father there is not the same distinction as between the eternal and temporal modes of the divine. It is true, as has been said already, that we cannot expect to understand the Person of God Incarnate. We only plead that our theory places the difficulty where we ought to expect to find it.

Thus temporally regarded God is known as Son and Spirit; as Son He achieves the perfect sacrifice; as Spirit He prompts and enables us to enter into it. God is thus our Leader in the way of life, and also our companion as we follow where he leads. Father, Son, and Holy Spirit are Three Persons, for what we know of each is incompatible in one personal life with what we know of Others. Yet these incompatibles are personal activities of an identity, which is perfect Love.

There is, no doubt, a danger lest such a conception may lead men to fix all attention on the Son while they fail to lift up their minds to the Eternal Father. There is an easy attractiveness and a fatal delusion in a religion which worships an Invisible King who is at work in History, while giving a perfunctory acknowledgement to a Veiled Being who abides in a remote Eternity. But to adopt any such attitude would be false to all man's deepest religious experience, which is always that of communion with the Eternal; it would also be contrary to the whole course of the argument by which we have come to this conclusion, for that argument consists in the double contention that Eternity must be conceived as requiring the actual historic process as part of its own content, and that History can only be understood in the light of Eternity. The Son is Lord of History only because He is the self-manifestation of the Eternal. Only through Him have we access to the Father; to Him, therefore, our immediate loyalty is given; but He claims that loyalty precisely in order that He may present us with Himself to the Father, so that, just because of our loyalty to the Son, the Father is Himself the supreme object of our adoration and service.

We have often used the word Love, but have attempted no definition. Nettleship's phrase lately quoted is not a definition but rather a statement of one element in Love. But Love cannot be defined; it can only be named; and its Name is threefold – Father, Son, and Holy Spirit. It abides constant in itself, and all its activities, while they are utterly essential to it, yet only express its constant nature; by its activities it calls itself forth even from where its presence is unsuspected. We know this quite well in our dealings with one another. What we have now found is that if we would understand God in whose Being all the universe is grounded, we must conceive that Value, which is real whenever two finite spirits find themselves in each other, raised to Infinity.

God is Love; therefore He seeks Himself in an Other; this seeking is the eternal generation of the Son, who is Himself the Other that is sought; the Son as the Divine Self-utterance is the agent of creation so that in Him all the universe is implicit; within the universe the Creator-Son lives a human Life and dies and rises again, so declaring to the universe the nature of its Creator; thus He calls forth from finite spirits the love which is theirs because He made them, though by self-will they had obscured it; so the creature becomes worthy of the Creator; and the same love which the Son reveals to men and elicits from them everlastingly unites the Son to the Father; this is the Holy Spirit. And this whole complex of related spirits is the Supreme Value or Reality – the Love Divine. (Note: Perhaps it is worth while to point out that for the full realisation of all the Values comprised in Love, triplicity is indispensable; there must be the Lover, the Beloved, and the Friend who rejoices in their mutual love. In the full reality of perfect Love, the three parts are interchangeable. Each is Lover; each is Beloved; each rejoices (as the friend of the bridegroom rejoices) in the others' mutual love. It is not true, therefore, as is sometimes supposed, that in principle only two centres are needed for the perfection of Love. Perfect Love is in principle Tri-une.) In God it begins, in Him it ends, and in Him moves whatever moves. His perfection is not coldly static; it is wrought out in struggle and agony and uttermost self-sacrifice. But neither is it precarious, for the historic process is the temporal form of an eternal perfection to which that process is essential.

To say that we can understand this Supreme Reality would be false; and if our view seemed utterly complete that would condemn it. But we find what we have a right to hope for; we find that, though the Supreme Reality transcends our grasp, we are not ever merely baffled. As we move in thought from point to point, the mind is never checked by a sheer obstacle. In thinking of God as Christians have learnt to believe in Him, the mind is always free; it is the finite before the Infinite, but its freedom proves its kinship. We are His children, and cannot fully understand Him; but He is our Father and we know Him enough to love Him. As we love Him we learn, for His sake and in His power, to love men. So loving, we become partakers of the Divine Nature, sharers in that divine activity whereby God is God.

Thus nothing falls outside the circle of the Divine Love. The structure of Reality when regarded analytically is a stratification wherein the lower strata facilitate the existence of the higher but only find their fulfilment as those higher grades inform them. The structure of Reality when viewed synthetically is the articulate expression of Divine Love. God loves; God answers with love; and the love wherewith God loves and answers is God: Three Persons, One God.

God is Love. But we miss the full wonder and glory of that supreme revelation if we let the term Love, as we naturally understand it, supply the whole meaning of the term God. There is a great danger lest we forget the Majesty of God, and so think of His Love as a mere amiability. We must first realize Him as exalted in unapproachable Holiness, so that our only fitting attitude before Him is one of abject self-abasement, if we are to feel the stupendous marvel of the Love which led Him, so high and lifted up, to take His place beside us in our insignificance and squalor that He might unite us with Himself. 'When I consider Thy heavens, even the works of Thy fingers, the moon and the stars that Thou hast ordained – what is man, that Thou art mindful of him?' It is a defective Christianity which has no use for the *Dies Irae*:

Rex tremendae majestatis,
Qui salvandos salvas gratis,
Salva me, Fons pietatis.

To omit the thought of God's Majesty, and to rebel at language of self-abasement in His presence, is not only to cut at the historic and psychological root of all man's religion, but it defeats its own object, for it belittles the Love which it seeks to enhance. If our first thought of God is that He always has a welcome for us, there is less thrill of wonder in that welcome than if we first remember His Eternity and Holiness, and then pass to the confident conviction, which remains a mystery commanding silent awe – 'Our fellowship is with the Father.'

But no; it does not merely remain such a mystery; this is itself the climax of mystery, which we apprehend (if at all) in an agony of joy and a rapture of fear. For the joy is shot through with the sense of our unworthiness, the rapture intensifies the fear that is our response to overwhelming greatness. So it is only half the truth to say that we must worship the Transcendent that we may appreciate the Immanent. God is never so transcendent as when He is most immanent. It was in the consciousness that He came from God and went to God that our Lord performed the act of menial service. It was when He acknowledged His earthly Name that the very soldiers went backward and fell to the ground. Nor is there any more august and awe-inspiring symbol of the supremacy of the Most High than the sublime and dreadful solitude of the Figure on the Cross – a spiritual loneliness made more intense by the physical proximity of dying malefactors and mocking crowds, for whom in His agony He prayed.

Christus Veritas: 'This is the true God and eternal life.'

5

Political Thought: Writings and Lectures, 1917–28

i. Liberty: Individual and Political

Temple did not restrict his philosophical enquiries to the philosophy of mind. In the chapter printed here, from Mens Creatrix, *with eloquence and confidence, he moved into moral and political philosophy. In these pages he makes connections between conceptual thinking and the issues and dilemmas of social and political life. In particular he lays down some important foundations for his practical social thinking, which later became the most influential element of all his work as an archbishop. Following the British Idealist philosopher T. H. Green, he argues for the importance of the positive role of the community and its order in allowing true freedom to flourish: all are responsible for the freedom of all. This leads him to argue that every national community should be responsible for its own life, so that Ireland should be granted home rule (it was still under British rule in 1917 when these words were written), and that workers were to be accorded respect as people and not just as 'hands'. There is also an eloquent case for respecting conscientious objection, which was very timely because it had not been accepted by the Government at the start of the First World War and some conscientious objectors had been imprisoned by the authorities or even, in the case of soldiers at the Front, executed by firing squad.*

Mens Creatrix, Chapter XVI, 'Liberty: Individual and Political', pp. 213–25

The people of Great Britain are as a rule ready enough to agree that the ideal State will rest upon freedom. A vast amount of popular sentiment is always available in support of that cry, but it appears after a very slight investigation that there are two quite distinct senses in which people use the word 'freedom', and that while no doubt these are connected at their root, they lead to the advocacy of very different forms of social order. The first and most elementary sense of freedom is simply the absence of external control. Without this there can indeed be no freedom at all. So long as a man's conduct, or the conduct of a State, is literally imposed by an alien authority freedom does not exist. In the case of an individual the abrogation of freedom may be complete. If, for example, I am standing on the edge of a cliff and somebody pushes me over, my fall is in no sense my own act. In the case of a State, on the other hand, freedom can never be entirely given up or suppressed so long as the State exists at all. No doubt it may sometimes be said that an action is forced upon the State, when what is meant is that the alternative was something which no set of persons could be expected to endure; none the less there is here still some element of choice and therefore of freedom. It is not possible actually to coerce a State as one can, by superior physical force, coerce an individual – literally seizing and carrying him off. But it is plain that the presence of such choice goes a very little way towards giving that freedom which men value. It is an indispensable condition of the kind of freedom that is precious; but in itself it may be no more than a choice between two evils, each so great that the selection of either is utterly contrary to the will which chooses. And this remains true, even where there is no external pressure. The man who is free to do what he likes, but has no control of the impulses which constitute his own nature, has not won effective freedom. The State which is subject to no alien rule, but which is driven into certain lines of action by the rebellion of an ungovernable minority is not in the complete sense free.

Liberty or freedom has no doubt often been regarded as consisting in this mere absence of control. Legislation is then regarded as a partial restriction of liberty for the sake of an increase of liberty on the whole. So, for example, Mill regards the matter. My effective liberty to go about my duties and pleasures is secured to me by the repression of the homicidal and predatory impulses in others; and their liberty is secured by the repression of similar impulses in me. This repression, being enforced by an external power, is a curtailment of liberty, but by means of it the greatest amount of liberty actually obtainable is afforded. This is very like the Social Contract theory as Glauco and Hobbes express it. The individual is the unit, and it is for his selfish interest that any order is constituted at all. The result of this doctrine in practice is the policy of *laissez-faire*, and liberty so understood is simply anarchism tempered by so much of government as may make it tolerable. Legislation therefore appears as a necessary evil, and should be reduced to a minimum. It seems probable that this position derives its attractiveness for some moral philosophers from the fact that they belong to the respectable and leisured classes. In their natural desire for simple illustrations they turn to elementary laws, such as the prohibition of murder and theft; being conscious of no temptation in themselves to commit these crimes, they easily regard the law as directed primarily against other people. This view derives further plausibility, and indeed much ground in fact, from a system under which a small section of the community controls legislation; for this section will tend to legislate against tendencies in the other rather than against its own. The old laws, and indeed even our existing laws, with regard to poaching, illustrate this point.

But it is to be observed that this kind of liberty may be complete in principle and yet negligible in result. There may, for example, be perfect freedom of contract in an industrial system; and yet the men have no real choice but to accept long hours, low wages, and bad conditions because the only alternative is starvation; the employers, on the other hand, may feel unable to improve the terms from fear of being driven from the market by others less scrupulous. Something like this was the actual state of affairs in the early part of the nineteenth century in industrial England. There was perfect freedom of contract but no effective choice, because of the available alternatives one was intolerable. For the law to step in and regulate these matters looks like a curtailment of liberty; the Factory Laws were opposed by John Bright and many others on precisely this ground. But we know now that the Factory Laws actually increased effective liberty by widening the area of real choice.

Moreover, quite apart from political and social problems, mere absence of external control will not confer true freedom upon the individual in his own personal life. A licentious man might be free in this sense of freedom; of him it would be true to say as Plato says of the tyrant, that he never satisfies his real will precisely because he can at every moment do what his fancy suggests, and so he gratifies one isolated impulse after another but never attains to peace and joy for his soul. This can only be won in a life which is dedicated to some purpose, wide enough to afford scope to every faculty of his nature, and lofty enough to claim the dedication of them all. The man who aims at being a great scholar or a great artist, having faculties that fit him to become one or the other, but who is unable to control appetites and impulses which blunt these faculties, has no freedom in any sense in which freedom is valuable. The freedom that is precious is to be found, not merely when a man can say of his act, 'I did it and no one compelled me', but when he can say 'I did it, and I am glad I did it, and if the opportunity comes I will do it again.' The act then not only springs from, but definitely expresses the man's personality; it is the externalisation of his own self; but to secure such freedom a man must first submit to discipline.

A child when he comes into the world consists of a whole mass of unrelated impulses and interests, and the purpose of the earliest education is to teach the faculty of attention, that is to say, of concentrating the mind upon some one object, however attractive may be other elements in the surrounding world. The child who is learning to read, or who is playing with sand upon a tray, is learning the elements of that power by which a man pursues a great goal ignoring all seductions and overcoming all obstacles, by which the hero dies for his country or a martyr for his faith. This is the real freedom which is worth having, and it is the direct product of discipline. At first indeed the discipline must be externally imposed. The chaos of impulses which constitutes our original nature cannot possibly organise itself; but gradually that faculty of purpose which we call the will is built up, and in proportion as this takes place, self-discipline becomes possible. Through this, advance is made to true self-control and to that perfect harmony of the soul where all capacities are used and all instincts satisfied in the pursuit of a life's purpose. That ideal may never be actually reached, but where it is reached it clearly constitutes a real mastery over the successiveness of Time, such as was described as the culmination of the development of Will.

In legislation we see the same process at work in the community. At first, for the sake of that degree of public order which is essential to an even moderate prosperity and happiness, a nation submits to a strong central government which is more or less autocratic. At this stage the control is mainly external. As the fundamental principles of social life become more widely accepted, authority is transferred to a body more and more representative of the whole community. Legislation then becomes a form of corporate self-discipline.

The essence of legislation, at least in a democratic community, is that the citizens condemn in advance any one of themselves who shall at any future time be guilty of certain acts. The only reason for doing this is that they know that these acts would be contrary to their real purpose and yet that they may be tempted to perform them. The motive for making the law is not only that it will be bad for each if someone else does the act, but that it will be bad for the man himself who does it.

Legislation with its penal sanction is like a resolution which an individual takes, except that it is more effective because the penalty enacted is more likely to be inflicted; and it is simply true in the ultimate sense that the criminal against whom the law is put in motion suffers by the act of his own real will (though it may be of course contrary to all his conscious desires), unless he has gone so far in criminality that he does not desire the maintenance of society at all. Legislation therefore need not preserve freedom in one by restricting it in another, but may directly increase real freedom all round by strengthening the deliberate purpose of our lives against the impulses as yet undisciplined, which would cut across and interfere with that purpose. For example, it is my deliberate purpose to be honest in all my dealings; but in a host of small ways I am perpetually tempted to dishonesty, and there can be little doubt that I am often saved from yielding to that temptation by the law, which, if I yielded, would involve me in varieties of inconvenience and inflict upon me the stigma of public censure. The true individual freedom then is found when the character is fashioned into so true a unity that in all its acts it expresses itself completely. Similarly liberty in the State is found when the citizens combine together in a common purpose which they are agreed in maintaining against any impulse, not only in others but also in themselves, which would thwart that purpose. In both individual and society *liberty is control of the parts by the whole which they constitute.*

It is perfectly plain that this formula can only stand for freedom if the whole is a spiritual unity in which the parts fully realise their membership. Otherwise a great deal of substantial tyranny may be carried out in its name. It is for this reason that the government of one race by another is always an evil, and may be an intolerable evil. The Polish subject either of the Kaiser or of the Czar does not at all feel that in submitting to the laws which the political government imposes upon him, he is realising himself by incorporation into a larger fellowship. (Note: Written in 1916. This and the following two pages deal with a political situation now ended, but the argument holds good.) The State for him is an alien force which so far as it secures good order provides a certain material benefit, but has no moral claim upon him. An Englishman lately said, in the presence of a number of such Poles, that his country had a claim upon all that he possessed and all that he was, because in each case everything was given to him by the country; he was not merely an individual, but essentially and fundamentally an Englishman. To be English was part of his essential self. One of the Poles replied that he did not understand this position at all; a man paid in taxes and the like for everything he received from the State, and he did not see how the State had any further moral claim. This complete divorce between governmental administration and moral loyalty is plainly an evil to which hardly any in the world is equal. For it strikes at the root of all real corporate life and tends to make the individual regard himself as an isolated atom whose rational course is to pursue his own interest, except so far as he may forcibly be checked, and whose self-sacrifice for the community, if his instincts lead that way, is from his own point of view sheer loss and no gain at all. Probably the inhabitants of Ireland in very large numbers feel much the same with regard to the United Kingdom. The fact that of recent years English government has at any rate attempted to be benevolent, may mitigate the bitterness of the feeling, but will not alter it. It is not the harshness, but the alien character of the government which constitutes the fundamental evil. In certain departments of life organised Labour has the same feeling towards the existing English State. The State is in fact so much controlled by men of a certain class and station that Labour perpetually feels itself to be in the position of a subject race. We see the result in the difficulties which the English Government had in introducing a measure of compulsory military service, and in their decision altogether to exempt Ireland from the operation of that principle.

In order that there may be real freedom the government must be the organ of a genuine moral unit, and for this reason frontiers should so far as possible coincide with national divisions. Here as elsewhere, when once sin has been committed, the right condition cannot be restored without atoning sacrifice. In Hungary and the Balkan States, for example, the claims of nationality were for centuries persistently ignored. There are now many Roumanians under Hungarian rule, but it may not be possible simply to transfer them to Roumanian rule because there are patches of Hungarian population scattered about in that territory which is predominantly Roumanian in race, and these will then be subject to Roumanian domination as the Roumanians are now to Hungarian. That would perhaps be better than the present situation, because the number of those subjected to an alien government would be far smaller; but to these Hungarians it will be a real injury none the less. There is also the permanent difficulty which besets a government that has ever been guilty of oppression; it has stored up against itself a bitterness of feeling which is very likely to retaliate when it is given liberty, and the oppression which began from sheer love of power may be maintained from fear of that retaliation. There seems to be no way out of this danger, except that the oppressed should be willing to wipe out the past, and voluntarily accept its sufferings without demanding recompense. In one way and another the only means by which sin can be obliterated is through the suffering of the innocent, and this may take the form of a voluntary acceptance of past suffering for the sake of future peace and fellowship. That government and people which has been guilty of oppression ought to do everything possible to alleviate the sufferings, and take their share, but if they are simply forced to accept a certain amount of retaliation from those whom they have injured, the evil process seems likely to be continued *ad infinitum*. No doubt the parties can to some extent meet each other half way. For example it is sometimes said that one difficulty about Home Rule for Ireland is that Ireland could not manage its own affairs without financial help from England; if that were all, as of course it is not, then let England give the financial help without demanding any supervision of its expenditure. That will be an act that may go far to mitigate the feelings of resentment still alive in Ireland which result from the bad old times. This illustration is of course given simply to suggest a principle; whether it is politically possible or not is a question that must be determined by those who have detailed knowledge of the facts. Anyhow two points stand out clearly: the right relation of government to governed is not a matter of administrative expediency, but of fundamental and spiritual principle, and when once that principle has been violated there is something present which can only be removed by the voluntary suffering of innocent persons.

But if this is all that can be said, we shall be left with the picture of a human race divided into a number of moral units, each free in itself but each attempting to be self-sufficient. This is the ideal of Nationalism. This attempt is, in the modern world, doomed to failure if only from economic causes. Every people upon the face of the earth is in fact economically dependent upon many others if not upon all others, and this is only the outward symbol of the spiritual unity which in fact binds all men together. Indeed just as the individual finds his freedom by personally realising his own membership in a community, so that community will only find its own self-fulfilment in realising its membership in humanity.

The principle of freedom seems urgently to require extension in two directions where hitherto it has been given little scope. So far as ordered freedom goes, which is very much the same as saying so far as civilisation goes, the national State has been almost its only expression. But, as we have seen, the national State cannot exist in isolated independence; and even within itself it is to be remembered that the national State does not by means of its regulations come into perpetual relations with the mass of individual citizens. These do, however, find their lives actually controlled by the regulations of the industry in which they work, These regulations invade their very homes and tell them when they may get up and when they may go to bed. Yet they often have no means of affecting these regulations except by the threat of a strike. Before we can be said to have a free society it will be essential that the control of industry shall pass largely into the hands of those immediately concerned. Here as everywhere else the extension of liberty is dangerous to material prosperity, though, if the experiment succeeds, it results in the increase of material prosperity, inasmuch as the enthusiasm of the workers is enlisted. But for the achievement of the spiritual ideal the extension of liberty is indispensable. The various great movements of recent times since the French Revolution, or the less spectacular but equally important industrial revolution in England at the end of the eighteenth century, have all had their real source more in the spiritual aspiration which is the distinguishing mark of man than in desire for more material goods. Very often the former expressed itself in terms of the latter, because it was economic bondage that fettered the life of the spirit; but the inner history of the movements shows plainly that the real energy came from spiritual discontent rather than from material greed. This has been most emphatically true of the Socialist and Syndicalist movements. Working men are not as a rule prone to self-analysis nor highly skilled in it. They may find great difficulty in stating where the seat of the trouble lies. But a sympathetic observer quickly detects that what really galls is not so much the small proportion of the results of industry allotted as the reward of labour, but rather the sense that the employees are treated as 'hands' and not as 'persons', so far as the industry is concerned. Their personality apparently is for their leisure time; only their productive utility counts in industry itself. But this is to say that for the greater part of their waking life they are treated as living chattels, which is Aristotle's definition of a slave. The economic maxim that labour is a commodity to be bought as cheap as possible by those who need it and to be sold as dear as possible by those who offer it, ignores the fact that a man's labour is inseparable from himself. I may sell my coat and another man may buy it without in any way affecting my personality; but I cannot thus sell my labour for my labour is simply myself labouring. The existing social organism is therefore felt to be unjust at its root, because it does not recognise the real and spiritual nature of man. Charity is no remedy. If all that labour asked were a fairer proportion of this world's goods, charity would be a remedy so far as it went; but as the demand is for recognition of the workers as rational and responsible beings, charity, far from being a remedy, is felt rather as an insult. As between equals it is only a foolish, and in fact weak, spirit that can be insulted by charity. A man ought not to shrink from receiving money or any other assistance from a friend, for he ought to believe that the friend is genuinely glad to give it. But when the relation of friendship is not there, and the charity is a working off of superfluity to satisfy the impulse of compassion, or is even the giving away of comforts in answer to a general and abstract sense of duty, there is involved the denial of true freedom to the person whose necessities can only be met in such a way. In political life sovereignty has had to be shared; the Crown which once governed has devolved its authority, no doubt under pressure, upon the representatives of the people. In the evolution of industrial freedom the private Capitalist and the Company must pass through the same process. If we are to have real freedom it must be an extension of our general principle to this sphere; the parts must be controlled by the whole which they constitute, and to that end must truly constitute the whole by which they are controlled.

It is clear, of course, that the association of Labour in the control of industry must be accompanied by a great extension of education; but that subject, as also the extension of the principle of freedom beyond the bounds of the National State, will occupy us in subsequent chapters. Before passing on, however, it may be well to remark that Liberty as we have defined it is bound up with Obedience. The principle requires both that the authority, governing the parts of the soul or the several citizens in the State, should be vested in the whole soul or the whole body of citizens, and also that the directions issued by this authority should be accepted and obeyed.

The State must also remember that it exists by no other right or title than that of all associations of men; it is bound therefore to recognise 'Personality' equal in essence to its own in all associations or corporate bodies within itself, whether they be religious, educational, economic, or of any other type. It must aim at their 'freedom' as it aims at the freedom of individuals, only claiming, in this case as in that, to be the supreme source of order in virtue of its including all other associations within itself. (Note: On this point, which is of capital importance in practice, see Figgis' *Churches in the Modern State*.)

What then is the place for the individual conscience? Is there no duty, or even right, of rebellion against corporate wickedness? Unless we can guarantee the moral perfection of the community – and of course that cannot be guaranteed – we must let the individual judge and act upon his judgment. But he must be sure that his objection is truly conscientious, or in other words that it is based on moral principle, which is the same as saying based on consideration for the highest attainable welfare of society as a whole. Nor must he raise any objection if the State puts its penalties in force against him. The State will do wisely to deal tenderly with the consciences of its citizens; moreover, if the position which we shall advance in Book II is accepted, the State must remember that its citizens are also children of God, owing an allegiance to Him which transcends all earthly loyalties, and having rights as free citizens in a Commonwealth of greater dignity than any nation or state. But the law-breaker has no right to expect exemption from penalty merely because he can plead conscientious objection to the law. He must be ready to follow his conscience to the point of martyrdom. Moreover, both he and the State must first of all remember that freedom rests upon law; frequent law-breaking and the contempt for law resulting from it is the way to chaos and the condition wherein the life of man would be 'solitary, poor, nasty, brutish, and short'. Frequent breaches of the law, however conscientious, are therefore disastrous to society, and if the 'objector' is to be truly conscientious he must have estimated as far as he can the harm which he does by weakening the authority of law. The true aim alike of State and individual is that condition which may be called either free order or ordered freedom; for this is the counterpart of that true fellowship which we defined as the life of free persons bound together by mutual love.

ii The Church and Labour

As a young man Temple had been angered and upset by the social conditions in which the industrial population were living at that time. He had become committed to working for social reform and this had been one of the main reasons behind his decision to offer himself to the service of the Church. Through his contact and work with the Workers Educational Association (WEA) this concern had, in his own words, 'made me as a person'. Furthermore, as he moved from post to post within the Church he continued with his work for the WEA even when there was intense pressure to concentrate on other things. Now, in 1918, he decided to join the Labour Party, and announced this to the Church of England's Convocation. He believed that this young party presented the best hope for social reconstruction at the end of the First World

War. The article printed below explains this decision, arguing that it expresses two key social principles: freedom and fellowship. Temple seeks to win others to the cause. While he would resign seven years later, over the inconsistency of the Party's policy in the Far East, and as a result of disappointment over its parliamentary achievements (Iremonger 1948, pp. 333, 509), he continued to feel more sympathy with the Labour Party's general programme than with that of any other political group (though he was not always ready to give Labour leaders the active help they sought from him: see Iremonger 1948, pp. 509–10).

Daily News, Tuesday 14 May 1918

Whatever else the Church is or ought to be it most certainly ought to be a fountain of idealism. And, historically regarded, so it is. Over and over again in history the Church has carried society forward by a great stride, because the spirit which is in it has kindled the soul of some prophet to see new visions and call men to their fulfilment. Very often the officers of the Church have suspected and opposed the prophet; and yet it is true that he drew his inspiration from the Church because by the spirit which is in it he was first set upon his course, and by its worship he was sustained throughout it. St Francis, Savonarola, Luther, Wesley, Newman, are all names of men who in greater or less degree were resisted by the official Church in which their ministry began; but from it they drew their inspiration, and the Church which once resisted learnt to honour.

But no serious Churchman can be content that the Church should throw up a prophet now and then. It ought to be itself prophetic. Theologians speak of it as being the 'Spirit-bearing Body'. It ought to give a united, a corporate witness to the Kingdom of God, the proclamation of which is the kernel of the original gospel. Above all, the Church ought to be quick to discern the signs of the spirits working in the world, to enter into these so as at once to give them the strength of conscious dependence on God, and also to keep them true to their own highest ideals.

Fellowship and Freedom

For corporate witness the Church is now incapacitated by its system of government. It has no organ of corporate thought or action. And because of this incapacity many of its members have combined to launch the

Life and Liberty Movement, which aims at making the Church an effective witness before the nation to the righteousness of God and to the life which is offered to men in Christ, and to this end demands for the Church without delay liberty in the sense of full power to control its own life.

One of the signs of the times that must give serious concern to any thoughtful Churchman is that, of late, the great movements of the Spirit have not even proceeded from the Church but seem to have gone on altogether apart from it. The Church has not been without prophets; much of what is now becoming accepted doctrine finds its origin in F. D. Maurice. Bishop Westcott was a prophet, as we become more sure with every year that separates us from his death. Lately we lost in Henry Scott Holland a man of the authentic fire and vision of the true prophet. Among the living are some who could be named in that noble company. And every one of these saw in what we now call the Labour Movement the working of the Holy Spirit who is given to the Church. Yet the Church as a whole still fails to see this.

There are two marks by which a truly spiritual movement may be known – freedom and fellowship. Freedom stands for the full development of personality; by itself it may lead to anarchy, conflict, and the break up of society. Fellowship stands for the unity of society, and by itself it may tend to blunt individuality, and so lead to mediocrity and stagnation. True progress depends on the interaction of the two. Where freedom expresses itself in fellowship you have love, the chief of the fruits of the spirit. Now the Labour Movement is essentially an effort to organise society on the basis of freedom and fellowship. As such it has a right to claim the sympathy of the Church.

Principle and Party

The Labour Party is a different thing: that is a political organisation, and the Church as a whole must not be attached to any political party – not even to the Tory Party. But Churchmen ought to consider very carefully the formulated programme of the Labour Party, and whether individually they should subscribe to it.

Here is a party who has at least put forward an outline scheme of reconstruction in national and international life. It is a scheme based on moral ideals. We must not support it merely because we sympathise with the motives behind it: but if we believe that those motives are, on the whole, applied with wisdom we have no right to stand aside, we must go in and help.

For if Churchpeople stand aloof from the Labour Party, however sympathetically, two great evils will result. The Church will suffer by alienation from a great movement of the spirit; that movement will suffer by lack of spiritual reinforcement and renewal, and will so fall beneath its own best aspirations. Most emphatically I do not say that all Churchmen should join the Labour Party. There should be Churchmen in every political party infusing into all its activities the Christian spirit. But with equal emphasis I say that the newly-constituted Labour Party claims our attention, and if we find ourselves in substantial agreement with it we are under a plain duty to join and help it both to keep its idealistic side uppermost and to press steadily forward to the realisation of its ideals.

iii The Power State and the Welfare State

We have already seen that Temple did not follow the great liberal philosopher J. S. Mill in believing that freedom was the simple absence of coercion (see pp. 72–3). He believed that freedom depended on society and, in particular, on the state fulfilling a positive role in the life of its citizens, especially through education, in equipping each of them for a purposeful and creative life in which they would play their part in moving society forward. While Bishop of Manchester, Temple was invited to give the Henry Scott Holland Lectures at Liverpool in 1928. This he did, using the lectures to develop and expand his view of the state, placing it in historical perspective. The lectures were published as Christianity and the State. *He saw the state as having an ordering and resourcing role in a person's life, though he was emphatic that the state had only a conditional authority and jurisdiction to do certain things: it could never be an ultimate object of political loyalty. What was especially significant in these lectures was the coining of the phrase 'the welfare state'. This came about through drawing a contrast between the pre-First World War Austrian and Prussian states, which coerced their citizens for the state's own ends, named as 'the power state', and the kind of state he was advocating, which is governed by law and exists to serve the community, now named as 'the welfare state'. This distinction would be drawn again in later publications, such as* Citizen and Churchman (1941) *and was adopted by other academics such as the economist Sir Alfred Zimmern. After the Second World War, of course, it came to be used widely as a description of the general package of reforms and initiatives put in place by the Labour Government of 1945–51. In these lectures, then, Temple unwittingly played a significant role in the evolving political life of the nation (see further p. 199).*

Christianity and the State, 1928, Chapter IV, 'The State in its External Relations', pp. 160–77

It is very commonly held that the State is most of all itself when dealing with other States; and the ground for this conviction is that its absolute sovereignty is then most apparent. There are, moreover, two Ways in which foreign relations appear to exhibit this Sovereignty in a special degree. First, those relationships themselves exhibit the fact that the State acknowledges no superior. It does not ask leave to make its decisions or to act on them; nor will it brook interference. Secondly, it is recognised to have the right to call on its citizens to obey its commands even to the death. What are we to say with regard to such claims?

I take the second first, because it is the most often challenged, and I believe it to be in principle beyond dispute. It is perfectly true that in war the State compels all other interests of men to be subordinated to the political interest. Commerce, culture, family ties – all count as nothing compared with the exigencies of State. This constitutes a great temptation. The statesman, like other human beings, is prone to magnify his office and to see life habitually in the perspectives apparent from the State's point of view; to him the sacrifice of all these other interests to the State is only an expression of the true order of their importance. This is one reason among very many why it is unsafe to be governed by statesmen to whom politics are the primary personal interest. It is well that they should be men who personally care more for other pursuits and administer the State from a sense of duty. No man who revels in power can safely be entrusted with it. In the claim of the State to use and sacrifice its citizens in its cause there is a fearful peril. And yet the claim, in principle, is just. The State is the only necessary organ of the community. The loss of any of its specialised associations would be an impoverishment; the collapse of the State is likely, at least, to break up the community itself. This is not necessary; it is possible to destroy the State and reconstruct it without destroying the community; but even so the loss is fearful. The State, as the organ of national unity, is so closely bound up with the community that it has almost as irresistible a claim as the community itself. (Note: Of course this does not mean that the Government always has this claim; but when the Government administers the State against the welfare of the community the normally right course is to turn it out, not to resist it while it remains the Government.) The political interest of men is not in itself so precious as their social and cultural interests; but it is in a special sense indispensable to these. Therefore the State is, in principle, entitled to subordinate these to itself for a sufficient reason; and it is, in principle, justified in calling on its citizens to die, and even to kill, for the preservation of what is necessary to it as the indispensable instrument of the nation's life.

There are many subsidiary considerations to be added in this connection, but they do not affect the main point. We pass to the first claim mentioned above – the claim that the State supremely exhibits its inherent sovereignty in foreign relations, because here, where it deals with its equals, it submits to no superior. This claim is commonly admitted to be valid; I believe it to be entirely false. Of course it is beyond question that States have acted on this claim, so that a theory which erects it into a principle is not to be refuted by historical facts. My contention is that the State in so acting has not exhibited, but has concealed, its true nature.

First we must notice that this theory depends for its plausibility on our adopting the national point of view. As soon as we take a European or broadly human point of View this claim to sovereignty appears just like the claim to total independence put forward by Hobbes on behalf of his imaginary human beings in the state of nature. Each was sovereign, and for that very reason life became unbearable for each and all. So since the Renaissance every State in Europe has claimed to be sovereign; its sovereignty is chiefly exhibited (the claim maintains) in the right to make War or peace. Many of us are beginning to feel that as a direct result of this precious sovereignty, 'the life of man is . . . poor, nasty, brutish and short'. In other words, the claim to sovereignty in this sense is, through the very exercise of sovereignty, leading to its own repudiation. That strongly suggests that the claim is false in principle.

Secondly, we have seen that the State is an organ of community and exists to serve its community. But what conceivable issue can arise the solution of which by arbitration would not better serve the community than the arbitrament of war? It is said that we cannot be sure of an impartial tribunal. Is war, then, so conspicuously impartial? When a dispute arose between Prussia and Denmark, in 1863, and each side held that the interests at stake were vital, is it so certain that that bloodiest of idols, the God of Battles, decided the issue according to justice? Is not that particular idol a notorious coward, always siding with the battalions? (Note: The fact that God can bring good out of evil is no reason for attributing evil directly to God's action.) This cant about the partiality of any international tribunal is peculiarly nauseating. Of course we cannot secure complete impartiality. We have not got it in the English Courts of Justice, nor in any tribunal that has been or can be set up on earth; but we know that it is better to let the courts decide than to appeal from them to force which does not even aim at impartiality or justice but only at 'superiority'. We are told that we could not submit to arbitration 'vital interests' or 'questions of honour'. But there can be few interests which do not suffer more through a victorious war than from a hostile award. And what honour is that which is satisfied by our divesting ourselves of the human and god-like faculty of reason that we may impose or accept the judgment of a force which is only not brutal because, being intellectually directed, it is devilish? So far as the State acts for its national community, it will always serve it best by resorting to arbitration, and by taking every possible step to forward such international arrangements as may secure that in all cases of dispute arbitration takes the place of war. Till those arrangements are completed, war may be a duty; but to complete them is as certainly a duty.

But, thirdly, it is when we consider the State as acting distinctively by law that we see how truly the logic of its own nature presses it on towards international organisation. After all, the State, we found, possesses force as the means of upholding the universality of law; and force is confined to the State in order that it may only be exercised under the control, and for the maintenance, of law. But war is the repudiation of law. If the State goes to war in preference to accepting arbitration, it follows its mere property of force in preference to its essential characteristic of law. It is not then most of all itself; on the contrary it is then false to itself. It shows its true nature when it promotes that international organisation which will secure the reign of law (its own true essence) in International relations.

Progress in this matter is being made, but it is long overdue. We find a fourth compelling reason for action in this direction in the relation of the State to the various associations through which men pursue the various interests of life. These grew up, we saw, within the national community; but the self-contained character of that community was an accident of history; it was due to the fact that, when means of communication were meagre, intercourse was geographically limited. We may well be glad of this, for it facilitated the development of a variety of national types. But it remains true that the national character of most human associations was always accidental. As soon as the external cause for this limitation of association was removed, all manner of international associations, economic, cultural and religious, sprang into effective life. This is one reason why modern war is so incomparably disastrous. It involves a reversion to the purely national point of view. When the nation comprised most human interests and activities there was comparatively little harm in this. Now it is a calamity beyond estimate. As the international ties are drawn closer, the opportunities of friction increase as well as those of friendship; and because all nations are linked together, none can stand aloof. The disparity between an international society and purely national States both precipitated the World War and added to its horrors.

> The age of competitive armaments and competitive alliances culminated in the World War... The struggle could not be localised because the nations were so interdependent, so bound up with one another. All the great nations of the World were embroiled... because a single system held them fast. Nothing was common save the catastrophe. In the words of Viscount Grey, 'it was a victory of war itself over everybody who took part in it'. The significance of this fact is simply that war has become an anachronism, an institution incompatible with the civilisation which has overspread the world. (R. MacIver, *The Modern State*, pp. 247–8)

And yet, as things were, it is hard to see how the new age could have dawned without the war. Men's political theory was in all nations so far removed from the actual facts of the new world that it is doubtful if they would have abandoned their idolatrous State-absolutism if it had not manifestly led them to calamity. Moreover, the whole conception of the State which finds its natural expression under modern conditions in the League of Nations is the extreme antithesis of that which had inspired Prussia since the time of Frederick the Great, or Austria from the time of the Thirty Years War, and it is almost inconceivable that a true League of Nations could have been inaugurated until the military monarchies of those States had been overthrown. The same is true of pre-revolutionary Russia. But history had made it necessary that the genesis of any League that was to work successfully should be among the Western European nations who had inherited that respect for law, which ancient Rome gave those who were fortunate enough to be conquered by her. A shrewd German observer said near the beginning of the war that it was a struggle between *Kultur* and the ideas of 1789. Fundamentally that is true, though the men of 1789, bemused by Rousseau, had so confused those ideas that it is often hard to disentangle them. The war was a struggle between the idea of the State as essentially Power – Power over its own community and against other communities – and of the State as the organ of community, maintaining its solidarity by law designed to safeguard the interests of the community. The Power-State might have yielded to shear pressure of circumstances in course of time; but it is contrary to the psychology of the Power-State to suffer conversion; it was likely to fight before it let a Welfare-State take its place. After all, it cost England two revolutions to reach the ideas of John Locke, unsystematic as they were; and it cost France another, equivalent in convulsiveness to our two put together, to secure ascendancy for the ideas of 1789. The Power-States of Austria and Prussia were not likely to yield to anything but power. The great objective issue in the war, vital for all peoples, was the issue between two theories of the State. It was no accident that the Italy of Mazzini and Cavour dropped out of the Triple Alliance to become the ally of French and British democracy; nor was it an accident that its place by the side of the military empires was taken by Turkey. If it is true, as I think it is, that 'the establishment of a League of Nations, directed towards the abolition of competitive armaments and the judicial settlement of international disputes, is not so much the institutional expression of an ideal as the belated adjustment of an institution to realities' (MacIver, *The Modern State*, p. 249), then it is also true that, before this adjustment could be made, the Power-State had to be swept into the limbo of forgotten idolatries. The issue of the victory of the Allies in the establishment of the League was no accident; it was the logical outcome of the principles which differentiated their political life from that of their opponents. Nothing is now so important as that the champions of those principles should be loyal to them.

The whole of this argument may be summed up very briefly. The State is an organ of community; community has mainly been territorially demarcated into nations; therefore the State has been national. Community is become very largely international; therefore the State must become international also.

We have found that the essential nature of the State and the immanent logic of its own development points towards the realisation of an international State, an Organ of the international community as the existing State is of the national community, promulgating law and possessed of force by which to secure for that law its essential characteristic of universality. But this international State will not be found already existing by the mere process of differentiating from it the other interests of mankind. It has to be deliberately constructed. There is need for a real Social Contract between the nations to lift them from the state of nature to the level of civilized community. Such a contract was never made by primitive mankind to found society or the State; but it was made in the Covenant of 1919 to found the League of Nations.

The League involves no supersession of the nation. The variety of the nations is good. A non-national cosmopolitanism, which would depreciate national distinctions, would thereby also abolish many valuable elements of our experience. But we can learn to rejoice in each other's peculiarities instead of detesting them. Only Germany could have given us Goethe; only Russia Dostoievski; only England Browning. Each can rejoice in the products of the others. We have to rise above the stupid alternative of identity and antagonism, of unison and discord, and help both to create and to enjoy harmony.

It still remains to ask how the argument that we have outlined is related to Christian principles. The doctrine of State-absolutism, at any rate, cannot be Christian, for it ignores or defies the sole absolute sovereignty of God. To Him the obedience of the State is due, as is that of all things in the created world. Before Him there are no rights which are not also duties. The State for a Christian may have the right to determine for itself what is its duty to God at a given time; it has no right to do anything except in accordance with His sovereign will. When Italy was considering whether or not to enter the Great War, statesmen and editors combined to say that of course she must determine the matter according to her own interest. That is false, unless indeed by 'interest' is meant her highest spiritual interest; and the way to serve that is to seek no interest at all, but only duty. Italy had no right to enter the war unless it was her duty to enter the war, just as we had no right to enter it unless it was our duty. I believe that, in all the conditions of that time, it was our duty; and if the conditions were repeated, it would be our duty again. For it was not a war of aggression, nor even (in the mind of the people at least) of self-defence. It was a war to keep our promise, to protect the independence of a small nation, and to secure not so much predominance as continued existence for 'the ideas of 1789' against an embattled *Kultur* already in arms against them. But though it would be again our duty to go to war if the same conditions were repeated, it is still more obviously our duty to see that those conditions never are repeated. That they existed at all was due to sin in our pre-war civilisation. Among nations that were Christian in all their dealings there could be no thought of war. The Christian's ultimate loyalty is due, not to his earthly State, but to the Kingdom of God, wherein all nations are provinces. If his loyalty to God conflicts with his loyalty to the State, it is the former that must prevail. The modern respect for 'conscientious objection' to what the State requires, whether that be military service or some other action which the conscience of an individual may condemn, is a great sign of progress. No doubt the poor human 'conscience' is invoked in relation to many matters with which philosophers will say that it has nothing at all to do; this is only one more illustration of the truth that man is not a rational animal, but only an animal striving to become rational. The fact remains that for the State to respect 'conscientious objection' is a recognition on its part that its citizens have a duty to something other and higher than itself, which Christians will call the Kingdom of God.

I do not share the conscientious objection felt by many to military service. I believe the State, when acting for the community, has a right to call upon me to be killed and even to kill in support of its cause, if that cause be just and can only be upheld by war. But the State has no right to call upon me to hate its enemies. There are those who have sneered at the fact that in the war men were more willing to give their lives than their property. But there is nothing to sneer about. It was only their animal lives – their mortal bodies – that they gave. Property is an expression of personality and is valued accordingly. Often it is valued blindly and foolishly, but it is not a purely blind valuation which prefers property, which can become the expression of personality for generations unborn, to the physical life which is anyhow bound to end before long. Yet the State has a claim on my property as well as on my body. But upon my character it has no claim. That belongs first and foremost to God and to eternity; and the State can only secure good service from it by recognising that it must not direct it. Those men best serve the State who are ready, if occasion come, in God's name to defy the State.

Now all experience shows that human nature has never in the mass so far appropriated the Grace of God that it can pass through the horrors of war with character unstained, even though to enter the War was at the time the only course of duty. If the argument for providing against war is strong on grounds of economic interest, on moral grounds it is overwhelming. To organise for peace is a most manifest Christian duty. And if we find, as we have found, that the very nature of the State presses us in this direction for the fulfilment of its own destiny, we cannot be in any doubt where the course of Christian statesmanship lies. It is the way of progressive international federation – the way of the League of Nations.

Perhaps it is still worth while to explode that hoary delusion which expresses itself in the Latin tag – *Si vis pacem, para bellum* – If you wish for peace, prepare for war. That was a quite sensible maxim as applied to the Roman Empire. The Empire comprised the whole civilised world; it had natural frontiers all round it – the ocean, the Rhine, the Danube, the mountains of Asia Minor, the Euphrates, the Desert. If such an empire were prepared for war, no one would make war upon it. The circumstances which made that maxim sensible were the very opposite of our system of competitive armaments. For us the sensible maxim has less literary attractiveness; it is – If you wish for peace, prepare for peace.

6

Reasonable Evangelism: The Oxford Mission of 1931

Temple not only developed a reasoned theology but sought to present it to students and others in a clear and cogent way. He would speak every summer at the Student Christian Movement gathering at Swanwick. He would visit different universities and address their Christian societies. He travelled abroad and lectured in the United States on three different occasions, speaking to students as well as to teachers.

The most famous of these encounters was the Oxford Mission of 1931. F. R. Barry, who was the vicar of the University Church, describes the background to the mission as being 'the disillusioned aftermath of the first war'. At Oxford, 'religious and moral life was at a low ebb. College chapels were virtually empty. Christianity was almost a dirty word. Christian belief was commonly regarded as the refuge of the mentally second-rate – few, anyhow, were prepared to take it seriously. The job of the University Church, in that context, was to get Christianity back on the map – to exhibit its relevance to the life of Oxford and as something intellectually respectable' (Christian Faith and Life, [1931] 1963, p. 11).

Temple spoke at the first mission to the University since the war. He spoke on eight consecutive nights in the church. He spoke without movements or mannerisms, with hands resting lightly on the lectern in front of him, standing motionless except for an occasional tilt of the head or the raising of a hand to adjust his glasses. He spoke of God's purpose for the world and how God had a purpose 'for us as part of His purpose for the world' (p. 126). As was so often the case, he allowed a sense of the sweep of history, past, present and future, to inspire and motivate his audience to make a committed response. He spoke of the place of Christ within this history, and of Christian morality, sin, repentance, the cross, the Holy Spirit, prayer, the sacraments, and the Church. Through all of this he was able to present the Christian *faith as a rational and coherent philosophy of life. And, apparently, he startled his hearers by his obvious and profound belief in aspects of Christianity that many of them had dismissed long ago. One of the undergraduates in the audience wrote the following description:*

> *The church was packed with hundreds of undergraduates, thronging to hear him. He was large of stature and the picture of this great figure, high above us in the pulpit, is one I shall never forget. Unlike many missioners, Temple was not an emotional preacher. His powerful appeal was primarily to the head. It aimed to challenge, deepen and straighten our Christian thinking, belief and standards of life, and only then to stir our emotions. In all his eight addresses there was this element of challenge and every night, following the address, there was time for quiet reflection – silence, punctuated by quotations from Scripture, which helped to shape our prayers and our resolve. The silence ended with a prayer and a blessing and we all went out into the Oxford night stimulated, challenged and deepened, many of us with a new approach to faith and life. (From notes by John Adam given to the author)*

On the last night Temple spoke of the need for his hearers not to practise their faith in isolation but to bring themselves into the Christian society, the Church. In some famous words he described the history of the Church, a description that seemed also to sum up what Temple was doing at Oxford:

> *And, remember, the supreme wonder of the history of the Christian Church is that always in the moments when it has seemed most dead, out of its own body there has sprung up new life; so that in age after age it has renewed itself, and age after age by its renewal has carried the world forward into new stages of progress, as it will do for us in our day, if only we give ourselves in devotion to its Lord and take our place in its service. (pp. 133–4)*

Then, right at the end, there was an unforgettable moment. When the hymn 'When I survey the wondrous cross' was being 'roared out' Temple stopped the singing and asked the students to read the words of the last verse to themselves. Then, if they meant them with all their heart to sing them loudly; if they did not mean them at all not to sing them; and if they meant them even a little and wanted to mean them more, to sing them very softly. There was silence while everyone read the words and then a spontaneous and hushed whispering of 'Love so amazing, so divine, demands my soul, my life, my all' (Iremonger 1948, p. 378).

Barry described how the mission touched and changed the lives of a large number of students, to the extent that many of them offered themselves for Christian ministry after leaving university. Adam was one of those. The mission *'was, indeed, a decisive moment in the history of that generation . . . It was when the tide began to come in'* (Iremonger 1948, p. 377). This is confirmed by Adrian Hastings who describes the mission as the first sign of a revival in Anglican Christian life after the scepticism of the 1920s (Hastings 1987, p. 257). It seemed to be, as well, a moment when Temple's own gifts and calling were perfectly matched with the task he was given. He was not only describing an ideal to an unbelieving world, in this case the Christian life to the students of Oxford, but moving his hearers towards it.

The text of his addresses also became very popular. It was reprinted 16 times between 1931 and 1957 and reissued again in 1963 and 1994, the last time in an edition sponsored by the author Susan Howatch. *Christian Faith and Life* gives one of the best summaries of Temple's religious outlook and demonstrates how it could be powerfully persuasive.

i A Call to Prayer

Chapter 7, 'Prayer and Sacraments', pp. 110–18

The aim of all prayer is the same as the aim of all life, it is union with God. Life and prayer should be as closely as possible intertwined. God is the ultimate reality who sustains all existence, including our own lives. To be in actual and living union with Him is the fundamental business of life; and everything else follows from that.

He has given us our duty in the world to do, and it is our duty to Him to perform it as thoroughly and effectively as possible. We shall do it best if, while we are engaged in the tasks He has given us, we give them our whole and complete attention; therefore, during that time, we cannot be specifically and directly thinking about Him. But, of course, we shall enter upon those tasks with minds perpetually refreshed by the memory of Him and of His love, and it is most desirable that not only on Sundays, not only at regular times of prayer, but also at any moments when our attention is not definitely claimed by the work we have in hand, our minds should go back to God as He is in Himself; and we shall thus be constantly remembering Him. There ought to be no sense of spiritual transition as we pass from any occupation which is our proper occupation at the time to the thought of God. We should feel, whether it be in performing the duty He has given us or in remembering Him who gave us the duty, that we are always seeking to deepen our union with Him. But the moments when we concentrate upon this purpose particularly are our times of prayer.

Let us be quite clear about what are not the aims of prayer. We are not, in our prayers, trying to suggest to God something He has not thought of. That would plainly be ridiculous. Nor are we trying to change His mind. That would be an enterprise blasphemous in the attempt, and calamitous in the accomplishment. He knows what we want before we ask it. Then why ask? Why, because there may be blessings which only are effectively blessings to those who are in the right condition of mind; just as there is wholesome food which is actually wholesome only to those who are healthy in body. If you give the best beef to somebody in typhoid fever, you do him great harm. The worst of all diseases of the soul is forgetfulness of God; and if everything that we need came to us while we forgot God, we should only be confirmed in our forgetfulness of Him, in our sense of independence of Him. It may be good for a man that a temptation which always beats him should continue, and continue to defeat him, rather than he should conquer it without knowing that the power in which he won his conquest was from God. So, over and over again, it will happen that, whether or not God can give the blessing which, in His love, He desires to give, will depend on whether or not we recognise the source from which it comes. The way to recognise that He is the source of the blessings, and that we need them, is to ask. This expresses our sense of dependence upon God for that blessing. And remember that the only object of using words in your prayers is to fix your own thoughts, not to give information to God. He can read your thoughts, but your thoughts are likely to be very vague and wandering unless you fix them by means of words. It is for your own sake, not for God's, that you put your prayers into words. That being so, in your private prayers, those are the right words which succeed in fixing your thoughts on the right objects. It does not matter whether they would assist anybody else to fix their thoughts there or not; it would not matter if you invented an entirely new language of your own for your prayers. The words that help you are the right words for you to use.

When we come to public worship, it is different. Here the worship gathers us together in a common aspiration and a common sense of dependence upon God. Here, then, the language should be the most beautiful we can find for the purpose, suggesting in its beauty the reverence we owe to the Divine Majesty. Moreover, it should very often express not only the things we do feel, but the things we ought to feel, so that we may, by our prayer, teach ourselves to feel those things more thoroughly than we have done.

But the aim is union with God, not changing His mind, but changing our own, in order that, as a result of our faith, our realisation that we depend upon Him, He may be able to do for us, or through us, what, until we are conscious of this, He cannot do. The proper outline of a Christian prayer is not 'Please do for me what I want.' It is 'Please do with me what You want.' That prayer will always be answered in proportion to its sincerity.

And in order that it may be prayer at all, it must be addressed to God. Those of us who try to say our prayers nearly all find times when they are very cold and dry. There are many reasons for this, but one of the commonest reasons is we have let ourselves slip into forgetting God even while we pray. We use His Name but do not stop to think what it means. Our minds are focused on the things we ask for, and not upon God. That is not praying; that is uttering wishes to no one in particular. I cannot imagine anything more tedious or more futile. Naturally, people who get fixed in that habit say they find their prayers are no good, so they give them up. What they were doing was no good; but it was not praying.

Praying is speaking to God; so the first necessity is that you should be directing your mind towards God. That is the best part and most important part of prayer anyhow, and without it all the rest is useless. The great aim is union with God, and the first need is that you should be, so far as you are capable, with open face gazing upon Him. And then, when you have remembered what you know about God (which is not difficult, because He has given us the portrait of Himself in Jesus Christ, and though you cannot see God you can always remember Jesus Christ; so you should never begin to pray until you have the figure of Christ before your mind, and should pray to God as you see Him there); then you turn to the things you will pray for, and this is to be after the manner of the Lord's Prayer. I wonder where most of you begin to mean business as you say the Lord's Prayer. I used often to ask that of boys at school when I was preparing them for Confirmation. Their answer, when they gave any, was always the same: 'Forgive us our trespasses'; but that is rather near the end. The reason, of course, was that this was the first thing they knew they wanted and knew they could only get from God. If they had been both hungry and hard up, I suppose they would have started with 'daily bread'. But our Lord says that when you come into the presence of God you should forget all about yourself and your needs, even your sins; you should be so filled with the thought of God that what you want above all things is that God's Name may be hallowed – reverenced – throughout the world. You are to ask for that first, because you ought to want it most. And next, that He may be effectively King of the world He has made, so that all men obey His law; and then, that His whole purpose of love shall be carried out unspoiled by the selfishness of men. We have got into a habit of saying, 'God's will be done', in a mood of resignation. That is blasphemous. It means that, having found we cannot have our own way, we are ready to put up with His as a second best. It will not do. We ought to say, 'Thy Will be done', in ungovernable hope, knowing it to be so much better than our own. Then you ask for freedom from anxiety, 'daily bread', to see your way one day ahead; that is little enough. Then, for the sense of His favour, without which you cannot serve Him with a full heart, and which you have so often forfeited; you must be forgiven if you are to serve him whole-heartedly. Then that there may be no unnecessary difficulties, 'Lead us not into temptation'. And there is some evil that has actually got hold of us now, we want deliverance from that. And all this is not because then we shall be good and happy, but because it is God's kingdom, power, and glory we are concerned about all the time.

It is the prayer you would want to offer if you loved God with all your heart and you may learn to love Him with all your heart if you realise what this prayer means, and try to enter into it. Never let it become for you a mere formula.

In our Lord's teaching about petitionary prayer there are three main principles. The first is confidence, the second is perseverance and the third, for lack of a better word, I will call correspondence with Christ. Confidence: you remember He used language so strong as to be almost violent about the confidence with which you are to pray. If only you believe you have the thing, if it is moving a mountain into the sea, you shall have it. He never took any pains to avoid being misunderstood. He wanted people to think out for themselves the application of the principles He gave; so He added no qualifications. But He went straight on apparently to something else which seems inconsistent: perseverance. When you pray, you are to be sure you will get the thing; and if you do not get it, you are to go on praying. He illustrates it by the parable of the unjust judge, who ultimately granted the woman's petition because she was becoming such a nuisance. This, of course, is one of those parables which derive part of their point from the fact that the suggested illustration will not work. We know that God does not grant our petitions to rid Himself of tedium at our persistence; and, amongst other things, our Lord is here saying that if you will think of God as first and foremost a Judge you will find Him a curious kind of Judge. He does indeed judge us. But He is not first Judge – He is first Father, and only judges as a father judges.

There is nothing that so much develops faith as to persevere in asking through disappointment. If you always get the blessing you seek at once, or something you recognise as corresponding to it, your faith will remain at about the level at which you started. The reason why God calls for perseverance is not, of course, that He wishes to test our faith. He knows exactly what it is worth. But He may wish to deepen it. The thing that will most deepen it is to persist with faith through disappointment. Many masters of the spiritual life have said it seemed to them, as a matter of experience, that at an early stage in the spiritual life God does answer some prayers quite directly, and then begins to stop. The next stage is one in which prayers do not often receive a perceptible answer. God always does answer prayer; He always acts in response to prayer; but often we cannot understand His actions. Your confidence in praying ought not to be chiefly confidence that you are going to get what you ask, because that will be confidence as much in your own judgment as in God. It has to be a real surrender to Him. You must pass from faith that God will give you what you ask, to faith that what He gives is better than what you asked.

Now these two first principles of confidence and perseverance our Lord gave in His public teaching; but to the disciples alone He added that the prayer always answered was the prayer that was offered in His Name. 'Hitherto,' He said, 'have ye asked nothing in My Name. Ask and ye shall receive.' What does asking in anyone's name mean? It does not mean only tacking on the words, 'Through Jesus Christ our Lord'. As Studdert Kennedy used to say, it does not mean that our Lord has signed a large number of blank cheques on the bank of heaven, and you can fill them in how you like. To act in anyone's name is to act as his representative. To pray in the name of Christ is to pray as He would pray – as He is praying now. He is first and foremost the great illustration of perfect submission to the Will of God. So we are led on to understand that, as the great purpose of prayer is union with God, so the thing we are to express in our prayer is complete submission to His will that He may do it for us, in us, through us.

The two sons of Zebedee once came to our Lord and started off with a quite exact illustration of the wrong way to pray: 'We would that Thou shouldest do for us whatsoever we shall ask of Thee.' He asks what it is; and it turns out to be something that is selfish in the radically bad sense; it is something from which, if they obtain it, other people are shut out; it is to sit on His right and left hand in His glory. Then comes the answer: 'Can you drink of the cup that I drink of and be baptised with the baptism I am baptised with?' They would have something for themselves; He asks whether they can share His sacrifice. Incidentally, He thus suggests to them what is the nature of that glory which they seek conspicuously to share. But that is not our main concern just now. God answers every prayer; but when you come praying after the formula, 'We would Thou shouldest do for us whatsoever we shall ask of Thee', there is only one answer you will get: 'Can you share my sacrifice?' If your prayer is selfish, the answer will be something that will rebuke your selfishness. You may not recognise it as having come at all, but it is sure to be there.

So all prayer, and the life of which it is the focusing point, becomes that offering of ourselves in union with the sacrifice of Christ, which finds its perfect expression in the Eucharist.

ii A Call to Holy Communion

Chapter 7, 'Prayer and Sacraments', pp. 118–24

There are very many ways in which we may approach the consideration of the Holy Communion. I say that because I shall, of course, be able to adopt only one. You must not suppose that, if the way in which I approach it does not help to make it more real to you, there is no other way of approach by which you might find it real and ever more real.

We [have] traced . . . the outline of our Lord's Ministry, and . . . considered the stages by which He challenged the authority of the High Priests and made it inevitable that they should either accept Him as the promised Messiah or pronounce Him a blasphemer, with the condemnation to death that would follow. After His conduct in the triumphal entry, and cleansing of the Temple, there was no avoidance of that choice.

During the last week, with the same careful pains with which He arranged for the triumphal entry, we find also He has arranged for His Last Supper. As you know, the New Testament contains accounts based apparently upon different chronologies, and there is some doubt whether the Last Supper was the Passover Feast or not. It seems likely at least that St John is right in maintaining that it took place, not on the proper day of the Passover meal, but the day before. It is agreed that the day of the feast that year fell on a Sabbath, and it would have been lawful and probable that the Passover feast had been transferred a day earlier. So it may have been the actual Paschal meal, though not on the actual day of the feast. This is comparatively of small moment.

His disciples ask what preparations they are to make. He tells them to go to the city and they will meet a man carrying a pitcher of water. Women as a rule carried water, so they would not make a mistake. He would say nothing, but would turn and walk to the appointed place, and they were to follow him. When they came there, they were to speak the password just as when they went to fetch the ass on which He would ride; they were to say, 'Where is My guest chamber, where I shall eat the Passover with My disciples', and he would show them the Upper Room furnished for them. Why are the directions given in this curious cypher? Surely the reason is evident; Judas must not know. He must not be able to bring the soldiers there. It would have been the easiest place to effect the arrest if only he had known for certain where the Lord would be; and there must be no interruption there.

The Lord has lived the perfect life of perfect love. In the threefold temptations He has repudiated the method of obtaining men's allegiance otherwise than by the free offering of love; and now there is one of His own friends who is meditating treachery. What shall He do? What took place in the Upper Room was the spiritual crisis of the whole ministry. It would have been the easiest thing in the world to give the order to Peter, and the rest, and have the traitor bound. So the Lord would have made His escape; and so He would have lost His Kingdom. He tells them, and in telling them, shows Judas that He knows his mind, and therefore ensures that what He is about to do shall not be misunderstood by him – He tells them that one of them shall betray Him; and the beloved disciple, leaning back on His breast, asks: 'Who is it?' and into his ear the secret is whispered. 'He it is to whom I shall give the first sop when I have dipped it.' He singles Judas out for special honour. He makes to him, without giving away his secret to the rest, the one appeal that love still can make, and watches the effect. St John, who knows the secret, watches also; and what he saw stands written. 'After the sop, then entered Satan into him.' He has seen the man's face go black; the Lord, too, has seen it. 'That thou doest, do quickly', and Judas passes out under his Lord's protecting silence. That was the great spiritual crisis: that was the moment when He had to determine whether He should be loyal to the whole principle on which He came to found His Kingdom, even though it must mean that nothing now could stop the arrest, trial and crucifixion. 'He then having received the sop, went immediately out; and it was night' – a glimpse, through the door of the lighted room, of the darkness into which the traitor went. And then the Lord did two things. First, He said, 'Now is the Son of Man glorified.' Whether they were the authentic words or St John's understanding of His mind it does not matter. We shall not get a better understanding of His mind than that reached by the writer of the Fourth Gospel. That was the moment when the Son of Man achieved His glory. When it was so easy and so innocent to desert the principle of His Kingdom and save Himself from all the anguish, He was loyal to the cause for which He came; and the Cross after this was, from one point of view, a mere consequence.

In that moment also He took the bread that was before Him; and said it was His Body; and broke it. For in that moment He had broken His Body, and in that moment He had offered His side to the soldier's spear. 'This is My Body.' What would they think? Remember this was late on Thursday evening; by nine o'clock on Friday morning He was on the Cross. As they looked back, the two things would seem very close together, and they would know that one thing at least that He meant was this: As I break this bread, so I am breaking My Body. But not vainly; I am breaking it to give it to you, that the sacrifice of which it is the vehicle may enter into you and be your own. In the Consecration Prayer the words are there: 'In the same night that He was betrayed.' What we do when we come to the Holy Communion is, among other things, at least also this, that we unite ourselves with the thing He did that night in the supreme spiritual crisis of His ministry in order that the meaning of what He did may become true of us as it was of Him – that His sacrifice may be ours.

How are we to think of the way in which He still offers Himself to us by this means? There is no complete analogy, but there are some that are not very remote. When you listen to beautiful music, where is the beauty? You do not create it: you do not invent it – you find it. And yet you will not find it unless you have the understanding of music which qualifies you to be sensitive to it. It is the same with beauty everywhere. Two men stand before some great picture. Both see the same colours and the same lines – one sees beauty, the other sees nothing significant. But the one who sees the beauty does not make it – the artist made it. And so in the Holy Communion Christ offers Himself in all His fullness of holiness and love to be ours, but whether you receive Him depends on the insight of your faith, on how far you are conscious of your need of Him, on how far you are sincere in seeking to be united with Him in His offering of Himself to the Father.

At least a great part of what is cared for by those who speak of the Real Presence is this, that Christ there offers Himself in the fullness of His self-sacrifice to you that you may receive Him; and the chief part of what those care about who dwell especially on His Presence in the faithful receiver, is that unless you come in the mind to be united to Him so far as you may, you will not receive Him. For it is a law of the spiritual life from which there is no escape, that we receive in proportion to what we give – much more than we give, thank God, or we should be in a sorry plight, but still in proportion.

If you come there giving nothing, with no intention that your life should be used by God and for Him, then you will receive nothing. He will be offering you His perfect life of love, but you will be shutting it out. When you come with those things about you which are the opposite of God, because they are the opposite of love – envy, contempt, resentment, spite – they make a block in the channel through which the life of Christ might reach you. And all of us are selfish, more or less; and none can perfectly receive that perfect gift. So we need to come there offering ourselves in His service, and seek to receive out of the gift which He offers in its completeness and perfection so much as we are able to receive, and then go out into the world to live by that, a little more loving, a little less selfish; then back again, able this time, because a little more loving and a little less selfish, to receive rather more fully that always perfect gift; until life and worship build one another up into a complete dedication, and you give yourself utterly to His service, and you not only aspire to mean but you do actually mean the words of the great prayer, 'Here we offer and present unto Thee, O Lord, ourselves, our souls and bodies, to be a reasonable, holy, and lively sacrifice unto Thee.' When you can say that, with nothing held back and with nothing forgotten, then you will receive the gift of the life of Christ in all its fullness, and will say with St Paul, 'I live, yet not I, but Christ liveth in me.' Until we can say that, and say it truly, we must no one of us be content. And there is no means by which we may so fully enter into the meaning of His Sacrifice as this which He has provided and which is adapted to our whole nature. For we are called upon to use our bodies as well as our spirits in the act by which we seek to receive the life of Christ to be our own, since while we are in the body our service will be unreal unless our bodies be given to it. And we recognise His gift for what it is, the life that is offered in sacrifice to God, wholly given to Him to be used by Him not for our own purpose but for His.

iii A Call to Serve Church and World

Chapter 8, 'The Christian Society', pp. 126–40

During this week we have been trying, so far as the time and limitations of capacity – yours and mine – might allow, to consider the character of God and His purpose for the world (for it is nothing less than that), and His purpose for us as the part of His purpose for the world with which each one of us is directly and immediately concerned. And it is always in that context that we ought to think of the life of Christ and of our duty in response to the call of Christ. If we think of it against a narrower background we may easily devote ourselves with enthusiasm to some course which, though effective in itself, is yet far less effective in the long run – which is, in the end, the only run that matters – than it might have been had we kept before us the true perspective in which God's revelation is always set throughout the Bible. If you have doubt whether that is indeed the right way for us to regard the life of Christ and His call upon us, then I ask you to read again the first chapter of St Paul's Epistle to the Ephesians. He sets forth the eternal purpose of God for which He made the world, as being to 'sum up all things in Christ'.

And, in the long course of that purpose's fulfilment, we have considered the supreme and crucial moment, the life and the death of Jesus Christ, and the new impulse which came into the world as a result of that revelation – the new power over the hearts of men which they found that God was exercising, and to which they gave the name Holy Spirit, afterwards reading back what they had learned through that experience into all other activities of God at work within nature and within mankind in fulfilment of His own eternal purpose and in response to the manifestation of His character. We have seen that the purpose of the life of our Lord was quite definitely the inauguration of the Kingdom of God, the rule of God in the world, but therein also the revelation of God who is King – a revelation which designates Him as perfect love, so that we may paraphrase the description of His purpose by saying it is the inauguration of the reign of love.

When His visible Presence was withdrawn from men's sight, what was left as the fruit of His Ministry? Not a formulated creed, not a body of writings in which a new philosophy of life was expounded, but a group of men and women who found themselves knit together in a fellowship closer than any that they had known, and who became the nucleus of the whole Christian Church. As the fellowship expanded, it drew within its bounds people of every type, every nation, every social class. And they found that so far as they were loyal to its inner purpose, and submitted themselves to that Spirit moving in it by which its life was constituted, all that separated them from one another became unimportant and negligible. There was neither Jew nor Gentile – the deepest of all divisions based on religious history, negligible; neither Greek nor barbarian – the deepest of all divisions based on education and culture, negligible; neither bond nor free – the deepest of all divisions in economic status, negligible; neither male nor female – even the distinction of sex on which the whole social fabric rests, negligible. The whole group of them constituted a single personality, because all governed by one spirit and purpose, and the centre of unity in any personality is its purpose. And St Paul sees that 'one man in Christ Jesus' growing from strength to strength as new races bring in their various talents and endowments, until all come to constitute the 'one man in Christ Jesus' full-grown; and that is the measure of the stature of the completeness of the Christ. For we shall never know what Christ is in the fullness of His power until He has all nations at His disposal to manifest through their peculiar gifts the various elements in His all-embracing purpose.

The name of this fellowship, which ought ideally to be so close as to constitute a single personality, is the Church. St Paul speaks of the Church as the Body of Christ, and what He means first and foremost by that is, of course, that as Jesus of Nazareth used the body of flesh and blood in order to live before men the life which interprets to them the very being of God, so the Church exists on earth to do the self-same thing. It is the means whereby Christ becomes active and carries out His purpose in the world; that is what it is for, and that is what makes it the Church – the life of His Spirit within it, rising out of its faith in Him. And that remains true of it even when the people who are the members of the Church from time to time become very feeble in their faith, so that the activity of His Spirit by means of them is very much hampered and limited. No doubt, as we look upon the actual Christian Church at many periods of history, including our own, we may find that in many respects it presents an uninspiring spectacle. That is because we are attending to things which are incidental, rather than to the things that make it the Church of Christ, His Body. Those things are the perpetual witness of the Gospel in its reading and its proclamation, the perpetual ministry of its sacraments, and supremely the Sacrament of the Holy Communion, of which we were speaking yesterday, where we do again the thing that Christ did at the supreme crisis of His Ministry in order that by imitation of His outward act we may be united in His spiritual self-giving. In the book of the Revelation, there is a vision of the Word of God going forth conquering and to conquer, and of the armies in heaven following Him. That is the true picture of the Church. And we have to remember that many of the fruits of the Church's existence and activity are to be found entirely outside its own specific organisation; for wherever you find the Spirit of Christ gaining hold among men, there you see the result of the continual activity of the Church across the ages.

Over and over again, no doubt, it may happen that there arises a group of people who think they can serve God very much better independently of this ecclesiastical organisation. Where did they learn about Christ? If there had been no organisation the knowledge of Him would never have reached them. When we take the long view, which we must take if we are thinking of God's eternal purpose to sum up all things in Christ, we recognise at once that organisation is completely and absolutely necessary, and our duty is not to cut ourselves loose from it, but to try to share the life which it exists to foster. And it is certainly true that no man can be a good Christian by himself. No man is able to understand more than a tiny fraction of the unsearchable riches of Christ; he needs the supplementing contribution of his neighbour's apprehension. And as it is true that no individual alone can be a really good Christian, so it is true that the full Christian life cannot be lived only in groups of like-minded Christians; for if they are like-minded they merely strengthen one another in those elements of Christian faith and experience in which they are already fairly strong. That is good as far as it goes, and these associations have their perfectly real place, for they generate a degree of enthusiasm and zeal which it is perhaps impossible to produce in the wider fellowship of the Church if it has no such lesser fellowships within it. But if such associations keep themselves apart from, and do not freely mingle with, other associations of people whose apprehension of Christ has been other than their own, they tend to stereotype their limitations as well as strengthen their faith, and in the end they may easily become causes of division, which weaken the whole Church in its witness, and so may even do harm as great as the good they do. It must be in the widest fellowship we can find, and a fellowship that bears the promise of permanence from age to age, that we are to fulfil the obligations of our membership.

As Christ's purpose was to found a Kingdom, so we should think of the Church as the army of that Kingdom. It is, no doubt, true that we have repeatedly substituted compromise for warfare and prudence for the spirit of adventure. The world in which the Church is set to work has, over and over again, made terms with it, which the Church of that period has most wrongly accepted. One of the commonest of the compromises that have been made is for the world to allow the Church to be at peace in proclaiming what may be called its philosophical paradoxes provided that it keeps quiet about its moral ones. And to some extent we have to confess that the Church, as we ourselves constitute it, has fallen into the snare. We have shown, no doubt, a disproportion of concern about the distinctive philosophical doctrines of Christianity as compared with the moral duties of all disciples of Christ. We have, for example, been much more silent than we ought concerning Christ's perfectly plain teaching on the subject of wealth and poverty. We have not driven home upon men His clear intuition that though, if wealth comes, it ought to be accepted and used as an opportunity, yet it must be recognised as rather a snare to the spiritual life than an aim which the Christian may legitimately set before himself to pursue. The ways in which this compromise has been effected have varied of course from one generation to another. The vital matter is that we in our time should try to be honest with ourselves about it. Inevitably, during this week we have been trying to see the Christian Faith, first and foremost so far as we may, as truth. Tonight we have got to see it, as far as we may, as duty. When you come to the thought of the society which Christ has placed in the world to represent Him, you are confronted with the challenge of Christian duty. If it seems to you that the Church as organised has somehow lost sense of proportion, remember that only through the Church has the Gospel ever reached you, and that only through the Church can it reach the ages far ahead. And you will do more service to the cause of Christ by bringing what reality you can into its life than you can ever render by staying outside and doing what seems possible to you, or you and your few friends, in isolation.

But the way in which we are to think of this society must never be primarily in relation to itself. An army does not exist for its own benefit; it exists for its kingdom and its king; and you must come to the Church not chiefly for what you can gain from it, but for what you can give to it. When you come like that, you will gain far more than if you come looking for gain. If you ever catch yourself saying, 'I got no good from it, so I gave up going', remember that only proves you were coming in the frame of mind in which you were not likely to get much good. Come to lend yourself as a member of the Body of Christ – one of His limbs, to be moved according to His will in co-operation with all the other limbs in His Body. That is the claim. And the issue that depends on the vitality of the Church, which you by your decision may a good deal affect, is at any given moment the great question of human history.

For in the last resort there are only two pivots about which human life can revolve, and we are always organising society and ourselves about one or other of them. They are self and God. In the great book with which the Bible closes, these two principles are set before us under the symbolic figures of the 'Lamb standing, as it had been slain' – the symbol of love that uses sacrifice as its instrument – and the great wild beast, the symbol of self-will or pride, whose instrument is force. And they work out into two civilisations. The principle of self and pride can only build up Babylon the Great, and Babylon the Great always comes tumbling down again. But by the activity among men of the principle of love, which must always show itself in sacrifice, there is built among men the heavenly City, the New Jerusalem which comes down, whensoever it comes, and in whatsoever degree it comes, out of Heaven from God. In every generation, but in a very peculiar sense in ours, the question has to be answered, What is to be built? There have been few moments in the history of mankind when the issue has been so naked as it is in ours. Which city is to be built? Babylon the Great, which has tumbled down so often, and will always tumble down again, or the City which you cannot build yourselves, but which God can build through you, if unitedly you give yourselves to be used by Him as its builders'? And the body that must answer this question is always the Church. No individuals can answer it; it must be the whole fellowship of Christ's disciples. And you can help towards the right answer just in the degree in which you associate yourself with it in its age-long effort.

And, remember, the supreme wonder of the history of the Christian Church is that always in the moments when it has seemed most dead, out of its own body there has sprung up new life; so that in age after age it has renewed itself, and age after age by its renewal has carried the world forward into new stages of progress, as it will do for us in our day, if only we give ourselves in devotion to its Lord and take our place in its service.

Now we come to the question, What are you going to do? You will feel quite rightly that what I am able to suggest is thoroughly pedestrian, and that is part of the test of our sincerity. It is rather agreeable than otherwise to expand the mind by the contemplation of an eternal purpose, and there is perhaps a certain amount of thrill and glamour about the conception of the age-long purpose of God now to

CHRIST IN ALL THINGS

be wrought out through His Church. But when we come to what we can do ourselves, it always seems so little, as, of course, it is. What each one alone can do is always very little, but the way great things are done is by all doing that very little unitedly. And it is the test of our sincerity whether we are ready to do the little things that are in our power – the things that have not about them a great thrill and glamour, the things that are rather dull, the things that we can only do, if we do them at all, because we are genuinely loyal and because we have a purpose that is firmly set, because we have a firm determination to serve Christ as we have the opportunity. Remember that the test which is coming to each one of you of the value which this week has been to you, is going to be found almost entirely in relation to quite small things, the multitude of which will carry their great weight in swaying the balance this way or that for the life of Oxford in the days that are coming.

While it is true that what each of you does is small, will you at least make up your minds whether all that you have been thinking of this week is genuinely your concern? The pressure of practical affairs in life is very great. If we are conscientiously to do the duty that lies before us, it often seems that it will claim nearly all our energy. Is it not enough that each man should do his own job thoroughly and conscientiously, and leave all this speculation (as he will call it if he is in the mood to talk like this at all) concerning the purpose of God for the world to other people who are interested in such things, and perhaps especially to those who may be regarded as being personally committed to that aspect of life, which means the clergy? But, is it not plainly true that the real value of your job depends upon the truth, speaking broadly at least, of those things of which we have been thinking this week? Is there not a grave possibility, if you leave that out of sight, that you are committing yourself to futility? Is it not certain that any man will do the job allotted to him with more understanding, and therefore more efficiently, if he understands a little the place which it takes in the general development of human welfare? And if it is true that God, the Almighty and Eternal, is watching over each one of us with the love that we see in Jesus Christ, is it, then, conceivable that it is not the concern of each one that he should know that love and consider what it means to him and for him? Will you first, then, genuinely think again, is it your concern? Can you even dare to say 'No' to that? And if it is, then the duty follows to reach a decision – not necessarily now, not necessarily this next week, but to reach a decision in time to be effective in your life. And you must realise that the greatest decisions always have to be taken before there is a complete sufficiency of evidence, because it is only after they have been made, and the experiment tried out, that the evidence can be there.

So when you have decided, as I urge you must decide, that this is your concern, your own individual concern, then what decision are you going to make about it? Are you going to hear and heed the call of Christ or not? And again, when you have answered, as you must, that you cannot set it on one side, there follows inevitably the duty of making Him known to your neighbours. The ways in which this may be done are infinitely various, but the duty is absolute and constant. His gift of Himself, that is to say of perfect love, is not something which you can have and keep. If you are keeping it, it proves you have not got it. Every Christian is a missionary, and if he is not a missionary he is not yet truly or deeply a Christian at all. He may be seeking to become one; but he is not yet one who has received the love of Christ in his soul; because that love is of such a kind that, wherever it is, it must go on to give itself to others.

We are most of us very shy about speaking of spiritual things. That has its root partly in real reverence; we do not wish to speak too easily or too unworthily about those things which we realise as greatest. And yet where people are on fire with any kind of zeal they can hardly keep themselves from some kind of speech, and most of us ought to conquer some part of our shyness and be ready to speak at the appropriate time. But at least all Christians have got to aim at being such people that our friends see in us a kind of life they would like to live and of which they want to know the secret. You have got to exhibit the winsome attractiveness of Christ. Individually, then, we must consider, is it my concern? Yes. Can I refuse its call? Assuredly not. If I obey then I am committed to making known what has come to me.

Now let us turn to more immediate action that you can take. First, let us gather in great numbers tomorrow at the Holy Communion to offer thanks for what God has done for us this week. We do not know what it is. Nobody knows what the upshot of this week is going to be, and nobody can know. But it is not conceivable that there should have been so many of you gathered here day by day to spend a little time at least in realising the meaning of Christ, and joining in prayer to God through Him, without result. What it will be we do not know; but let us give thanks at least that God did gather us together and make the opportunity for us, and let us dedicate ourselves in His service that that opportunity may be used. Then try to recall some parts at least of what you have heard this week. Think it over and decide how far you can accept it. I hope there will be groups in colleges and other places to discuss these subjects. The way you may most easily open your minds to receive the truth of God more fully is to see how far you agree with what has been put before you and to make that much your own. Then I would especially urge that you should consider together the use that might be made of that wonderful endowment which we have in Oxford for the furtherance of its spiritual life, in the college chapels – both by attendance at services now being held, and through thinking out what would meet your need in some other way, and consulting with the chaplain of the college how that may be done.

Take the opportunities that come. I would plead that whatever is done as a direct continuation of this Mission should be kept as wide at least as the Church of England. It is right that there should be other associations representing special points of view and the determination to follow special kinds of Christian activity, because in them men generate a keener enthusiasm; but let them not be separated from the whole wide fellowship in which we strengthen and enrich one another.

It is inevitable that the suggestions made should seem pedestrian and small; only remember that your first duty while you are here is preparation for the life that is to come. Your first duty is not forthwith to be rendering in full form the kind of service to which your life is to be given, but to make yourself ready for that service when the time comes so that it may be as effective as it can. Because that is your duty, therefore the opportunities for these more specific forms of Christian service must be comparatively limited. But you are preparing for a life which you mean to live for Christ. You must look forward to it as this, and seek to do the will of God in and by your work. Never imagine that vocation is to the ministry alone. Every man has his own vocation, and must try to find it. The work which has now to be done for God in the world is not work for the clergy alone; it is the work of the whole Church, the whole body of the disciples of Christ, in which every man must be finding God's will for him, and doing that.

But if you are in doubt how you may best lay out your life, and if you are quite clear in your acceptance of Jesus Christ as your Saviour and your God, then the mere circumstances of the time constitute a call to the Church's direct service in its ministry which you must face; for there is no sphere of life in which a man can more certainly lay out all his talents in the service of God. It will call for every capacity; it will bring you into touch with human beings in every conceivable relation. There is no life so rich or so full of all those joys which come from serving people at the point of their greatest need. But these things are for you to think over. What is clear is that the King is calling, and you must answer. He calls not to comfort nor to power, as the world reckons power; He calls for heroic service. Has it occurred to you that you will search the Gospels in vain for such words as these: 'If any man will come after Me, I will deliver him from the pains of hell and give him the joys of Heaven.' It would have been quite true; but He did not say it. He did, indeed, say: 'Come unto Me all ye that labour and are heavy laden, and I will give you rest.' And if you are weighed down under the burden of the evil in your own soul and in the world, that invitation is addressed to you. But that is not the nature of His appeal for followers. That appeal is to deny yourself and take up your cross and follow Him. It is the appeal of the heroes of all ages.

You know how Garibaldi saved the Roman republic in spirit, though its body perished. The little state that had been founded in Rome was falling before the combined assault of the corrupt states round about it. The siege had lasted for more weeks than the experts thought it could last days, but at last the day of surrender had come, and into the great concourse of citizens there rode the man whose faith and heroism had sustained it all the while. He said, 'I am going out from Rome. I offer neither quarters, nor provisions, nor wages; I offer hunger, thirst, forced marches, battles, death. Let him who loves his country with his heart and not with his lips only, follow me.' And they streamed out after him into the hills, and because of his heroism and theirs, there is a kingdom of Italy today. It was a paraphrase of the appeal of Christ. 'I offer neither quarters, nor provisions, nor wages'; 'if any man will come after Me, let him forget about himself and be ready for whatever it involves, and follow Me.' And if we would stream out after Him, there might be a Kingdom of God in Oxford tomorrow.

The King is calling, and you must answer; for to give no answer is to answer 'No'. That is the thought I want to leave with you. You have heard – however poorly expressed – His call: and you must answer, because to give no answer is to answer 'No'.

But you will answer 'Yes', and so take your place in the great fellowship of worship and of service, the eternal Church, the communion of saints, the army in heaven which rides in the train of the Word of God as He goes forth conquering and to conquer.

7

Philosophical Theology: *Nature, Man and God* of 1934

Temple returned to the interface of theology and philosophy in the Gifford Lectures delivered at Glasgow University between 1932 and 1934. It was a good moment for him to give this prestigious series of lectures. He was now well established in his new role as Archbishop of York and he and his wife were happily settled in their new home at Bishopthorpe. He was freed from the time-consuming work of administering a large urban diocese. He had a certain amount of time for reading and writing, though apparently he was in the habit of writing out his next lecture on the train from York to Glasgow. He was aware that his previous essay on the philosophical foundations of theology, Mens Creatrix, had been written in disconnected moments of a busy life in London and had suffered as a result. He would have been keen to make another attempt to express the pre-eminent intellectual concern of his life.

In the Preface to the printed version of the lectures Temple explains that his method is not to construct, stage by stage, a philosophical fabric where each conclusion becomes the basis of the next advance. Something more complex is being attempted: 'My own endeavour is rather to provide a coherent articulation of an experience which has found some measure of co-ordination through adherence to certain principles.' Later he explains what he means by drawing a comparison with the dialectical materialism of Marx, Engels and Lenin, who, he recognizes, make a strong appeal to the minds of his contemporaries. He wishes to present a dialectic that has a greater range of apprehension than that of Marxism and is more thorough in its appreciation of the interplay of factors in the real world (pp. ix–x). In other words the spiritual as well as the material dimension of life is to be included.

The method he was proposing can be explained by returning to the common root behind both Marxism and Temple's own Idealist philosophical background, namely Hegel's philosophy and especially his belief in historical development being fundamental to reality (sometimes called historicism). Hegel claimed to present a way of interpreting and unifying human experience and the reality behind it. He did this through positing the concept of 'Geist', a kind of controlling spirit of human culture, at work through human affairs and historical development. He saw the conflicts, struggles and resolutions of human history as the working out of an overarching dialectical process, involving the three steps of thesis, antithesis and synthesis at every turn.

Marx and his disciples retained the grammar of Hegel's philosophy, as it were, while replacing the vocabulary. They continued to see an unfolding dialectical process that will bring unity to history, but saw the controlling concept behind this as the struggle of the working classes for a class-free society. History was still seen as purposeful and progressive, but in a materialist rather than a cultural or spiritual way.

Temple also thought easily and naturally within the historicist grammar of Hegelian philosophy. His project was the attempt to update its Idealist vocabulary, as it were, with ideas and ways of thinking drawn from Christian belief, and to do so in a way which accounted for a greater range of human experience than Marxism. He was also seeking to improve on the outlook of A. N. Whitehead's Process and Reality, *which he respected greatly. Temple agreed with many aspects of Whitehead's process thought but felt that at crucial points in the argument Whitehead did not sufficiently recognize the separation of the Divine Mind from the world.*

The areas he included in his study of dialectical realism, as he now called it, were similar to those he discussed in Mens Creatrix. *In the first half of the book he began with the fact of evolution as shown by science. He sought to trace the scope and limits of human knowledge within this evolutionary process, and the likelihood of a unifying Mind (his equivalent of Hegel's 'Geist') lying behind the unfolding reality of the terrestrial world. He discussed the place of truth and beauty within this scheme, and the key significance of value as a concept which can explain why things are the way they are. He traced the place of freedom and determinism for individuals within the evolutionary process. Towards the end of the section he concluded that this evolutionary reality gives grounds for believing in a transcendent Mind or, as he now says, a personal Spirit, over and above the process of development.*

Then, in the second half of the book, he worked in the other direction. He began with the premise of a transcendent Mind at work through the whole cosmic process, and sought to trace the ways it is immanent within that process and can be known by finite minds. He discussed the nature of a particular revelation, which he famously defined as not being a set of propositions held as truths, but as the coincidence of divinely guided events with minds divinely illuminated to interpret those events (p. 312; see Section i below). In evenly balanced and thoughtful discussions he returned to the issue of human finitude and the relationship of divine grace and human freedom, and to the nature of eternal life. In characteristic form he also argued that transcendent Mind can be seen in the way all values ultimately exhibit a commonwealth of value. In one of his most impressive and key discussions, on the meaning of human history, he considered the relationship of this history with eternity, which is always a pressing issue for Christian historicism. Drawing on an evocative analogy of the relationship between the characters in a play, who acquire their own characters and fashion the play, and the writer of the play itself, he argues that while human history ultimately exhibits a dependence on eternity, history is necessary and essential to the eternal, and that in an important sense it 'makes' eternity (pp. 448, 451; see Section ii below).

Then, in his penultimate lecture and chapter he summed up his view of cosmic reality. As he worked his way to this summary he made a brilliant and now famous aside: as a deliberate rebuff to Marxism he presented Christianity as 'the most avowedly materialist of all the great religions' (first presented in 'The Christian Conception of History' in the journal The Pilgrim, *October 1925; reprinted in* Personal Religion, *1926, pp. 15–26). In other words, it does not ignore the material side to life or deny it, but roundly asserts its reality as well as its subordination to the spiritual. He then quoted John 1.14 as an example of this principle: 'The Word was made flesh.' 'By the very nature of its central doctrine Christianity is committed to a belief in the ultimate significance of the historical process, and in the reality of matter and its place in the divine scheme' (p. 478; see below Section iii).*

Later in the chapter he summed up his view of reality with the powerful and evocative concept of the sacramental universe. He defined a sacrament as 'the spiritual utilisation of a material object whereby a spiritual result is effected' (p. 491). In other words, it is an instance where matter becomes an 'effectual expression' or 'symbolic instrument' of spirit: the spirit is first and last, with the matter as its vehicle. He then applied this idea to the whole of the created universe: 'the view of the universe which I have called sacramental asserts the supremacy and absolute freedom of God; the reality of the physical world and its process as His creation; the vital significance of the material and temporal world to the eternal Spirit' (p. 493; see below Section iii).

In these passages it is clear that Idealist philosophy has given way to Temple's own religious faith as the controlling influence on his thought. And this illustrates an important comment on Nature, Man and God *made by Emil Brunner in a letter to Temple. Brunner argued that Temple had failed properly to distinguish true natural theology, which relies simply on logical argument and generally accepted facts, from Christian theology and dogmatics, which are regulated by Christian beliefs:*

> *So, for instance, your conception of religion is determined* a priori *by Christian faith, and is deduced from it; the same applies to your concepts of sin, love, personality, etc. This means, however, that in these passages your natural theology is natural only in appearance, whilst it is in truth Christian. In the third and final part of your book, your expositions are substantially, even predominantly, nothing more nor less than Christian dogmatics, even though the difference in method is repeatedly stressed. (Iremonger 1948, pp. 531–2)*

In this important set of lectures, then, Temple had again blended his philosophy with theology, which means Nature, Man and God *would not convince the unbeliever of the truth of Christianity. Nevertheless it still has great value. The physicist and theologian A. R. Peacocke has described William Temple's percipience in detecting those broad features in the new knowledge of his day, mostly from the sciences, that theology needed properly to respond to (Peacocke 1983, p. 29). And Dorothy Emmet, in an acute and sympathetic review of the book, states that Temple's philosophical writings stand as an impressive exposition of a reasonable faith (Iremonger 1948, p. 535). In other words, Temple may not convince the sceptic but he certainly impresses the sceptic and makes him or her seriously engage with the issues of religion. Furthermore, Emmet suggests, some aspects of Temple's scheme could be carried forward even if his metaphysics ultimately fail. She quotes a letter that Temple wrote to her in 1942, which shows Temple now thinking that the Gifford Lectures do not describe reality as it is, but reality as it will become in God's own time:*

> *The particular modification (in my thinking) to which I am feeling driven is not substantial, though I think it is very important. It is a much clearer perception of what is worked out in the Gifford Lectures about process and value. What we must completely get away from is the notion that the world as it now exists is a rational whole; we must think of its unity not by the analogy of a picture, of which*

all the parts exist at once, but by the analogy of a drama where, if it is good enough, the full meaning of the first scene only becomes apparent with the final curtain; and we are in the middle of this. Consequently the world as we see it is strictly unintelligible. We can only have faith that it will become intelligible when the divine purpose, which is the explanation of it, is accomplished . . .

All this is really there in the Gifford Lectures, but I don't think the total presentation in that book or in Christus Veritas *sufficiently gives this impression of a dynamic process and leaves too much that of a static system. (Iremonger 1948, pp. 537–8)*

Temple still believed in a profound and unifying meaning within the universe, but now he saw that this would only become clear in the future (a position not unlike that of Teilhard de Chardin). Nature, Man and God *could still contribute to this future-orientated view of the world, but its argument would now have to be read as an extended description of the contours of such a hoped-for world, a world which would eventually produce a society of spirits united in a commonwealth of value. And the belief in the universe being sacramental would now have to be understood as a description of the universe not as it is but, tantalizingly, as it will become.*

i How Revelation Occurs

Lecture XII, 'Revelation and its Mode', pp. 301–27

From page 304

The whole course of our argument forbids us to draw any sharp distinction between the works of God so as to regard some of these as constituting His self-revelation and the others as offering no such revelation. We can make no truce with any suggestion that the world for the most part goes by itself on its own way while God intervenes now and again with an act of His own. The course of thought, which enables us to hold together religious faith in the living God and the picture of the world with which science provides us, renders the whole notion of such divine intrusion from without intolerable and incredible; for this course of thought has perpetually recurred to the insistence that all occurrences find their ultimate ground in the Divine Volition. But if we stopped here we should only have affirmed that in the entire course of cosmic history there is to be found the self-revelation of God; and that, no doubt, is true; but as no man can ever hope to contemplate that history in its entirety, it cannot be said to afford a revelation to us or for us. Moreover, this affirmation by itself concerns cosmic history as a whole, as though it proceeded on its course uninfluenced by any agents within it who are completely or partially free to influence that course. If there is ground for holding that such agents exist, then we must expect to find instances of divine action relevant to the situations which their free acts create, and while such action will be no more divine than the constant purpose which sustains all things in being, it will have a specially revelatory quality, because it is an expression of the divine character in face of critical situations, and not only an episode in the age-long energy of God. It is always in dealing with persons as persons that personality most truly expresses itself. It tells us something about a man's character if we know that he rises from bed every day at the same hour; it tells us much more about him if we know that he even once rose a great deal earlier to do some act of kindness. The main field of Revelation must be in the history of men, rather than in the ample spaces of nature, though it is also true that if nature were so severed from God as to offer no revelation of Him at all, it would mean that there was no Being fitly to be called God, and therefore no revelation of Him either in human history or elsewhere.

We saw at an earlier stage that man's relationship to Truth, to Beauty and to Goodness is such as to imply that in each of these a Personal Spirit is calling to him and claiming him. This prepares us for a more intimate expression of what thus receives august but not unfamiliar intimation. The revelation to which Religion in many of its historical forms appeals is therefore nothing alien from such a view of the world as we have been led to form, but is something very much more than is discoverable except in such supposed revelation. Here the Divine Mind in which all Nature is grounded speaks direct to that Human Nature which, of all Nature known to us, is nearest to itself because, like itself, it is personal and spiritual. The personal God can only be adequately revealed in and through persons; but then such revelation must be distorted by any defects in the persons through whom it comes. The revelation given in the majesty of the starry heavens may be perfect in its kind, though its kind is markedly inadequate; the revelation given through the reason and conscience of men is more adequate in kind, but in that kind is usually imperfect.

We have not yet spoken of the problem of evil except to refer to it as the distinctively religious problem among all those which call for intellectual solution, and the discussion of it must be postponed until we can give undivided attention to it. But the existence of evil in its worst form, that of sin, introduces a defect, and it may be a distortion, into all revelation given through the medium of human personality, unless there be found an instance of this which is free from sin. This defect or distortion is something more than limitation in fullness or completeness; it affects the quality of the revelation in ways that are not capable of ascertainment in advance; and this fact must be borne in mind in any attempt to set forth the general conditions of the possibility of revelation.

[Temple's italics:] *We affirm, then, that unless all existence is a medium of Revelation, no particular Revelation is possible; for the possibility of Revelation depends on the personal quality of that supreme and ultimate Reality which is God. If there is no ultimate Reality, which is the ground of all else, then there is no God to be revealed; if that Reality is not personal, there can be no special revelation, but only uniform procedure; if there be an ultimate Reality, and this is personal, then all existence is revelation. Either all occurrences are in some degree revelation of God, or else there is no such revelation at all; for the conditions of the possibility of any revelation require that there should be nothing which is not revelation. Only if God is revealed in the rising of the sun in the sky can He be revealed in the rising of a son of man from the dead; only if He is revealed in the history of Syrians and Philistines can He be revealed in the history of Israel (Amos 9.7); only if he chooses all men for His own can He choose any at all; only if nothing is profane can anything be sacred. It is necessary to stress with all possible emphasis this universal quality of revelation in general before going on to discuss the various modes of particular revelation; for the latter, detached from the former, loses its root in the rational coherence of the world and consequently becomes itself a superstition and a fruitful source of superstitions. But if all existence is a revelation of God, as it must be if He is the ground of its existence, and if the God thus revealed is personal, then there is more ground in reason for expecting particular revelations than for denying them.*

From page 311

[What, then, of the revelation found in Scripture?] The Historical Figure in whose career the story finds its culmination, and who is acclaimed as its crown and illumination by those whose theory is under review, is in nothing more remarkable than in His unfailing respect for the spiritual liberty of those with whom He had dealings. Though the record presents Him as capable of miraculous action, and as having recourse to it for purposes of mercy, it also presents Him as steadily refusing to allow such acts to become the basis of men's adherence to Him or to His cause. He appears as desiring none but willing disciples; and to them He gave teaching designed rather to stimulate and direct their thought than to provide formulated doctrines claiming acceptance on His authority. The revelation, if given at all, is given more in Himself than in His teaching, and the faith in which His early followers believed that they had found salvation did not consist in the acceptance of propositions concerning Him nor even in acceptance of what He taught in words concerning God and man, though this was certainly included, but in personal trust in His personal presence, love and power. Doctrinal or credal formulae had their importance as pointing to Him, by trust in whom His followers had found peace; they were not themselves the revelation, but sign-posts indicating where the revelation was to be found.

All this was in line with the earlier and supposedly preparatory revelation. For this, as has been already suggested, consisted primarily in historical event and secondarily in the illumination of the minds of prophets to read those events as disclosing the judgment or the purpose of God. What we find in the Old Testament Scriptures is not mainly, if at all, authoritative declaration of theological doctrine, but living apprehension of a living process wherein those whose minds are enlightened by divine communion can discern in part the purposive activity of God.

Revelation so conceived is the full actuality of that relationship between Nature, Man and God which throughout these lectures we are seeking to articulate. First there is the world-process, which, in its more complex components, if not throughout, is organic in principle; secondly, we have the fact that certain organisms, to wit ourselves, occurring as episodes of the world-process, are able to apprehend and in part to comprehend that process; thirdly, we infer from this that the process, in order to give rise to such episodes in its course, must be regarded as itself grounded in a mental principle; fourthly, enquiry into that interaction of the intelligent organism with its environment which we call thought, compels the assertion that the principle in which the world-process is grounded, is not only mental but spiritual and personal; fifthly, this leads us to the conviction that the process itself and all occurrences within it – including the intelligences of men – are due to the purposive action of that Person whose reality has been established as the governing fact of existence. *He guides the process; He guides the minds of men; the interaction of the process and the minds which are alike guided by Him is the essence of revelation.*

But His action in guiding the world is not constant in a mechanical sense; rather its constancy, as that of all personal action, is found in its infinite adjustability to present conditions. It is true that the conditions are themselves due to the divine action, but that does not affect the argument if we recognise two facts: first, that the divine action in or upon the world is not the essentially dead action of an immanent principle, but the essentially living action of a transcendent Person; and secondly, that among the conditions are the attitudes adopted by, and the situations created by, the relatively free acts of finite intelligences like ourselves.

Much of the divine action which sustains the world is such as to produce apparent uniformity in the world-process. We have already seen why this should be so, even from the standpoint of human interests. But of course this apparent uniformity may itself be due to an elaborately designed balance of multiform adjustments. If those scientists are right who regard recent developments as having introduced indeterminacy into the basis of Physics, so that laws of causation are to be understood, not as real uniformities but as statistical averages (a sociologist may know how many people will commit suicide in Great Britain next year, but he cannot know which individuals will do so), the theistic philosopher will be prepared with the account of the (physically) indeterminate behaviour of electrons and of the resultant constancy of natural processes, which has just been offered. If on the other hand the older scientific view of uniform causal processes ultimately prevails, for this also the theist has his explanation, both in the constancy of the Divine Nature which will vary its activity only for sufficient reason, and in the need for substantial uniformity as a basis for moral action. The more modern view supplies a greater measure of that continuity between different stages of evolutionary complexity, and this may recommend it to theists who share the common scientific interest in such continuity. The Natural Theologian [such as Temple] is not concerned in the dispute; either alternative is equally agreeable to him.

Whatever be the final view of that matter, it will remain true that, while the apparently uniform process of the world is in its measure a revelation of God for those whose minds are alert to its significance, it is less fully revelatory than specially adapted activities for the meeting of such contingencies as give sufficient ground for such activities.

It is therefore not unnatural or inappropriate that the term Revelation should be commonly used with a specialised reference to these occasions. But these must be understood as particular and conspicuous illustrations of the principle of revelation already stated – the interaction of the World-process and the minds, both being alike guided by God. In these events too – be it a deliverance of a nation from bondage in despite of all calculable probabilities, be it the Incarnation in a human life of that Self-Utterance of God which is the ground of the created universe – there is no imparting of truth as the intellect apprehends truth, but there is event and appreciation; and in the coincidence of these the revelation consists.

There is obviously neither need nor possibility to draw any dividing line between the revelation which is continuously given in the whole course of the world-process as men's minds are enlightened to appreciate this, and the revelation which is given in special and signal occasions. Among the events which are conspicuous in the record accepted by Christendom as in a special sense Revelation, those which accompanied or facilitated the Exodus or the retreat of Sennacherib may be more easily referred to normal processes, while those which preceded the birth or followed the death of Jesus Christ are more difficult to classify under that head. Yet even here, for those who start, not from efficient causation but from divine intention and efficacy, it may be that we have the most strictly natural way of bringing about a divine self-incarnation, and a strictly natural issue of the bodily death of humanity when rendered sinless by divine indwelling. If we make the mistake of beginning with the thought of God as normally acting by way of immanence, while holding His transcendent resources in reserve against emergencies, we may fairly be challenged to say under which heading any particular occasion should be classified; and scientifically trained minds then appear to have some justification for the protest, to which they often are inclined, that it would be more consonant with divine Majesty so to order the World that no interventions disturbing to its order should be required. But if the contention of the last Lecture is sound, and divine immanence is always and only the activity of a transcendent Personality, and operates, after the manner of personal action, by infinitely various adjustments which exhibit constancy of character in face of varied situations, then there is no need for any dividing line, nor any possibility of drawing one. All things are grounded in the divine volition, which acts on each occasion as is appropriate for the fulfilment of the divine purpose. All therefore is alike revelation; but not all is equally revelatory of the divine character. We find revelation at its highest where God finds occasion for unusual action, and we find it then both in the choice of occasion for such unusual action (for the divine character is revealed in its estimate of such and such an occasion as sufficient) and in the mode of action taken.

But whether we think of the unceasing revelation afforded in the whole world-process or of the occurrences which constitute revelation in the specialised sense of the word, *the principle of revelation is the same – the coincidence of event and appreciation.* (The appreciation need not be contemporaneous with the event. But till it comes, the event, though revelatory in its own character, is not yet fully revelation. If no one had recognised Christ, the Incarnation would have occurred, but it would have failed to effect a revelation of God.) Here we have at its fullest development that living intercourse of mind and world-process which we found to be the true life of thought. For here the mind, which arises within, and out of, the process, apprehends the process for what it truly is – the self-expression of that Creator-mind in the kinship of which created minds are fashioned. From the occurrence of our finite minds within the process we were led to believe that the process which contains them must be grounded in mind; the finite mind in developing its intercourse with its environment finds itself the subject of intellectual judgments, aesthetic appreciations, moral obligations, thus becoming aware of the reality of Truth, Beauty and Goodness in that environment; considering these experiences it finds in all of them evident marks of personal relationship, and learns to recognise the environment as the self-communication to itself of a personal Creator. In the characteristic moments of revelation this apprehension and appreciation is at its highest point of development.

Its essence is intercourse of mind and event, not the communication of doctrine distilled from that intercourse.

ii   The Relationship of History with Eternity

Lecture XVII, 'The Meaning of History', pp. 427–51

From page 441

In entering on this task let us premise that we do not expect complete success. The essence of the enterprise is that we who are finite are seeking to comprehend the infinite, in order to define its relation to our finite selves. In such an attempt apparent success must be certain failure.

Further, our method must be one of analogy and not of demonstration; for the Eternal ever eludes us, and we cannot without certain error form a definition of it which might be the starting-point of logically cogent argumentation. But by analogy we may make progress, and our hope will be that if we reach a stark antinomy, this may arise in regard to that which we know we cannot comprehend, and that at all other points our difficulties may be such as to give way before us even though we never reach their ultimate solution.

[There are three points to hold on to]: the complete and all-controlling supremacy of the Eternal; . . . the ultimate importance of History and its moral choices; . . . the expectation of a climax of History inaugurating a new world-order. With these in mind let us turn to our analogies. We naturally direct our attention to that human activity wherein the mind launches into being, as it were, a miniature history. Dramatists have declared that when once they have set their several characters in motion, they have no further control over the conduct of those characters. Indeed in so far as a dramatist creates after the fashion of those poets who apprehend their own thought in the act of expressing it, it must be so. Yet in another sense the dramatist retains an absolute control, even to the extent of cutting short the composition and destroying it. His thought, active in self-expression, is immanent in the play; the play is made by it, and apart from it no episode in the play takes place; further, the vitality of every episode comes from the relation of that episode to this thought. Yet the dramatist himself is absolutely transcendent in respect of the play. Upon him it depends whether there shall be a play at all. The play depends upon him for its existence; he does not in that sense depend upon the play at all. But because his vocation is to be a dramatist, he fulfils his nature by writing plays; if he did not write them he would be untrue to himself. The self-expressing thought through which the play comes into existence is part of the principle of his being. Consequently the play itself, and its content, is of vital consequence to him.

We now turn to another form of human creativity, which we have the highest religious sanction for regarding as an analogue of the divine. The father in a human family is to his children at once the source of their existence and a present Providence. Because they will represent before the world the results of his training of them, because they bear his name and may bring to it either honour or shame, but most of all because of his love for them, prompting him to give up what he values most if so he can serve their welfare, their doings are of vital concern to him. He gave them being; to a great extent he shapes their circumstances; perhaps his influence over them is so great that they will never knowingly act against his wishes; yet they are free to respect his wishes or not; if they do so, it is because it appears to them good to do so; when he controls them, he does not coerce them, because his control is effective through their wills and not either apart from or against their wills.

The analogy of the dramatist breaks down because his creations are not substantially alive; the analogy of the human father breaks down because the father himself is only another finite spirit, subject to successiveness in the same way as his children. But if we can think the two analogies together we find ourselves adumbrating a conception which seems to meet some at least of our requirements. Let us attempt the articulation of that conception, knowing that we can only speculate, and accepting a 'likely tale' (Plato, *Timaeus* 29.d) concerning a theme too great for our scientific apparatus.

We start then with the conception of the Eternal God, perfect in the plenitude of Being. We know that He creates, for here is the world, and to attribute it to any other source than to Him is to attribute to Him finitude and limitation. In that case we should have to assume something greater than God, to wit, God plus the world, or whatever that may be in which both are grounded. The insuperable difficulties of this way of thinking have already been indicated. We can only understand the world at all if it is grounded in the Will of the living God. He is therefore known to us as Creator. That He should create cannot be a mere accident of His being; it proves Him to be of such a nature as to create. Following our analogies of human creativity, we may connect this with the sheer satisfaction of creative activity – which is not by itself the highest even of human motives and therefore is not by itself an adequate of the divine action – and with the desire for self-communication. This latter, suggested by Plato as the motive of creation, is an expression of love, and coheres with the essential condition of good as the finding by mind of itself, or its kin, in its object.

In the inorganic world we may imagine that the divine mind takes delight, as that world in vast expanse and tiny detail expresses the perfection of quantitative relationships. It is a delight both scientific and aesthetic, and if here perhaps the scientific preponderates, we may assume that there is preponderance of aesthetic satisfaction in the loveliness exhibited by every form of organic life from the 'Tyger! Tyger! burning bright' (William Blake) to the delicacy of a butterfly's wing, so that in every changing phase of nature 'God renews his ancient rapture' (Browning, *Paracelsus*). 'He looks upon His own creation and finds it very good' (Genesis 1), and therein also finds the fulfilment of the purpose with which He made it. It is His work, and in it He finds the counterpart of His own mind, so that the human student of creation is, in Kepler's words, 'thinking God's thoughts after Him'.

Upon one planet attached to a certain sun (whether also elsewhere or not we have no knowledge), His creativity expressed itself in beings able in some measure thus to enter into His mind and understand His work, so that in them He found a fuller counterpart than elsewhere of His own being. Rooted in nature they yet are not swayed only by natural forces, but by that which appears to them good, that is to say, by that in which they find themselves as God seeks to find Himself in them. They, like all else, exist only in dependence on His will. But since He has thought it good (that is, has found Himself in determining) to fashion them in so complete a resemblance to Himself, He must now control them according to the law of their being which He has imposed on them; He must control them through what appears to them good and their power to appreciate it – that is, through their unforced affection and will. Thus He Himself does not know *beforehand* exactly how they will respond to the various modes of His manifestation of Himself to them. So far as He is Himself at work within the process of Time, the precise mode of the future is unknown to Him, though its general issue in the fulfilment of His purpose is secure. Yet, all the same, because He is not in His own nature within the Time-process any more than the dramatist is personally within the play, and all that happens utterly depends on Him, He knows it all with utter certainty. To Him the contingent is still contingent, as not being compelled by its own past; yet the whole is necessary, and therefore also all its parts; and the whole is the expression of His will. So He knows the contingent as contingent and yet knows it with certainty.

There is something here which we cannot fathom; but the difficulty arises where it ought to arise, in our attempt to understand the divine nature itself. The profoundest religious intuitions do not here lead to a scheme of thought perfectly comprehensible by men; they do, however, lead to apprehensions germane to the speculations which we have sought to follow out. In many religions they have led to some form of Trinitarian doctrine. In Christianity they have led to a form of Trinitarianism which may consonantly with our line of thought be presented as follows:

The Eternal God is such as to communicate Himself; co-eternal with His ultimate Being is His Word, which is His mind in self-expression.

The form of that self-expression is the created universe, as the form of Shakespeare's self-expression is the scheme of words that constitutes each of his poems and plays. The divine and creative Word was not uttered once for all, but it receives perpetual utterance in the radiation of light, in the movements of the stars, in the development of life, in the reason and conscience of man. So soon as there is life, there is self-determined response to environment, though at first the part played by the 'self' in this process is very small. Where it occurs, there is a transition from purely efficient to efficient plus final causation. Action is now governed in some measure by the apparent good. The good which appears, as being objectively given, is an activity of the divine Word – that self-expressed mind of God wherein man's mind gropingly finds itself, with many distortions and errors, but never without some reality of correspondence. This discovery or recognition shows itself in man as a more eager appetite of that good, and this responsive appetite is felt also to be divine and is called by Christians Holy Spirit. It was hardly recognised as distinct from the Word until the Word was uttered in a new fullness of expression, as Christians believe, in the historical Person, Jesus of Nazareth. That fuller objective self-manifestation of the divine called forth a new potency of responsive aspiration to which, as an experienced fact, was given the name Holy Spirit. This power of God within the soul, responding to God self-manifested in Jesus Christ, could afterwards be recognised in the responsive reaction of all life to the good wherever manifest.

But this response is not mechanically evoked; the degree or direction of it cannot be calculated in advance by reference only to the appeal offered to it. In this field it is not true that 'action and reaction are equal and opposite'. The living, self-determining organism is an uncertain entity until its response is made. Therefore life has taken many lines of development that lead nowhere, and living objects, from parasitic worms or beetles up (or down) to self-seeking men of high intelligence, seek their good – that is, their true selves in what brings loss to others. Every time this happens it brings disappointment to God at work in the process of time; for God Himself, so far as His experience is temporal, has not absolute knowledge when the response that gives Him full sovereignty will be made; so that it is said 'Of that day and of that hour knoweth no man, neither the Son' who is the divine Word, God self-manifested in the created process. But God is not only known as the Word who makes God manifest, nor as the Spirit who makes response to that manifestation, but as the Father, the fount of Deity and therein of all else, with whom a thousand years are as one day, and whose

PHILOSOPHICAL THEOLOGY

Love – that is, giving of self to rejoice in the self-gift which answers – is fulfilled in Word and Spirit, with all that in redemption and sanctification issues, from the eternal creativity. This is not all that Christians have meant by the doctrine of the Triune God, but it is that part of it which coheres with our present line of enquiry.

Does History then make any difference or not to the Eternal? In one sense, it manifestly does not. The question is framed in the language of succession. To make a difference is only possible in a literal sense where one phase succeeds another. And the Eternal is not successive. But in another sense History makes a great difference to the Eternal; for if there were no History, or if History were other than in fact it is, the Eternal would not be what the Eternal is. God the eternal is such as to sustain His own fullness of being, with the self-giving and the reality of victorious sacrifice which Religion apprehends as the heart of that fullness of being, through the historical process which supplies to these elements in His nature an opportunity of actualisation not otherwise conceivable. History does not make a difference to God in the sense of making Him different at one time from what He was at another; but it does make a difference to Him in the sense of being so vitally united to His eternal essence as its inevitable self-expression that if it were annihilated, or even changed, that would involve a difference in Him as compared with what, as author, over-ruler, and fulfiller of History, He is.

It may be legitimate to put this in the terms of traditional Christian belief. The Nativity, Death and Resurrection of Christ did not, according to that belief, make God other than He was before. They did, indeed, enable Him to treat mankind in a new way, and so in a real sense altered His active relationship to men; manifestation of what human selfishness means for divine love rendered morally appropriate a new method of action on the part of the divine love. But the love itself was unchanged. This does not mean, however, that the Eternal Life of God was unconcerned with the historical life of Christ, which merely exhibited it. On the contrary, that historical life is so intimately one with the eternal which it makes manifest, that if it could be annihilated, the eternal life would be different in quality. It is not incidental to God's eternity that (if the Christian Gospel be true) He lived and suffered and triumphed in the process of time. If that happened, then His eternal being is such as to necessitate its happening, so that its not happening would prove His eternal being to be other than Christianity believes. The quality of God's eternal life is such that 'it behoved the Christ to suffer'; and if either there were no History, or History contained no divine passion, that quality would be other than it is. *The eternal is the ground of the historical, and not* vice versa; *but the relation is necessary, not contingent – essential, not incidental.* The historical is evidence of the eternal, not only as a shadow is evidence of substance, but as a necessary self-expression of a Being whose essential activity is at once self-communication and self-discovery in that to which He communicates Himself.

To enter upon any discussion of the meaning of actual human history as known to us is to leave the field of necessary connexions for the contingent. For owing to the nature of spirit, contingency is itself a necessary characteristic of human history. But we can lay down certain principles even here. If our whole account of the nature of Value is true, or even only contains truth, then the meaning of History is found in the development of an ever wider fellowship of ever richer personalities. The goal of History, in short, is the Commonwealth of Value. From this standpoint the formation of the League of Nations marks an epoch of significance not only for our historical period but for History itself when viewed in relation to Eternity. And the difficulties of the enterprise are part of its significance. For those difficulties represent the claims of the several units to fullness of independent life within the fellowship. The goal is neither richness of individuality without recognition of the claims of fellowship, nor width of fellowship established between units that have little depth of individuality; the goal is individuality in fellowship where each term is heightened to the maximum. It is idle to speculate which of the two terms is the more important in principle; but it may well be held that we have now reached a stage in the development of warfare at which hostilities are so disastrous to all parties that the cause of national individuality can never be served by such national individualism as may involve war. Certainly in the last resort the two terms are necessary to one another. There can be no richness of individuality for men or for nations without fellowship, and there can be no fellowship apart from individuality nor depth of fellowship apart from rich variety of individuality.

But this History of nations is an affair of a few generations. Its whole drama is enacted upon a planet which is losing its power to sustain life. Astronomers seek to comfort us with the thought that for many millions of years life can continue, and there is plenty of time for our enterprise of progress. That thought brings comfort if the harvest of the world is to be gathered into some eternal store; but it is sheer lack of imagination to suppose that a vista of a million million years can give more significance than a week or a fortnight to our moral strivings, if at the end it is all to be as though we had never been at all. If that is the end for the race, and all its members pass out of existence, then it is in such a futility that the Eternal finds expression, and nothing can check the attribution of the futility to the Eternal there expressed. Yet what is the alternative? Mere prolongation of existence for individual spirits points either to an everlasting stagnation or to an unending restlessness; and neither is very satisfactory. What would give meaning to all the movement of History is the attainment of that synoptic vision of its process which at once appreciates the process as such and yet enables the mind to compass it instead of being immersed in it. Such a serene relationship to the occurrences of Time – entering into them with sympathy but yet detached from them because possessed of the principles (or the Spirit) which shape them – is perhaps one part of what has been called the Peace of God. The reality of that Peace, and its availability to finite spirits, would give to History a meaning; if there is no such condition, or if finite spirits cannot reach it, then History is indeed 'a tale Told by an idiot, full of sound and fury, Signifying nothing' (*Macbeth* Act 5).

Here we recall the intuition of Religion at its deepest that History moves to a climax which is historical because it occurs in, and crowns, the course of History, but which is in its own nature a transition to a new order of experience. That order is not one which has no relationship to the historical. The 'things above' on which this hope would bid us 'set our affection' (Galatians 5.22) are none other than the things on earth which are 'the fruit of the spirit' (Colossians 3.1). 'Life eternal' (John 13.3) is such that it is attainable before as well as after the catastrophe of death. Yet the order of experience which death makes possible is new, and unpredictable by those whose experience is of the historical order only. Therefore we are not only unable to anticipate the experience that awaits us, but are for that reason unable fully to understand or to justify the historical order itself. The historical order together with the climax which is a transition to something more and other than history is, on this view, one of those unities where the principle of unity is in the whole, so that even what precedes is fully intelligible only when what follows has completely developed the ground of the necessity of every part. This type of unity, as we have seen, is perfectly familiar in every good poem or drama. From the standpoint of the end, necessity governs the whole; from any earlier standpoint, there is contingency and indeterminacy. We are living out such a drama – the drama of which the plot is the creation of finite spirits by divine love, and the fashioning of their initially selfish individualities into the Commonwealth of Value. *The end is not predictable from the beginning; and the beginning can only be understood in the light of the end.*

Consequently our apprehension of the Meaning of History is very meagre. But we apprehend these two points. It can only have meaning at all if Eternal Life is a reality, and the meaning then is one which we do not so much discover as actually make. For human History is nothing other than ourselves; and we make its meaning by living out its process in the power, already available to us, of the Eternal Life which is at once the source of that meaning and its culmination.

iii   The Sacramental Universe

Lecture XIX, 'The Sacramental Universe', pp. 473–95

From page 478

It may safely be said that one ground for the hope of Christianity that it may make good its claim to be the true faith lies in the fact that it is the most avowedly materialist of all the great religions. It affords an expectation that it may be able to control the material, precisely because it does not ignore it or deny it, but roundly asserts alike the reality of matter and its subordination. Its own most central saying is: 'The Word was made flesh', where the last term was, no doubt, chosen because of its specially materialistic associations. By the very nature of its central doctrine Christianity is committed to a belief in the ultimate significance of the historical process, and in the reality of matter and its place in the divine scheme.

From page 481

It is clear that . . . we are trying to frame a conception which is not identical with any of the commonly offered suggestions concerning the relation of the eternal and the historical, and are now extending its application so as to include the relation of the spiritual and material. It is not simply the relation of ground and consequent, nor of cause and effect, nor of thought and expression, nor of purpose and instrument, nor of end and means; but it is all of these at once. We need for it another name; and there is in some religious traditions an element which is, in the belief of adherents of those religions, so close akin to what we want that we may most suitably call this conception of the relation of the eternal to history, of spirit to matter, the sacramental conception.

No doubt the term 'sacrament' covers a wide diversity of meaning; but there is always a central core which is found in all interpretations of supposed sacraments. If we attend to this, and to some at least of the diverse views which it holds together by their relationship to itself, we may find that we have in familiar religious experience exactly what is wanted as a clue to our metaphysical problem. The interpretation of sacraments is notoriously a focus of contention among rival schools of theology. But we are only concerned with two points, on one of which there is no disagreement, and the other of which is supremely valued by those who find most value in sacraments. The first is that, within the sacramental scheme or order, the outward and visible sign is a necessary means for conveyance of the inward and spiritual grace, but has its whole significance in that function. It is not maintained that the spiritual grace cannot be imparted in any other way; but it is universally agreed that when it is otherwise conveyed – as for example through instruction, through personal influence, or through mystic rapture – there is no sacrament. What in that case is the special importance of sacraments is a question for the dogmatic rather than for the natural theologian. But the use of sacramental rites is a common feature of human religion; it is especially prominent in Christianity; and, whatever may be thought about the comparative merits of sacramental and non-sacramental religion, it is agreed that if there is to be a sacrament there must be the material sign. We are confronted therefore with this fact: in many forms of religion, and conspicuously in the most extensive tradition of Christianity, prominence is given to rites in which the spiritual and the material are intimately intertwined. That proves nothing; but for those who on other grounds expect to find in religion guidance for the ultimate interpretation of reality it is suggestive.

Further, among those traditions which give most prominence to sacraments in the ordering of religious practice, the sacramental rite is regarded as effectual *ex opere operato* [it confers grace irrespective of the merits of the minister or recipient]. This is said, of course, not by way of contrast with the doctrine that the benefit of the sacrament is received by faith alone, for in one form or another this is again common ground; it is said in contrast with any notion that the sacrament is effective *ex opere operantis* or through the personality of the administrant, though it is required that he have the intention to 'do what the Church does'.

There is here an assertion – not indeed of identity, as that word is commonly understood – but of the unity of matter and spirit which is even more suggestive than the intimate relationship between them which is asserted by all use of sacraments whatsoever. But those who have clung to this conception as an interpretation of sacramental experience as an element of worship have seldom used it as a clue to the general interpretation of the universe. It is precisely this that we desire to suggest, always bearing in mind the constant and irreducible difference between man's utilisation of existent matter and God's creation of matter *ab initio*.

A sacrament, regarded as effective *ex opere operato* in the sense explained, is not regarded as only or chiefly a stimulus to a psychological process issuing in some spiritual apprehension; it is this, but it is also an actual conveyance of spiritual meaning and power by a material process. We find a real analogy to this in the familiar use of written or spoken language, when this takes the form of poetry. A word is in itself only a noise or a set of marks on paper. But by a social convention it is secured that, when one man speaks or writes a word, another apprehends his meaning. In so far as the word only denotes some object, this is an instance of sheer occasionalism operating by means of a convention. The meaning here is not in the word at all. It is first in the mind of the speaker, and then, on the occasion of his utterance, it is also in the mind of the hearer. But when a poet takes words as his instruments, that account of the matter becomes inadequate. The very sound of the words is now part of the meaning; that meaning can never be apprehended or recovered except by re-hearing physically or in imagination the actual sound of the words. It is not the sound apart from the meaning which exercises the magic spell; it would not exercise any such spell upon a person ignorant of the language used. Nor is it the meaning apart from the sound, for that simply does not exist; in the divorce of one from the other the meaning vanishes away. It exists as significant form or sound. Here we are near to a sacrament; but the sound that is thus filled with spiritual quality remains (for the physicist) no more than a movement of inorganic particles. The conferring of spiritual quality upon inorganic matter, of which the bare possibility is sometimes denied, is one of the commonest experiences of life; the phrase is almost a definition of Art.

But to convey meaning is not to convey the self. A sacrament is something more than a divine poem, because it conveys (as is believed by those who make use of it) not only God's meaning to the mind, but God Himself to the whole person of the worshipper. No doubt it is 'Grace' which is commonly spoken of as thus conveyed; but Grace is not something other than God, imparted by Him; it is the very Love of God (which is Himself) approaching and seeking entry to the soul of man. How can this intimately spiritual process be mediated by a material rite *ex opere operato*? We here come to a point where the sacraments of religion are unique. The finite spirit can impart his thought through a physical, even an inorganic, medium; he cannot so impart himself. But the divine spirit can so impart Himself, because He is the omnipresent. All things are present to Him, and are what they are by His creative will. In and through all of them He is accessible; there is therefore no contradiction in the supposition that in and through certain physical elements, by methods which He has chosen because of their appropriateness to our psycho-physical nature, He renders Himself in a peculiar degree accessible to those who seek Him through such media. Whether in fact He does this, only specific experience can decide – not, indeed, the momentary experience of the individual worshipper, but the whole experience of the adherents of a religion which finds in sacramental worship its focal points.

We are not now concerned to justify the religious use of sacraments, still less the particular sacraments of any positive religion, but only to vindicate the principle on which belief in sacraments reposes, in order that we may be secure in using it as a clue to the understanding of the relation of spirit to matter in the universe. From two sides there is a constant pressure to separate these two as widely as possible. From the scientific side pressure is exerted by the proper and necessary insistence that physical phenomena shall be accounted for in physical categories, and that reference to spirit – to determination by the good rather than by efficient causes – shall be excluded from physical enquiry. If this demand of the scientist be pushed to the uttermost, spirit is made to appear an alien sojourner in this material world, and its connexion with its physical counterpart is a mystery not only unsolved but demonstrably insoluble. From the religious side there is constant pressure to keep the spiritual free from what is felt to be the contamination of the material world, which is regarded as in some way gross and unworthy. Because the life of the spirit is characterised by determination by the good, the physical World of mechanical forces and chemical compounds is regarded as merely alien from it. But this results, as logic would lead us to anticipate and history proves to be the fact, in leaving the physical to go its own way unchecked by spirit, so that the vaunted spiritual exaltation has its counterpart in bodily immorality. In either case the unity of man's life is broken; the material world, with all man's economic activity, becomes a happy hunting-ground for uncurbed acquisitiveness, and religion becomes a refined occupation for the leisure of the mystical. *It is in the sacramental view of the universe, both of its material and of its spiritual elements, that there is given hope of making human both politics and economics and of making effectual both faith and love.*

It is to such a view that our whole course of enquiry has been leading us; and it is such a view which affords the strongest hope for the continuance in reality and power of religious faith and practice.

From page 491

Now a sacrament, as understood by those who prize sacraments most highly, is an instance of a very definite and special relationship of spirit and matter. We have already distinguished it from mere conventional symbolism such as we find in ordinary speech or (more accurately) in nomenclature. We have also pointed to the less marked distinction which separates it from the 'essential symbolism' of poetry. It is a spiritual utilisation of a material object whereby a spiritual result is effected. Its operation is not independent of symbolism or of the psychological processes set in motion by symbols; but its operation and effectiveness does not consist in these. Indeed many of those who set special store by the sacramental mode of worship value it because of their belief that the efficacy of the sacramental rite is totally independent of any conscious apprehension or other form of spiritual experience at that time. When faith exists as a struggle to believe in spite of empirical and temperamental pressure to unbelief, when the whole life of feeling is dead, when nothing is left but stark loyalty to God as He is dimly and waveringly apprehended to be – then the sheer objectivity, even the express materialism, of a sacrament gives it a value that nothing else can have. And when faith revives its ardour, and feeling is once more aglow, when the activity of prayers spoken and praises sung is again a natural expression of devotion, the rite which is believed to have retained its efficacy when all else failed becomes a focus of grateful adoration to the God who therein offered grace – that is, His love in action – to a soul that could receive Him in no other way. All turns, of course, on the conviction that in the sacrament God acts, fulfilling His own promise. This distinguishes the sacrament from magic, of which the essence is that man through the rite puts compulsion on the god, while it also endows the sacrament with the virtue and potency which magic falsely claims to offer.

In the sacrament then the order of thought is spirit first and spirit last, with matter as the effectual expression or symbolic instrument of spirit. That is the formula which we suggest as an articulation of the essential relations of spirit and matter in the universe. Our enquiry starts from matter, or at least from physical process. But that process produces centres of spiritual life, which, once manifested, displays its true nature as logical *prius* as well as temporal resultant. Consequently we reach, from the consideration of the world as apprehended, and without any reference to the data of distinctive religious experience, the scheme familiar in the religious interpretation of the world: (a) God, supreme, and perfectly free to express Himself according to His own nature of perfect spirit; (b) the world, at first in its crudest material form of inorganic matter – or at least of matter not yet perceptibly or effectively organic; then organic matter exhibiting the activities of life; then mind directing vital activities by selection of appropriate means to an end fixed by its correspondence to the nature and needs of the organism; then mind forming free ideas, and thus becoming capable of self-determination in accordance with apparent good, making selection among ends presented by outward experience and ends held in thought and imagination as true ideals or principles of conduct; (c) the world, thus understood as a sphere of finite spirits self-expressed through their own physical organisms, now transformed into the Kingdom of God by the uniting of finite spirits in a fellowship which reproduces in the creature the love which is the essential being of the Creator. Thus we pass from God through the world of process and history to God. But God is God in the activity which sustains the process and directs the history. If He did not create He would still exist, for He is not dependent for existence on His creation. But if He did not create, He would not be what He is, for He is Creator.

Thus the view of the universe which I have called sacramental asserts the supremacy and absolute freedom of God; the reality of the physical world and its process as His creation; the vital significance of the material and temporal world to the eternal Spirit; and the spiritual issue of the process in a fellowship of the finite and time-enduring spirits in the infinite and eternal Spirit. Matter exists in full reality but at a secondary level. It is created by spirit – the Divine Spirit to be the vehicle of spirit and the sphere of spirit's self-realisation in and through the activity of controlling it.

This conception does not only mean that a mind of sufficient insight can detect the activity of God in all that happens if it be seen in its true context and perspective, so that the sublimity of nature is an expression of the divine majesty, and its beauty of the divine artistry, and love's sacrifice (wherever it be offered) of the divine heroism. That is true and precious. But more than this is involved. The world, which is the self-expressive utterance of the Divine Word, becomes itself a true revelation, in which . . . what comes is not truth concerning God, but God Himself. This . . . does not exclude the possibility of special revelations; rather it is the condition of that possibility. The spiritually sensitive mind can be in personal communion with God, in, and by means of, all its experience. It is probable that no adequately sensitive mind exists, and that all must deepen their insight by periods of adoring contemplation, which alternate with periods of activity inspired and guided by what is then apprehended. But the goal is to fuse action and worship into the continuous life of worshipful service; in the holy city which came down from God out of heaven the seer beheld no place of worship because the divine presence pervaded all its life (Revelation 21.22). The significance of this conception from the side of the historical process we have tried already to adumbrate. We must also attempt to grasp its significance, in what restricted fashion we may, from the side of the eternal and divine. One aspect at least of the Divine Glory is the triumphant self-sacrifice of love. This is God's very being – not perhaps its entirety, but truly a part of its essence. That fact determines the dominant issue of history, which is the prevailing and increasing supremacy of love in all its forms over self-centredness in all its forms – a supremacy both won and sustained by love's own method of self-sacrifice. This is the divine glory whereof the heaven and the earth are full. If heaven and earth did not contain this, it could not be the glory of God who is creator of earth and heaven. It is in and through being such as we find Him in the course of history at its greatest moments to be, that He is eternally love and joy and peace. Even to the eternal life of God His created universe is sacramental of Himself. If He had no creatures to redeem, or if He had not redeemed them, He would not be what He is. Neither does His historical achievement make Him eternally Redeemer, nor does His eternal redemptive love simply express itself in history while remaining unaffected. But each is what it is in and through the other, like spirit and matter in a sacramental rite, yet so that the eternal and spiritual is first and last, with the historical and material as its medium of self-actualisation.

The thought seems tangled. Yet I believe that is only because we are attempting the inevitable, yet impossible task of expressing in conceptual terms what is nothing less than life itself. Let us take an analogy from an enquiry apparently remote. The question has lately been revived whether thought most fitly precedes action, to determine its direction, or follows it, to account for what has occurred. If our whole position is sound we shall repudiate the implied dilemma. Thought and action, if separated from one another, are abstractions and falsifications; the real fact is active rational life; and this is best expressed in rational activity, where thought and conduct are inextricably united. The man of trained and disciplined mind spontaneously acts in relation to an emergency in a manner quite different from that adopted by the thoughtless or undisciplined man. He may not consciously think for a single moment about the situation; perhaps there is not time for thought; yet his action is rational, and he can, if desired, afterwards articulate its principles. Here the logical, if not also the temporal, order is thought first and thought last with physical movement as its mode not only of expression but of self-actualisation. This complete integration is not always attained; when it is lacking, the question whether thought or conduct takes precedence must be settled by circumstance. But action without understanding is likely to be misguided, and abstract thought in detachment from the detail of the concrete situation is sure to be misleading. Thought is most of all itself in and through the process of determining rational action in face of the complexity of a given situation.

So God, who is spirit, is His eternal self in and through the historical process of creating a world and winning it to union with Himself. His creation is sacramental of Himself to His creatures; but in effectively fulfilling that function it becomes sacramental of Him to Him-Self – the means whereby He is eternally that which eternally He is.

8

Seeking Christian Unity: Addresses and Sermons

In the 1930s Temple became one of the leaders of the nascent ecumenical movement. His addresses and sermons in this chapter come out of and reflect that leadership. The background to this work was his understanding of the vocation and destiny of the Church to which he belonged, the Church of England. Its vocation, he believed, was derived from the way it was heir to the continuous history of Christendom and, also, heir to the 'new birth' of the Reformation: 'Both of these must be borne in mind, for both of them are equally essential to the constitution, doctrine, and work of the Church of England as it has constantly represented itself from the time of the Reformation onwards' (Essays in Christian Politics, 1927, p. 192).

From the historic tradition of the undivided Church, the Church of England had inherited its sacramental and especially eucharistic ministry. But for Temple the Reformation marked the recovery of two fundamental principles of Christian life: the supreme authority of Scripture, and the duty of private judgement (or what he prefers to call the freedom of the individual religious life). Temple described this as the duty of everyone 'sincerely to make up his mind what it is that God says to him through the Scriptures'. But Temple did not see this as taking place by means of the individual alone. The believer will do it 'in the fellowship of his fellow-seekers in the Church; he will allow to the witness of the Church's authority, if he is wise, a weight which will override any mere whims of his own mind' (Essays in Christian Politics, 1927, p. 198).

For Temple these principles were embodied in the Church of England. Its vocation and destiny was to live by them and in them: 'to offer the fullness of God's help to every soul but never to dictate to any soul precisely how that soul may best receive the benefit'. And this vocation meant that the Church of England was in an excellent position to understand and appreciate both the traditional Catholic churches of East and West, and the Protestant churches of the Reformation. It was a vocation that would include reaching out to both traditions: 'we have a position unique in Christendom, the full value of which can only be realised for the universal Church so far as we are true to both sides of our own tradition' (Essays in Christian Politics, 1927, p. 206).

Ecumenism, then, should have a natural place in the life of Anglicanism because this tradition was based itself on the coming together of different traditions. Anglican leaders would need to reach out, interact in dialogue and draw more closely together with the leaders of other churches because that was the inherent nature of Anglicanism. Ecumenical commitment, for Temple, was part and parcel of being an Anglican Christian.

In the late 1920s and 1930s Temple did just this, extending his hand to both the Catholic and Reformed traditions. It is important to rehearse the key moments in this work. His first encounter with the ecumenical movement had been as a steward at the Edinburgh Conference in 1910. This made him aware of the emerging call among missionaries for the churches to work more closely together in the evangelization of the world. He was also involved with the ecumenical Student Christian Movement, having become one of its most regular speakers at the annual Swanwick conferences. Many of the student leaders of the SCM in the 1920s and 1930s were also inspired by Temple to work for unity among the churches, among them Lesslie Newbigin, Ambrose Reeves, Oliver Tomkins and Ronald Preston.

The Faith and Order movement was created to bring the Protestant churches together in discussion about core theological matters, in order that the churches might move more closely together. The first significant Faith and Order conference was at Lausanne in 1927, with the second in Edinburgh in 1937. Temple was present at both. At the first it was agreed that the Apostles' Creed and the Nicene Creed expressed the faith of all the churches represented, and that a future unity must rest on the basis of the historic episcopate. Temple considered these achievements to have been very significant. He remained fundamentally committed to the episcopate, which some of his Protestant friends found difficult. He thought carefully about this stumbling block to some, and in one of his charges to the clergy of York Diocese he carefully and extensively presented his reasoning (see Section i). This was an aspect of Anglicanism that Temple was not prepared to surrender in ecumenical discussions. He welcomed the exchange of pulpits between ministers of *the different churches, but he could not accept the interchangeability of eucharistic ministry. On his belief that, ultimately, the eucharistic ministry of the non-Catholic churches was not fully authorized, and that episcopacy was necessary to the preservation of the true order of the Church, he was vigorously challenged by Reinhold Niebuhr (see Niebuhr's fascinating account of their discussions in Iremonger 1948, pp. 493–4).*

In 1929 he was elected to be the chairman of the Faith and Order continuation committee. Thereafter he never failed to attend its annual meetings, mostly on the continent of Europe, and to chair the executive committee, at which most of the important preparatory work was done.

Temple's considerable skill in guiding discussion and producing comprehensive statements at the end resulted in his then being elected the chairman at the world Faith and Order conference in Edinburgh in 1937. This meant that he preached the key note sermon at its opening service in St Giles' Cathedral, Edinburgh, in 1937 (see Section ii). The sermon was a rousing call for renewed commitment to Christian unity in the increasingly bleak environment of Nazi-dominated Europe.

During the 1930s Temple also played a key role in the development of the idea for a world council of churches. He worked closely with two influential figures in the international ecumenical movement: J. H. Oldham, a Free Church of Scotland secretary of the International Missionary Council, who later became chairman of research in the 'Life and Work' arm of the ecumenical movement; and William Paton, an English Presbyterian who had been a missionary in India and was Oldham's forceful successor at the International Missionary Council. Oldham, Paton and Temple have been described as 'the ecclesiastical statesmen of Protestant Europe, dexterously creating the structures for the Church of the future' (Hastings 1987, p. 302). Of the three it was Temple who became the public representative. (A letter of Paton to Temple is printed in a postscript to this chapter.)

The idea of a world council of churches was developed during an informal meeting at Bishopthorpe in May 1933, at which ten people representing different international ecumenical bodies talked together and developed a new sense of shared leadership. At another informal meeting at Princeton in 1935 Temple took the lead in proposing an 'interdenominational, international council representing all the churches'. Then in July 1937 he chaired the so-called Committee of Thirty-Five meeting at Westfield College, London, which formulated the precise proposal for a 'World Council of Churches'. This was subsequently accepted by the international ecumenical 'Life and Work' conference at Oxford (chaired by Bishop Bell of Chichester) and by the Edinburgh conference that summer. The next year, at Utrecht, Temple was elected chairman of the provisional World Council's central committee, with Wim Visser 't Hooft, Oldham's assistant, as one of two general secretaries, and Paton as the other.

As Archbishop of York he was the most senior church leader to be involved in these discussions, and this partly explains his rise to leadership of the movement. But his rise was also due to his considerable skills as an advocate of the idea and, underlying all, to his own theology of the Church which, as we have seen, was one that accepted other churches as fellow pilgrims along the way. Adrian Hastings writes that 'It is unlikely that the World Council would have been proposed, agreed to, and brought into existence without his combination of authority and persuasiveness' (Hastings 2004). If Temple had lived he would almost certainly have become the first president of the World Council of Churches when it was formally constituted in 1948. His Christmas message to the churches of Germany of 1942 (see Section iii) gives a glimpse of what this leadership would have been like.

At the same time as the plans were being laid for the WCC, the churches in the British Isles were also reaching agreement, after protracted discussions, on the establishment of a British Council of Churches (but without the Roman Catholics). Temple was part of these discussions and supported the plans. In 1940 he had proposed a resolution to the Church Assembly of the Church of England welcoming the establishment of the World Council and paving the way for its counterpart in the British Isles, and this had been passed. Then at the climax of this process, in September 1942, he preached at the service of the inauguration of the BCC in St Paul's Cathedral. His sermon explained why it was so important that the different churches, which had distinctive principles and commitments, should nevertheless come together in a body like the British Council of Churches (see Section iv). It was an impressive culmination of all his efforts, national and international, to call the churches together over the previous 15 years. The work showed that in this respect he was not just someone who talked about a future Christian unity in a theoretical way, but gave equal attention to the practical business of convening, chairing and implementing the process of bringing it about.

i Reunion and the Place of the Episcopate

A Charge delivered to the Diocese of York, printed in *Thoughts on Some Problems of the Day*, 1931, pp. 88–132

The Committee of the Lambeth Conference [1930] on Unity contented itself with affirming its conviction that 'the unity of the Church is the will of God' almost without argument. For its own purposes this was sufficient, but it is worth while, in addressing the Home Church, to set out some of the calamities which result from our disunion; for we have become so accustomed to many of them that we now take them for granted.

First, then, is the hindrance to the fulfilment of the purpose and prayer of our Lord 'that they all may be one' (John 17.21). It is impossible for a divided Church to gather together in the unity of one fellowship the multitudes of mankind.

Second is the paralysis of witness. The chief evidence which Christians are to give of their discipleship is their love for one another; through their unity the world is to be won to Believe (John 13.35). But the world cannot see even such unity as exists among Christians so long as they are unable to join together at the Table of the Lord. Where there are many Churches in the same place, they obscure instead of manifesting the one Christ.

Third may be set the perpetual hampering of practical activities. A vast amount of the material resources available for the Work of the Christian Community is frittered away through the overlapping of organisation, the needless multiplication of places of worship with consequent waste of man-power, and the loss of efficiency through the need to weigh irrelevant considerations. One Secretary of a great Christian organisation has lately declared that he can seldom consider who is the best man for a particular piece of work, because he has to consider which denomination has a claim to the next appointment.

Fourth, and equally important with any, is the injury to our apprehension of truth. Every division, through the very controversy which causes it and to which it afterwards gives occasion, leads each of the separated bodies to pay exaggerated attention to the points about which difference arose. Thus, to take the example nearest home, I am convinced that the Anglican Communion is right to maintain its insistence on the Historic Episcopate, but I am equally convinced that Anglicans think far too much – not necessarily too highly, but assuredly too often and too long of that same Episcopate. It would be far better for us if we could take it for granted and give our undistracted thought to other matters.

It is very important to notice that the greatest divisions of Christendom are geographical, and correspond with, if they do not spring from, certain temperamental types. The first great division was that of East and West, which was between a mentality dominated by metaphysic and a mentality dominated by law. The next was within the West between North and South, between a traditional love of local autonomy and a traditional love of centralised unity. In each of these both parties were the losers, both by lack of what the other possessed and by exaggeration of what each retained. Northern Protestantism needs the Roman instinct for order to save it from the chaotic license of fissiparous sectarianism; Rome needs the Northern love of liberty to save it from the petrifaction of a bureaucratic despotism; the practical and efficient West needs the mysticism and philosophy of the East to save it from materialism; while the subtle and penetrating philosophy of the East seems to need the ethical energy of the West to save it from stagnation or brooding inactivity. But it is necessary to qualify all comments on the Eastern Church by the recollection of the long oppression that most of it has suffered at the hands of Sultans, Tsars or Bolsheviks; where there is no liberty of action there can be no censure of inactivity.

The urgency of reunion cannot be exaggerated. And yet there are prices too high to pay. The severed parts of the Universal Church are trustees for the treasures of their own spiritual tradition, and must bring these with them to the reunited fellowship of the future.

> We must not, for the sake of union, barter away our special heritage, for we hold it in trust for the whole Body of Christ; and we recognise also that those with whom we seek to be in fuller unity must equally safeguard the special treasures of their own tradition. (Lambeth Conference 1930, *Report on Unity*, p. 112)

What of the episcopate?

In the Book of the Acts and subsequent story of Christendom ... what was found existing after the withdrawal of [the Lord's] physical presence was a fellowship of believers with the Apostolate as its focus of leadership and authority. Neither did the Apostles gather the Church about them in obedience to an authority which they independently possessed, nor did the society of believers confer upon the Apostles an authority originally inherent in the body as a whole. But the Church was born with the Apostolate as an integral part of it, providing leadership and exercising authority with a general consent that was grounded in a universal sense of what was fit. This was the inevitable and unquestionably (as I think) intended result of our Lord's own action in forming the Apostolate; thus the differentiation of Clergy and Laity within His Church is of His own making.

By one means or by many the Church sought to remain in full continuity with its life in those early days; and after a few generations had passed, if not throughout, it is found universally agreed in using the Episcopate, 'in its continuity of succession and consecration' (*Report on the Ministry* of the Lausanne Conference on Faith and Order, p. 115), as its central principle of Order. The Anglican Communion still uses the Historic Episcopate in that way.

To this no one objects. No one asks us to abandon episcopacy for ourselves. But we are asked why we should insist upon its acceptance by others before we can establish full intercommunion with them. In order to give the necessary background to the inquiry we must go back to the function of the Church itself.

It is fundamentally and essentially a sacramental organism. It exists to be the 'repository and trustee' of the Gospel (Resolution 1 of Lambeth 1920); not what it actually is in the person of its members, but what it potentially is by reason of the Spirit always at work in it, is the clue to the understanding of it. It is what it signifies, not what it has at any time become.

The supreme Christian Sacrament is the Incarnation itself, wherein, by the act of becoming flesh, the Word of God achieved both self-manifestation to men and sovereignty over their hearts such as were otherwise impossible. In Christ's Humanity there is a revelation of Deity such as our sin prevents from being given through ours: yet it is the whole meaning of the Church as His Body that His Divine Spirit should, by subduing our selfish wills and binding us into the unity of love, declare His nature and fulfil His purpose through the ages and across the world, as that nature was declared and that purpose fulfilled in Palestine by means of the Body born of Mary.

Christ now acts in the world through His Body the Church. All particular Sacraments belong to the Church, and have their meaning within its corporate life. If we are to understand them we must consider their place in the corporate life of the Christian society and proceed from this to their value for the individual. To invert this process and ask first (for example) what is the spiritual difference between a baptised infant and an unbaptised, is to confuse the problem in advance. Our first problem is, not chiefly to determine how this Christian or that may be sure of obtaining grace today or tomorrow, but how we may maintain and express the essential character of the Church as a society founded by the act of God in the Incarnation and perpetually offering to men the grace and truth which came by Jesus Christ, as distinct from an association of individuals who are agreed in a desire to serve and follow Him. Its ground is not in the acceptance of Him by our wills as our Lord, but in the act of His will calling us through Himself into fellowship with the Father.

In no age have the human members of the Church been completely responsive to their calling, and for that reason the actual Church on earth has never completely become what it signifies. This is in itself a most potent reason for maintaining all those elements in the Church's life whereby its significance, as the God-created channel of God-given life, is expressed. If we could all be perfect saints, these things would matter less. The world would see in our lives what now one can only show them by pointing beyond ourselves to all that proclaims the Church as the channel, not of man's aspiration, but of God's call upwards (Philippians 3.14) and His gift of power to obey. The possibility of corruption in the earthly Church is one ground for insisting on those elements – the distinctively Catholic elements – which witness to the transcendence of Him whose Body it is.

But in fact the corruption has sometimes gone so far that to the best men of the time it has seemed necessary, if witness was to be given to the grace of God at all, that it should be given in separation from the body as it had come to be; for this body smothered the Spirit which it existed to manifest. At the Reformation, in particular, the first great Reformers would gladly have preached their freshly apprehended truth within the Catholic Church; but the authorities of that Church would not permit their preaching of it at all. No doubt there were grave faults in the Reformers also, which gave to the authorities an occasion for their repressive action. But it does not seem to me possible to doubt that the Reformers were bound by loyalty to Christ to preach the truth in Him as they had newly come to know it, and if that could not be inside the unity of the Church, then it must be outside. So there were formed new fellowships of Christians not in fellowship with one another.

These new fellowships were bound to provide as wisely as they could for the maintenance of their own spiritual life. To begin with, they all had the Scriptures, the Creeds, and the use of the two Sacraments of the Gospel. Some also had the continuity of ministerial succession; for some that was lost by force of the very circumstances that led to their separation. Where it was retained, as in England and in Sweden, the four chief witnesses to the super-natural character of Christianity were all preserved. Where it was lost, as over most of Protestant Christendom, what are we to say concerning the sacramental character of the group concerned?

Now if it be held that episcopal ordination confers a power of making sacraments, so that when an episcopally ordained priest celebrates the Eucharist something happens in the world of fact which does not happen on any other condition, then these bodies have no real Sacraments. But that is a theory to which I find myself unable to attach any intelligible meaning. It is admitted that the peril to which strong sacramental doctrine is most liable is that of falling into conceptions properly described as magical; and this theory seems to me to lie on the wrong side of the dividing line. What is conferred in Ordination is not the power to make sacramental a rite which otherwise would not be such, but *authority* (*potestas*) to administer Sacraments which belong to the Church, and which, therefore, can only be rightly administered by those who hold the Church's commission to do so. The objection to lay celebration is not that it is in its own nature inoperative, but that it is a usurpation by one member of what belongs to the whole Church. Strictly speaking, I submit, we should not say that a layman cannot celebrate, but that he has no right to celebrate, and it would therefore be wrong for him to do so.

But, it will be urged, we are not concerned with lay-celebration, but with ministries accredited in their own parts of the Church. That is for the most part true; but the first point on which it is necessary to be clear is whether we regard the action of the Church in Ordination as so related to the Sacraments that where there is no episcopally ordained priest there is no real Sacrament. I find that position untenable, and even in the last resort unintelligible. Moreover, the Church recognises Lay Baptism, though of this Sacrament as of others the bishop is the proper minister, 'or he to whom the bishop may entrust it'; he does this by the very act of ordaining a priest, and gives authority to a deacon to baptise 'in the absence of the priest'. It is hard to see any difference in principle in the case of the Eucharist. But Lay Baptism is only permitted in extreme emergency, and in the case of the Eucharist the emergency can only arise in the very rarest circumstances, for the individual believer can make a spiritual communion if there is no duly accredited minister to offer him sacramental communion, and in the strength of earlier communions can continue to feed upon Christ in his heart with thanksgiving.

If, however, there *can* be a real Eucharist where there is not an episcopally ordained priest, we need have no difficulty in acknowledging the reality of the Sacraments administered in at least some non-episcopal communions. Further, the great bodies of which we are now thinking were separated from the historic Church mainly through that Church's fault; they sought to live as Christ had taught; in their worship they set themselves to do what He commanded, believing that He would give what He had promised. It is impossible without blasphemy to doubt that their Sacraments were, and are, effective means of grace to them. Moreover, history is the witness that God has accepted and used those ministries. To me it would seem shocking presumption to question the reality of the Sacraments administered, for example, in the Presbyterian Church of Scotland or the Lutheran Church of Germany. As Christian disciples, the members of those bodies belong to the soul of the Catholic Church; by Baptism they are admitted to membership in its body. But it is not only as individuals that they form part of the Catholic Church. These bodies themselves are not mere religious societies, of which the several members are, by virtue of their faith and baptism, members of the Universal Church. They are, as their fruits have shown, parts and organs of the Universal Church. We recognise in their achievements the works of Christ which can only be done through His Body. And if all this be so, then in the Eucharist as celebrated and ministered among them Christ offers Himself as in our own Churches to all those for whom the ministries employed are authorised organs of the Church. We cannot, in my judgment, refuse to recognise that 'within their several spheres' the ministries of such non-episcopal communions, 'ministries which imply a sincere intention to preach Christ's Word and administer the Sacraments as Christ has ordained, and to which authority so to do has been solemnly given by the Church concerned, are real ministries of Christ's Word and Sacraments within the Universal Church' (George Bell, *Documents on Christian Unity*, i, p. 159). 'Yet,' as the document in which those words occur goes on at once to say, 'ministries, even when so regarded, may be in varying degrees irregular or defective.' In other words, though real ministries within the Universal Church, they may still not be ministries of the Universal Church with a commission from the whole fellowship to all its members. Our claim is that where a living Church acts through duly consecrated Bishops we have assurance that there Christ bestows His commission, which is a commission of Ministry to and on behalf of the Universal Church. If some part of the Church refuses to recognise it, that will constitute a defect in the effectiveness of the Commission, but will not destroy it as a Commission of the

Universal Church. For it is Christ who gives the Commission through the Church, His Body.

Let us consider what would be the antithesis to the true conception of the Church's Ministry. Perhaps the person most remote from a true minister of the Word and Sacraments would be one who should begin to preach and lead in worship of his own motion, and to conduct forms of worship for whatever followers he might collect. Such a man might be a prophet, and it might be the duty of the Church to offer him opportunities for the delivery of his message. But if, of his own motion, he celebrated the Eucharist, he would be dispensing what had never been entrusted to him; he would be a usurper of the rights of the whole Church.

Scarcely, if at all, less remote from the true conception of the Ministry would be the action of a group of persons who should select one of their own number to say to them the things which they desired to hear.

The Church is the repository and trustee of God's self-revelation. Its ministers do not represent a local group; they are the appointed agents of the Universal Church for the proclamation of the revelation and dispensing of the means of grace which are entrusted to that Universal Church. An essential part of their testimony is directed to that Universal Church which is alone the 'pillar and ground of the truth' (1 Timothy 3.15). Where the full system of the historic Church has been maintained, their very office bears this testimony. The priest who preaches and celebrates does so as the organ of the Universal Church; the office of the Bishop who ordained him is, in part of its very essence, constituted by, the commission to commission others on behalf of the Universal Church. When in the Eucharist we lift up our hearts to the Lord, it is with Angels and Archangels and all the company of heaven that we laud and magnify God's glorious Name. The congregation with which we worship is not the handful of people in the same building at the same time; it is the 'innumerable hosts of angels, the general assembly and Church of the firstborn who are enrolled in heaven' (Hebrews 12.22). No doubt this experience is possible, and often actual, apart from the historic Order of the Church. But in fact it is observable that this conception of worship, and especially of Eucharistic worship, is most frequently found and cherished where there has been preserved that historic Order of the Ministry which by its very nature represents and proclaims the binding in one of all races and all generations by the chain of the laying on of apostolic hands.

Now if the fruit of the Reformation were found to be a few great Churches united by their use of the Scriptures, the Creeds, and the two great Sacraments – united also by their sense of the Ministry as an organ of the Universal Church, but divided in so far as some had, and some had not, been able at the crisis to preserve continuity of succession – then certainly the problem of Reunion would be not only simpler but in its essence different. There would still be need to unify the different ministerial streams by general acceptance of that Order which is 'historic in a sense in which no other now can ever be'. But mutual relations during the process could be far more intimate. In fact, however, we find that the communions which trace their separate existence to the Reformation exhibit every grade of deviation from historic Order, even to a point hardly distinguishable from the position of the two hypothetical cases suggested as the extreme antithesis of the true conception of the Ministry. And we find, as might be anticipated, that where Church Order is not accepted as a thing given, as distinct from a thing to be constructed, there is often a reluctance to accept the Revelation in Christ as a thing given, or to be given. In spite of Luther and Calvin, some branches of Protestantism have developed a degree of Pelagianism which is to my mind inconceivable in Churches of the historic Order.

History, as it seems to us, makes manifest the spiritual value of the historic Order. There are points where the bodies from which we are now separated have much to give to us. That very Pelagianism which appears in some of them is the reverse side of their zeal for righteousness in which they have often put us to shame. And who shall say that zeal for righteousness is in God's sight less pleasing than completeness of sacramental Order? But it is Order, not righteousness, which is in question here.

> Appreciation of spiritual devotion affords ground for desiring reunion, but agreement upon Faith and Order is the essential matter, in the sense that to secure a common Faith and Order is in itself to accomplish reunion. (Lambeth Conference, 1930, *Report on Unity* p. 114)

Not every group of Christians who organise their Worship on one pattern can be regarded as corporately a part of the Universal Church. God created His Church as an organism with a structure appropriate to its function. Some groups, which have been unable to maintain that structure in completeness, are none the less true parts of the Church. Some may be essentially societies for edification, on which the blessing of God has rested because they consisted of good men sincerely doing what seemed to them best. In such a situation unity can rightly be recovered only by general return to the historic structure of the organism of the Church.

Now we are often urged to unite in the Holy Communion as an expression and seal of the fellowship which is so richly enjoyed at Conferences and the like where we co-operate with members of other denominations. But that seems to put the matter on the wrong basis. Among fellow-Christians so assembled there is a most precious reality of fellowship in Christ. But if they mean to persist in maintaining their divisions, it is spiritual only; in other words, it is not sacramental fellowship. It is not as a detached individual Christian that I receive the Holy Communion. It is as a member of Christ's Body, the Church. What I need – (I do not say 'desire', but what I spiritually need) – is to escape from any such narrowly limited fellowship as depends on feelings of the moment, that I may be helped to the realisation, so far more difficult, of fellowship in the whole Communion of Saints. A large part of the value of sacramental worship is its independence of 'feeling', or present consciousness of gifts received. It is in the conviction that, as I accept what is given me by the Universal Church through its Minister commissioned as a steward of its mysteries, I am indeed 'fulfilled with grace and heavenly benediction' – it is in this faith, quite apart from all warmth of feeling, though that too may come, that I find the special value of the sacramental as distinguished from other modes of worship. Feeling and conscious realisation are greatly to be welcomed when they spring out of the due performance of the appointed rite. But they must not be made the basis of the rite, if only for the reason that the rite essentially stands for a fellowship qualified to be universal, while every fellowship based on human sympathy has narrow limits.

How then can I rightly seek the means of grace from ministries which have not received their commission through channels representing to me the Universal Church when ministries that do represent that whole fellowship are available? I do not call in question the reality of the grace conveyed to those for whom these ministries are normal and accepted; on the contrary, in the case at least of the great Reformed Churches I assert it. But I observe, as I think, that the defect of authorisation leads to a lowered sense of the spiritual importance of authorisation, and in extreme instances to such neglect of it as involves spiritual individualism and self-assertiveness even towards God. Still more important than this is the fact that the means by which those ministries have been commissioned are not such as to make a claim that the commission is that of the whole Church Universal. If I seek the means of grace at their hands, while there is no intention of unifying the ministries, I seem to assert that this defect of commission or authorisation is unimportant, whereas my whole conception of the place of Sacraments in the life of the Church is such as to make its importance very great and to certain true spiritual interests fundamental.

If the means of grace are at any time for a long period not available through the channels which for us have full authorisation, we find ourselves temporarily in such a situation as arose locally in Northern Germany (for example) after the Reformation; it may then very well be justifiable to avail ourselves of those means of grace which have the authorisation of the only Christian community that is accessible . . . To make such an exception in exceptional circumstances is a way of affirming the general rule, and even of safeguarding it; for nothing so much imperils a general rule as to enlist in opposition to it the generosity of human nature by a rigid enforcement that takes no account of special circumstances.

But it may be urged that to give this place to the question of authorisation is contrary to the spirit of the Gospel. Cannot the disciples of the Lord join at His Table in the meal of fellowship without concern for such arid and bewildering requirements? To which I answer that the Eucharist is not first and foremost a meal of fellowship. No doubt it was instituted in the midst of a meal of fellowship, but in itself it is something more and other than that. The Last Supper as a whole was a meal of fellowship, whether it was the Passover meal or not. But if this had been the essential note, it would have been enough for the Lord to say, 'Do this in remembrance of Me', which it is not quite certain that He did say. There would have been no need for the tremendous and unquestioned words: 'This is My Body; this is My Blood of the New Covenant.'

I must reserve for another chapter any discussion of Eucharistic Doctrine beyond what is strictly necessary for the present discussion. But one main element in Eucharistic worship is our incorporation into the One Body in which Christ makes His eternal self-oblation to the Father. The bonds across time and space are here definitely more important than the realised fellowship of the present congregation; and while the unity which those bonds represent may be apprehended without their aid, yet it appears that this aspect of the Eucharist, and even of the Christian fellowship, tends to be neglected where those bonds are missing; and the bonds in question are the ministerial succession through ministers whose commission includes, and always has included, the right to give commission to others.

Sacraments are in their very nature external, as well as spiritual, and by universal consent certain specified externals are requisite for the rite to exist at all. If there is neither Bread nor Wine, there cannot be the Sacrament of Holy Communion. There may still be the spiritual apprehension and appropriation of all that that Sacrament represents and conveys; but the Sacrament itself would be lacking. Consequently there must be agreement about the external conditions of the Sacrament if people are to join in sacramental worship. This is connected with the two great merits of such worship; for it is by means of their formal correctness that Sacraments bring us the assurance which is independent of feeling; and it is by their materialism that they can represent and promise the complete control of the physical by the spiritual, the complete expression of the spiritual through the physical. That is why a purely spiritual unity which does not look for or intend organic union should not be given sacramental expression in the Holy Communion. There are countless ways of expressing a spiritual unity which falls short of demanding organic union; we must not give away for this purpose the only means we have for expressing and realising organic union itself . . .

The question of spiritual hospitality is different – I mean the welcoming of members of non-episcopal Churches to receive the Holy Communion with us. Here the chief questions are those of pastoral expediency. Any baptised Christian may present himself at the altar, and if he does he may not be repelled, unless he be personally excommunicate. But many who would themselves desire to do this, yet hesitate if they feel that they are thrusting themselves upon us. We surrender no essential principle if we let them know that they are welcome; but if we do this at large, we shall obscure what is at least a part of the central significance of the rite, the incorporation of all not only into one spiritual fellowship, but into one body. Accordingly, it seems wise that only those who have the status of communicant in some Christian denomination should be welcomed, and that this should be only when either the ministrations of their own communion are not available, or when there is some special condition tending to foster at least the spirit of unity. And for myself, that I may honestly lay bare my mind, a chief reason for desiring to offer such a welcome is the belief that it will be a powerful means of increasing the desire for full organic reunion on the basis of the Historic Ministry.

A practical consideration to be borne in mind is that a reunited Christendom must include both the Eastern Orthodox and Rome. It is inconceivable that either of these would enter into union with churches which did not maintain the Historic Ministry. But that is comparatively unimportant. What is important is that they would be right to refuse.

I have said much with which friends of mine will disagree, and part of what I have said will cause pain to some of them. But it seems to me that we must make a new effort to understand each other, even if the first result is to find that we differ more than we hoped or thought. Then we can in conference and discussion seek the way to combine the treasures of our various traditions. We must teach and learn from one another not only what it is to which we cling, but why we cling to it. And if it be said that this is all very complicated and the ways of Christ are simple, I answer that His way indeed is simple, but these complications are not of His making; they are part of the entanglement of sin – that sin of disunion of which the guilt rests upon us all, not less on those who have maintained the historic order and failed to commend it than on those who for conscience' sake broke away from it . . .

I make no claim to perfection for the Anglican Communion. I know that we are the poorer for lack of gifts which our Free Church friends possess in greater abundance. I do not claim that our ministry is fully representative; the refusal of recognition by Rome, even though we believe it to be mistaken, would alone prevent that. For the only fully representative Ministry would be one 'acknowledged by every part of the Church as possessing not only the inward call of the Spirit, but also the commission of Christ and the authority of the whole body' (Lambeth Conference 1920, Resolution 9.6).

We must discharge [the stewardship of our ministry] at once with loyalty to the tradition for which we are trustees, but also with charity and with minds attentive to the work of God accomplished apart from that tradition. I do not claim or hold that through bishops apart from any living Church the commission of Christ is given. The bishop is the agent of Christ in His Church. But it is of the essence of episcopacy that the bishop acts for the whole Church, not for any section of it. Where any great part of the Church refuses to recognise a bishop or the commission bestowed through him, the commission is to that extent defective, not in authority (which comes from Christ alone) but in effectiveness. If some part of the Church has failed to maintain the episcopate in its continuity of office and consecration, it has lost the agency through which the claim to issue the commission of the whole Church is made. God may (and we know He does) bless the ministries serving those parts of the Church, and also those serving bodies which are in origin and form societies for edification but which have been honestly accepted as Churches by their members. But this does not constitute the commission given to and on behalf of the Universal Church, and to treat the two as identical is the way, not to secure union, but to new disunion whenever some strong conviction is formed by any group of Christians.

Neither continuity of consecration apart from the living body of the Church, nor any body of Christians without the historic episcopate as its organ, corresponds to the true requirement for Church and Ministry. As the primitive Church was a Society of believers with the Apostolate within it as its focus of authority and unity, so it is through the fellowship of the Church and by means of the episcopate within it that Christ gives his commission to administer the Sacraments, which are His gifts and have their place and meaning within the organic life of the Church.

ii A Call for Christian Unity

Sermon at the opening service of the Second World Conference on Faith and Order, St Giles', Edinburgh, 3 August 1937, in the William Temple Papers, vol. 68, pp. 207–26

Ephesians 4.13

The unity of the Church, on which our faith and hope is set, is grounded in the unity of God and the uniqueness of His redeeming act in Jesus Christ. The 'one body and one spirit' correspond to the 'one God and Father of all'. The unity of the Church of God is a perpetual fact; our task is not to create it but to exhibit it. Where Christ is in men's hearts, there is the Church; where His Spirit is active, there is His Body. The Church is not an association of men, each of who has chosen Christ as his Lord; it is a fellowship of men, each of whom Christ has united with Himself. The Christian faith and life are not a discovery or invention of men; they are not an emergent phase of the historical process; they are the gift of God. That is true not only of their historical origin, but quite equally of the rebirth to that faith and life of each individual Christian. Our unity in dependence for our faith upon the unique act of the one God is a perpetual and unalterable fact. If we are Christians, that is due to the activity of the Holy Spirit; and because He is one, those in whom He is active are one fellowship in Him – 'the fellowship of the Holy Ghost'.

But there is no human heart possessed wholly and utterly by the Holy Spirit; and most of us, 'who have the first fruits of the Spirit', are still governed also by self-will. Our surrender is not absolute; our allegiance is not complete. Consequently the historical form and outward manifestation of the Church is never worthy of its true nature. What marks it as the Church is the activity within it of the Holy Spirit – the Spirit of the Father and of the Son. But in the Church as an actual society in history this is not the only power at work; the various forms of human selfishness, blindness and sloth are also characteristics of those who by the activity of the Holy Spirit are united to Christ. It is as though a lantern were covered with a dark veil. It is truly a lantern, because the light burns in it; yet the world sees the light but dimly and may be more conscious of the veil that hides it than of the flame which is its source. So the world may see the sin of Christians more clearly than the holiness of the Church, and the divisions which that sin has caused more clearly than the unity which endures in spite of them.

When that happens, and in whatever degree it happens, the witness of the Church is weakened. How can it call men to worship of the one God if it is calling to rival shrines? How can it claim to bridge the divisions in human society – divisions between Greek and barbarian, bond and free, between white and black, Aryan and non-Aryan, employer and employed – if when men are drawn into it they find that another division has been added to the old ones – a division of Catholic from Evangelical, or Episcopalian from Presbyterian or Independent? A Church divided in its manifestation to the world cannot render its due service to God or to man, and for the impotence which our sin has brought upon the church through divisions in its outward aspect we should be covered with shame and driven to repentance.

We do not escape from sin by denying the consequences of our sin, and we cannot heal the breaches in the Church's outward unity by regarding them as unimportant. To those who made the breaches, the matters involved seemed worthy to die for; it may well be that in the heat of conflict, such as tormented the sixteenth century, men so zealously upheld what seemed to them neglected truths that they became blind to supplementary truths which were dear to their opponents. It is seldom that in any human contention all the truth is on one side. We may look back with a calmer wisdom and see how here or there a division which occurred could have been avoided by a more conciliatory temper and a more synthetic habit of mind. But it does not follow that we should now take all the divisions as they stand and merely agree to co-operate while still maintaining separate organisations. For in practice those separate organisations are bound to become competitors, however much we wish to co-operate; and the separation will hinder the free interchange of thought and experience which should be a chief means of the process whereby the Body of Christ 'builds itself in love'.

So we come to the second great evil of our divisions. The first is that they obscure our witness to the one Gospel; the second is that through the division each party to it loses some spiritual treasure, and none perfectly represents the balance of truth, so that this balance of truth is not presented to the world at all. God be thanked – we have left behind the habit of supposing that our own tradition is perfectly true and the whole of truth, and are looking to see what parts of the 'unsearchable riches of Christ' we have missed while others have them; and so we are learning increasingly one from another. This mutual appreciation is the way alike of humility and of charity; and it is leading us to perpetually fuller fellowship.

In part our progress is due to the presence of the needs of the world. It is not the task of the Church to solve political problems or to devise contrivances for mitigating the effects of human sin. But it is the Church's task to proclaim that the most oppressive evils under which the world groans are the fruit of sin; that only by eradication of that sin can these other evils be averted; and that the only Redeemer from sin is Jesus Christ, 'Very God of Very God . . .' – To Him . . . we call the world that it's sins may be removed, that it's divisions may be healed, and that it may find fellowship in Him.

That proclamation, that invitation, we are bound as a Church to make. And the world answers:

> Have you found that fellowship yourselves? Why do your voices sound so various? When we pass from words to action, to what are you calling us? Is it to one family, gathered round one Holy Table, where your Lord is Himself the host who welcomes all His guests? You know that it is not so. When we answer your united call, we have to choose for ourselves to which Table we will go, for you are yourselves divided in your act of deepest fellowship, and by your own traditions hinder us from a unity which we are ready to enjoy.

What is our answer to that retort? Is it not true that Christians who have lately been converted in heathen lands, and even the ordinary lay-folk who are rather detached from our denominational pre-occupations, are more ready to come together in face of the resurgence of paganism than are the leaders of ecclesiastical organisations, intent upon the maintenance of their tradition and upon keeping their organisation in being and in working order? If it is true that in its deepest nature the Church is always one, it is also true that today it is so-called 'Churches' rather than any forces in the secular world which prevent that unity from being manifest and effective.

Here is matter for deep penitence. I speak as a member of one of those Churches which still maintain barriers against completeness of union at the Table of the Lord. I believe from my heart that we of that tradition are trustees for an element of truth concerning the nature of the Church which requires exclusiveness as a general rule, until this element of truth be incorporated with others into a fuller and worthier conception of the Church than any of us hold today. But I know that our division at this point if the greatest of all scandals in the face of the world; I know that we can only consent to it or maintain it without the guilt of unfaithfulness to the unity of the Gospel and of God Himself, if it is a source to us of spiritual pain, and if we are striving to the utmost to remove the occasions which now bind us, as we think, to that perpetuation of disunion. It should be horrible to us to speak or think of any fellow-Christians as 'not in communion with us'. God grant that we may feel the pain of it, and under that impulsion strive the more earnestly to remove all that now hinders us from receiving together the One Body of the One Lord, that in Him we may become One Body – the organ and vehicle of the One Spirit.

While there is much on our side for which we must repent, there is also much wrought by God for which we should give thanks. The record of the last ten years, since the former Conference in Faith and Order met at Lausanne, has been a time of progressive unification. That period can fitly be called, in the title of the Report presented on that subject, 'a decade of objective progress in Church Unity'. The consummated unions are chiefly, as is natural, between Churches of similar polity; but there is also a growth of understanding and appreciation among Christians of deeply sundered traditions. We shall speak of these things later in our Conference; but let us here at the outset take note of them and give thanks to God; for we enter on this second World Conference with great encouragement from what God has done for us since the first.

Moreover, side by side with progress in the specific task entrusted in part to us, we must rejoice in, and give thanks for, the perpetual growth of other manifestations of the *Una Sancta* despite its divisions. The sister Conference at Oxford has profoundly impressed the world; and it has approved a method whereby, if we are also led to approve it, the *Una Sancta* will be provided with a more permanent and more effectual means of declaring itself and its judgment than at any time for four hundred, perhaps for eight hundred years. We deeply lament the absence from this collaboration of the great Church of Rome – the Church which more than any other has known how to speak to the nations so that the nations hear. But the occurrence of the two World Conferences in one summer is itself a manifestation of the *Una Sancta*, the holy fellowship of those who worship God in Jesus Christ and look to Him as the only Saviour of the world.

In this world movement of Churches towards fuller unity and more potent witness we have our own allotted task. In what spirit do we approach it? How shall we seek to express in this enterprise the graces of faith, of hope, and of love? Of these love is the greatest, but in part at least it is rooted in faith and sustained by hope. Love, for us who are assembled here, means chiefly two things – an ardent longing for closer fellowship, and a readiness both to share our own spiritual treasures and to participate in those of others. Ten years ago our main concern was to state our several traditions in such a way that others should understand them truly; and that must still be our aim. But the divisions which we seek to overcome are due to the fact that our traditions are just what they are and none other; division cannot be healed by the re-iterated statement of them. We are here as representatives of our Churches; true; but unless our Churches are ready to learn from one another as well as to teach one another, the divisions will remain. Therefore our loyalty to our own Churches, which have sent us here, will not be best expressed in a rigid insistence by each upon his own tradition. Our Churches sent us here to confer about our differences with a view to overcoming them. As representatives of those Churches each of us must be as ready to learn from others where his own tradition is erroneous or defective as to shew to others its truth and strength. We meet as fellow-pupils in a school of mutual discipleship. The Churches desire, through us, to learn from one another. That is the humility of love as it must be active among us here.

It will be sustained by hope. Hope springs from the experience of the last ten years. But even were it otherwise, hope should be strong in us because the goal which we seek is set before by God Himself. The hope which arises from that knowledge is altogether independent of empirical signs of its fulfilment. Even if our cause were suffering defeat on every side, we should still serve it because that is God's call to us, and we should still know that through our loyal service He was accomplishing His purpose even though we could not see the evidence of this. But in His mercy He has given us not only the supreme ground of hope, which is His call, but also the manifest tokens of His working in the Churches that are spread throughout the world.

Let us never forget that, though the purpose of our meeting is to consider the causes of our divisions, yet what makes possible our meeting is our unity. We could not seek union if we did not already possess unity. Those who have nothing in common do not deplore their estrangement. It is because we are one in allegiance to one Lord that we seek and hope for the way of manifesting that unity in our witness to Him before the world.

Thus our hope is based upon our common faith. This faith is not only the assent of our minds to doctrinal propositions; it is the commitment of our whole selves into the hands of a faithful Creator and merciful Redeemer. If the word be thus understood we are already in one faith, but also alas! – and this perhaps is the more relevant to our purpose – one in the weakness and incompleteness of our faith. We are one in faith, because to commit ourselves to Him is the deepest desire of our hearts; we are one in the weakness of our faith, because in all of us that desire is overlaid with prejudice and pride and obstinacy and self-contentment. 'Lord, we believe; help thou our unbelief.'

Meanwhile our witness is enfeebled: the true proportion and balance of truth is hidden from the world because we cannot unite in presenting the parts enshrined in our several traditions. We still wait in hope and faith for the movement of the Spirit which shall bring us all to a perfect man – the 'one man in Christ Jesus' grown to full maturity – who shall be the measure of the stature of the fullness of Christ.

Our faith must be more than the trust which leads us to rely on Him; it must be the deeper faith which leads us to wait for Him. It is not we who can heal the wounds in His Body. We confer and deliberate, and that is right. But it is not by contrivance or adjustment that we can unite the Church of God. It is only by coming closer to Him that we can come nearer to one another. And we cannot by ourselves come closer to Him. If we have any fellowship with Him, it is not by our aspiration but by His self-giving; if our fellowship with Him, and in Him with one another, is to be deepened it will not be by our effort but by His constraining power. 'The love of Christ constraineth us.' To that we come back. Because He died for all, all are one in His death. Not by skill in argument, not even by mutual love that spans like a bridge the gulf between us – for the gulf though bridged is not closed by any love of ours – but by the filling of our hearts with His love and the nurture of our minds with His truth, the hope may be fulfilled. It is not by understanding one another, but by more fully understanding Him, that we are led towards our goal. We can help each other here, and learn one from another how to understand Him better. But it is towards Him that our eyes must be directed. Our discussion of differences is a necessary preliminary; but it is preliminary and no more. Only when God has drawn us closer to Himself shall we be truly united together; and then our task will be, not to consummate our endeavour but to register His achievement.

O Blessed Jesu, Love and Truth of God incarnate, cleanse us from all that hinders or distorts our vision of Thee. So fill us with trust in Thee that we cease from our striving and rest in Thee. Thou light of the world, so shine in our hearts that the rays of thy brightness, now known to us in our separation, may be gathered into the pure radiance of Thy glory manifested through us in our unity in Thee. Thou Lamb of God, that takest away the sin of the world, wash our spirits clean from sin. By the mystery of Thy holy Incarnation, by Thine Agony and Bloody Sweat, by Thy Cross and Passion, by Thy glorious Resurrection and Ascension, and by the Coming of the Holy Ghost, unite us within Thyself and in Thyself with one another, that we may be one with and in Thee as Thou art one with the Father, that the world may believe that Thou only are its Saviour, God-blessed for ever.

iii   Christmas Broadcast to Germany

Broadcast 25th December 1943, in *Is Christ Divided?*, 1963, pp. 112–13

I am most happy that it falls to me as Chairman of the Provisional Committee of the World Council of Churches in process of formation to add these closing words of greeting to our fellow Christians in Germany. The project of the World Council is a result and expression of that growth in fellowship which, all over the world, has been uniting Christians to one another in ever-deepening unity. Thirty years ago it could not have been conceived as possible: now it is an achievement on the point of being consummated.

Through those thirty years we have watched the Christian Church take root in one country after another throughout Asia and Africa. We have seen these native Churches grow up into full and equal partnership with the Churches of Europe and America, to whose missionary efforts they owe their origin. The daughters are become the companions of the mothers.

Largely under the inspiration of this missionary movement, the older Churches also have drawn together in two great movements, the Faith and Order Movement and the Life and Work Movement. It was these two which, at the World Conferences held in 1937, gave birth to the project of a World Council of Churches.

Those of us who have taken part in either of these movements, or any part of the Oecumenical Movement, as it is justly called, have received a great enrichment of our understanding of the one unchanging Gospel through our friendships, there formed, with Christians of other communions and of other nations. I think of many very dear German friends, whom I yearn to meet again, knowing that when we meet it will be to find our fellowship in allegiance to Christ unbroken and undiminished.

For this unity of the Christian people in every land is not a construction of human beings. It is not, in the ordinary sense, an international fellowship. That phrase suggests that we start from our various human groupings and seek ways of drawing these nearer to one another. But Christians do not begin in that way at all. They do not construct their unity, nor develop it out of their aspirations. They find that they are united across all barriers or gulfs of division; and this unity is in their one Lord Jesus Christ. Those whose hearts are open to Him are by Him united in heart to one another.

How we long for the time when we can together call the world to that obedience to Christ which is the only way of peace! How eagerly we look forward to the day when fighting will cease and all the Christians of the world can join together in proclaiming to all nations of the world the glad tidings of Christmas – that 'God hath visited and redeemed His people', and calls us, children though we be, to 'go before the face of the Lord to prepare His ways, to give knowledge of salvation unto His people in the remission of their sins through the tender mercy of our God, whereby the day-spring from on high hath visited us, to give light to them that sit in darkness and in the shadow of death, and to guide our feet into' that way which all men long to find, 'the way of peace'.

iv Unity in the British Isles

Sermon at the inauguration of the British Council of Churches, 23 September 1942, St Paul's Cathedral, in the William Temple Papers, vol. 69, pp. 59–62

Today we inaugurate the British Council of Churches, the counterpart in our country of the World Council, combining in a single organisation the chief agencies of the interdenominational co-operation which has marked the last five years . . .

There is no compromise of our distinctive principles in our coming together. But there is a choice involved between two different directions of attention, two different points of emphasis. In days when Christianity itself in its fundamental principles is unchallenged it may seem natural to lay most emphasis on the points which distinguish one communion from another. But in days like these when the basic principles of Christianity are widely challenged and in many quarters expressly repudiated, the primary need is for clear and united testimony to Christianity itself. The difference between Catholic and Protestant is very small as compared with the difference between Christian and non-Christian, between those who do and those who do not believe that in Jesus Christ God hath visited and redeemed His people.

Our differences remain; we shall not pretend that they are already resolved into unity or in harmony. But we take our stand on the common faith of Christendom, faith in God Creator, Redeemer and Sanctifier; and so standing together we invite men to share that faith and call on all to conform their lives to the principles derived from it.

As we co-operate with one another, so we shall be ready to welcome into co-operation with us in our particular enterprises all those who share the hope which inspires each enterprise, whether they share our basic faith or not. For there are many who wish to live by the principles which we claim as Christian who are as yet unable to accept the Christian faith in which we are persuaded that those principles are grounded. We shall need their help for the fulfilment of our hopes; and through their association with us we may lead them to the faith which as yet they have not found.

We owe united witness as a duty to our nation and to the hope of Christian civilisation. But we owe it still more to Our Lord Himself. While we show ourselves to the world only as divided, we alienate men from Him. Only as we unite to present Him to men as the one Lord of life, our life and theirs, can we be true witnesses to Him. That is the conviction which above all else gives us courage and inspiration today.

'Speak unto the children of Israel that they go forward.' The new opportunity is dawning – the opportunity for adventure in the name of Christ, for uplifting Him as the Redeemer of social as of individual life. To us is given the high honour of sounding the call.

'Wherefore cry thou unto Me?' If prayer be a substitute for action, then our choice must be for action. But indeed we must cry unto the Lord, not that He would do for us what He bids us do ourselves, but that He would uphold us as we go forward, sustaining our courage, and bracing our will for endurance. The promised land awaits us. Our Leader has trodden the way before us. He calls us to follow. By His enabling grace, we will.

Postscript: Temple's Ecumenical Leadership

From the Revd William Paton, the Free Church ecumenical leader

World Council of Churches,
Edinburgh House,
2, Eaton Gate,
London, S.W.1.
January 20th, 1943.

Private

My dear William,
I have had it on my mind to write and say one thing to you which is borne in on me as I wander up and down the country. I wonder if you realise the extent to which your leadership is accepted by the Free Churches, and (I might almost say, 'even') by the Church of Scotland. I find on all hands that, whatever may be the case among the bankers and the army colonels, there is an enormously widespread acceptance of your general lead and that Nonconformists in England do in fact accept you as the spokesman of the whole Church in a way which is quite new in our experience. When I was in Scotland in December I was

interested to find the same thing there and it has attracted the attention of some of the Scottish church officials. I think you are probably too humble a person to believe this easily but I think it is right to tell you of this widespread feeling, for it is a new thing in this country and very valuable and precious.

I think all this bears, and I imagine you do too, upon the kind of auspices under which you make your most important pronouncements. I think everyone understands that, as head of the Church of England, you must give a lead to your own communion. At the same time there is no kind of doubt that a wider platform, such perhaps as the British Council of Churches could afford, would in your case be universally acceptable, not as a mere gesture of inter-confessional friendliness, but as a simple, natural, realistic expression of what is a fact. I desperately badly want this to happen. The Free Church Federal Council is a body which has never done very much. Nobody wants it to get into the market with Free Church parallel action. Everyone, on the other hand, does want to back you up and I know you won't mind my writing to say so.
Yours affectionately,
William Paton

9

Meditating on Scripture: *Readings in St John's Gospel*, 1939–40

While at York, Temple did not only produce philosophical theology. He also sought to restate the truth of the incarnation through an exposition of the Fourth Gospel. He wrote that 'for as long as I can remember I have had more love for St John's gospel than for any other book', and that 'with St John I am at home'. His exposition, which had begun to be formulated at St James', Piccadilly, was especially developed when he addressed clergy on retreat or laity at conferences and in services. He came to write the exposition down in the late 1930s 'in odd half hours', as he admitted, and it was published in two parts, the first in 1939 and the second in 1940, as Readings in St John's Gospel. *It is not an approach that drew especially on the New Testament scholarship of his time and so did not attempt to resolve critical and exegetical questions surrounding the Gospel. It was deliberately a reading of the text as it stands and drew, for its inspiration, on Temple's own living experience of Christ as on the text itself. In his comments on one passage in the Gospel he gave a description of what the whole book was doing. Writing on John 1.14 he comments:*

> as we read the story, though it all happened long ago, we apprehend present fact. It is not only the record of a historical episode that we read; it is the self-expression of that God 'in whom we live and move and have our being'; so that whatever finds expression there is true now, and the living Jesus who is 'the same yesterday and today and for ever' still deals with our souls as He dealt with those who had fellowship with Him when He tabernacled among us. Our reading of the Gospel story can be and should be an act of personal communion with the living Lord. (p. 14)

This is what the whole book presents. Through its exposition of the unfolding story of Christ's ministry, death and resurrection, and the dialogues that intersperse it, in the Authorised or King James version of the Gospel, the book uncovers and describes not only the ways Christ related to his disciples but also the ways he relates to believers today. Using the text of the Gospel as a peg, Temple draws on his own and others' experience of Christ to present the living truth of the Christian gospel, which is Christ himself. In the Introduction he describes his method of reading and writing in the following terms: 'I am chiefly concerned with what arises in my mind and spirit as I read; and I hope this is not totally different from saying that I am concerned with what the Holy Spirit says to me through the Gospel' (p. xiii).

While this kind of reading does not remove the need for philosophical theology, because on its own it does not convince the unbeliever, it does lead the believer far beyond the results of philosophical theology. Temple describes how this type of reading leads to a direct encounter with the truth itself, because that truth is a living person. Writing on John 14.6 and the words 'I am ... the truth', he states:

> *Truth is the perfect correlation of mind and reality; and this is actualised in the Lord's Person. If the Gospel is true and God is, as the Bible declares, a Living God, the ultimate truth is not a system of propositions grasped by a perfect intelligence, but is a Personal Being apprehended in the only way in which persons are ever fully apprehended, that is, by love. (p. 223)*

The use of the intelligence was not the way, ultimately, to know God: such knowledge would come through a loving relationship, taking as much time and involvement as any other kind of committed relationship. God in Christ would be known through ongoing attentiveness to him:

> *'He that hath seen me hath seen the Father.' Those are the words that we long to hear. We cannot fully grasp that supreme truth, as we should if our discipleship were perfect. We need to hear them over and over again, to let the sound of them constantly play upon our ears, the meaning of them perpetually occupy our minds, the call in them unceasingly move our wills ... In adoration, in supplication, in dedication, let us take care always to address ourselves to God as He is seen in Jesus Christ. Never ask in prayer for any blessing till you are sure your mind is turned to Jesus Christ; then speak to God as you see Him there. (p. 225)*

The truth of the incarnation, then, was to be grasped in the same way that the disciples came to know Christ, by means of accompanying him through his life, death and resurrection. The incarnation was to be known in its depths through the practice of faith rather than in just the description of faith. The story within the Fourth Gospel, as it unfolds in Temple's hands, provides a model of such practice.

Readings in St John's Gospel has proved to be one of Temple's two most enduring books (the other being Christianity and Social Order *of 1942). It was not his most popular book when it was published (this was to be* Christianity and Social Order*) but it is the one that remained in print for the longest (for 60 years after being published). It was a presentation of the Christian faith that made sense to a growing number of people, even when some aspects of its style and presentation became dated. It was not a volume that set out to convince the sceptical of the truth of Christianity, and nor did it, but it helped those who wanted to believe, to believe with more confidence and assurance. And so, surprisingly, it was this volume, rather than the more weighty* Christus Veritas *or* Nature, Man and God, *that went furthest to fulfilling an early ambition to restate Christian belief in a convincing way for his contemporaries.*

i   The Prologue: John 1.1–14

Readings in St John's Gospel, pp. 3–15

1, 2. *In the beginning was the Word. And the Word was with God. And the Word was God. The same was in the beginning with God.*

'In the beginning.' Of course the words take up the opening of Genesis. But they do this so as to suggest at once the transition from temporal event to eternal reality which is the essence of this Gospel. For the Greek Words can also be translated 'In principle'. It is a great mistake to suppose that, when a Word in one language is represented by two or more in another, it is always necessary to choose one or other of these; very often a word covers several meanings because the meanings really are connected together, and the mind easily passes from one to the other without consciousness of movement. So the word really means both things; and here the expression used means both 'in the beginning of history' and 'at the root of the universe' . . .

The term 'Logos' [Word] was in general use in the Hellenistic world; among Hellenised Jews the intellectual currents represented by Philo inevitably exerted an influence. The Evangelist is not here proclaiming unfamiliar truth; rather he is seeking common ground with his readers. It is of no use to tell the Hellenistic Ephesians that the Messiah is come; they are not expecting any Messiah and would not be interested; it would be like trying to excite an English audience by proclaiming the arrival of the Mahdi. Moreover he wants a term that carries thought nearer to the heart of all reality. He finds it in this word 'Logos', which alike for Jew and Gentile represents the ruling fact of the universe, and represents that fact as the self-expression of God. The Jew will remember that 'by the Word of the Lord were the heavens made'; the Greek will think of the rational principle of which all natural laws are particular expressions. Both will agree that this Logos is the starting-point of all things. It exists as it always did *en arche* – in the beginning, at the root of the universe.

Moreover its very essence is a relationship to God such that it is truly divine. The term 'God' is fully substantival in the first clause . . . it is predicative and not far from adjectival in the second . . . Thus from the outset we are to understand that the Word has its whole being within Deity, but that it does not exhaust the being of Deity. Or, to put it from the other side, God is essentially self-revealing; but He is first of all a Self capable of being revealed. This same Word, or Self-revelation, is then again said to exist in essential relationship to God.

St John has thus established common ground with all his readers. If they are Jews they will recognise and assent to the familiar doctrine of the Old Testament concerning the Word of God. If they are Greeks they will recognise and assent to the declaration that the ultimate reality is Mind expressing itself. To both alike he has announced in language easily received that the subject for which he is claiming their attention is the ultimate and supreme principle of the universe.

3. Through its agency all things came to be, and apart from it hath not one thing come to be.

The Greek pronoun may be either masculine or neuter. In the mind of the evangelist, no doubt, it is masculine but not in that of a contemporary reader; ground has not yet been given for attributing personality to the Logos, so it seems better for languages which must choose one or the other to choose the neuter. The supreme principle of the universe is not only its bond of unity, but its ground of existence. In other words, only because it is God's Nature to reveal or communicate Himself is there a world at all; everything in it, every single occurrence in time and space, is subject to this controlling fact, that the world exists as the arena of God's self-revelation. Of course St John knows that he is stating the religious principle of God's supremacy, the philosophical principle of ultimate unity, in the way that most of any [principle] throws the problem of evil into relief. The reference to 'darkness' about to follow shews his awareness of this. But he makes no comment now. The story which he is about to tell contains comment and even his solution of the problem (13.31–32). But as there is no real solution except in the light of that story he will not comment now. He will only assert, in the strongest terms that he can find, his assurance that all things exist or come to be as a result of God's activity by self-expression, knowing that he thus provokes in its acutest form the gravest of all religious difficulties. Just so the hymn of the Elders in the *Apocalypse*, 'Worthy art thou, our Lord and our God, to receive the glory and the honour and the power, for thou didst create all things, and because of thy will they were, and were created', introduces the interpretation of that Book of Destiny in which the chapters are Conquest, War, Famine and Death. And there, too, the interpretation is the same (Revelation 4.11; 5.9; 6.1–8).

4, 5. What came to be in it was Life, and the Life was the light of men, and the light shineth in the darkness, and the darkness did not absorb it.

Here the interpretation for Christian and non-Christian begins to diverge.

(a) For non-Christians the words would mean that within that supreme principle is, and always has been, Life. Life is not said to be a product of its agency as the world is, but rather to be one of its own inherent characteristics. When we pass from the inert thing to the living creature we reach a stage where there is something in common between the creature and creative principle besides bare existence. And in this vital energy – for it is Life in that sense that the word implies! – is the beacon by which men are guided. The impulse to move is also the guide of our movement. Its direction is not yet disclosed; but in the fact that the vital impulse is an element in the divine manifestation we have the assurance that correspondence with the mind of God will be the true satisfaction of that impulse.

(b) But for a Christian reader a new suggestion is already present. He would notice the difference in the prepositions used. 'Through its agency all things came to pass'; but they are not said to be all of them Life.

'What came to pass in it was Life.' But only of one occurrence is it true to say that it took place not only through but in the Logos; that is the nativity of Jesus. All other existing things, though owing their existence to the Logos, and never escaping its final control, yet shew some deviation from it. The Cosmos lieth in evil, not in the Logos. Only Jesus is wholly in the Logos. And only Jesus is truly Life – so that all true Life in us is drawn from Him. As He alone is truly Life (11.25; 14.6), so He alone is truly Light (8.12). In all periods, but supremely in the period of Christ's earthly ministry, *the light shineth in the darkness, and the darkness did not absorb it.*

Imagine yourself standing alone on some headland in a dark night. At the foot of the headland is a lighthouse or beacon, not casting rays on every side, but throwing one bar of light through the darkness. It is some such image that St John had before his mind. The divine light shines through the darkness of the world, cleaving it, but neither dispelling it nor quenched by it. The word translated in the Authorised Version 'comprehended', in the text of the Revised Version 'apprehended', and in its margin 'overcame', is a word of two meanings; literally it is 'to take down or under', and may thus mean 'to take right into the mind' (apprehend) or 'to take under control' (overcome). In this context the two meanings are direct opposites, for to apprehend light is to be enlightened by it, and to overcome light is to put it out. Yet the word truly means both of these. The darkness in no sense at all received the light; yet the light shone still undimmed. So strange is the relation of the light of God's revelation to the world which exists to be the medium of that revelation.

St John is not yet, as I read him, thinking only of the Life of the Word Incarnate, though what he says is true also of that Life. He is thinking of the period covered by the Old Testament, with the light of the revelation to Israel piercing the darkness of the heathenism by which Israel was surrounded; and this is to him an illustration of a universal principle. It is always so. Take any moment of history and you find light piercing unillumined darkness – now with reference to one phase of the purpose of God, now another. The company of those who stand in the beam of the light by which the path of true progress for that time is discerned is always small. Remember Wilberforce and the early Abolitionists; remember the twelve Apostles and the company gathered about them. What is seen conspicuously in those two examples is always true; and as we think of the spiritual progress of the race this truth finds a fresh illustration. As we look forwards, we peer into darkness, and none can say with certainty what course the true progress of the future should follow. But as we look back, the truth is marked by beacon-lights, which are the lives of saints and pioneers; and these in their turn are not originators of light, but rather reflectors which give light to us because themselves they are turned towards the source of light.

This darkness in which the light shines unabsorbed is cosmic. St John is most modern here. The evil which for him presents the problem is not only in men's hearts; it is in the whole ordered system of nature. That ordered system is infected; it 'lieth in the evil one' (1 John 5.19). St John might have had all the modern problem of the callousness and cruelty of nature before his mind. Anyhow, his approach is the modern approach. He does not conceive of Nature as characterised by a Wordsworthian perfection, which is only spoilt by fallen mankind. To his deep spiritual insight it is apparent that the redemption of man is part, even if the crowning part, of a greater thing – the redemption, or conquest (16.33), of the universe. Till that be accomplished the darkness abides, pierced but unillumined by the beam of divine light. And the one great question for everyone is whether he will 'walk in darkness' or 'walk in light' (1 John 1.7; 2.10, 11).

6–8. There came a man sent from God – the name of him John. This man came with a view to witness, in order that he might give witness concerning the light, that all might believe through him. That one was not the light, but was to bear witness concerning the light.

Here is one of those who act as beacons for pilgrims by reflecting the divine light. But he did more than reflect it; he pointed to it and bade men follow, not him, but it. His whole function was witness or testimony. He was a voice. He would direct attention away from his personality to his message. He pointed to one whose message directed attention to Himself; for He, to whom John pointed, was the light itself.

9–13. There was the light, the true light, which enlighteneth every man – coming into the world. In the world he was; and the world through his agency came into being; and the world did not recognise him. To his own home he came, and his own people did not receive him. But as many as received him, to them gave he the right to become children of God – to those that believe on the name of him who was born, not of blood, nor of the will of the flesh, nor of the will of a man, but of God.

We now approach the new revelation. From the beginning the divine light has shone. Always it was coming into the world; always it enlightened every man alive in his reason and conscience. Every check on animal lust felt by the primitive savage, every stimulation to a nobler life, is God self-revealed within his soul. But God in self-revelation is the Divine Word, for precisely this is what that term means. What is constituted within that divine self-communication, as one element composing it, is the energy of Life; this is what urges all kinds of living things forward in their evolution; and this is what is fully and perfectly expressed in Christ. So it may be truly said that the conscience of the heathen man is the voice of Christ within him – though muffled by his ignorance. All that is noble in the non-christian systems of thought, or conduct, or worship is the work of Christ upon them and within them. By the Word of God – that is to say, by Jesus Christ – Isaiah, and Plato, and Zoroaster, and Buddha, and Confucius conceived and uttered such truths as they declared. There is only one divine light; and every man in his measure is enlightened by it.

Yet this light is not recognised for what it is. If it were, its fuller shining would always be welcomed. But it is attributed by each tribe or group to some historic or legendary founder or pioneer of their own, so that each claims to have a monopoly of the light itself, when in fact each has only a few rays of that light, which needs all the wisdom of all the human traditions to manifest the entire compass of its spectrum. Moreover it has to shine through veils of prejudice and obsession, so that even the rays received by each group among mankind are not clear and pure in the illumination which they give.

So the light itself is unrecognised; and when it blazes out more fully, men refuse it, even though it is that by which they already walk. For these reasons it is true both that Christ is indeed the Desire of all Nations, and yet that He is always more and other than men desire until they learn of Him. To come to Him is always an act of self-surrender as well as of self-fulfilment, and must be first experienced as self-surrender.

But there was one nation specially prepared for the reception of the light in its fullness. Israel had received the light in a measure so full as to be called its own home, its own people. But when He came – (and here for the first time a pronoun unmistakably personal in its reference is used) – His own people were as completely unable to receive Him as any others had been to receive light fuller than that to which they were accustomed.

With this direct reference to the coming of the Christ to Israel the drama of the Gospel opens. It is throughout its course the picture of His rejection by His own people generally, and His reception by the few.

Over and over again the Evangelist will draw this moral with reference to the various episodes that he relates (cf. 7.40–44; 8.30, 59; 10.19–21; 11.45, 46. These are perhaps the most conspicuous instances, but similar comments are frequent). This is in one aspect a Gospel of Judgment. By their reaction to the impact of Christ men are judged, and take their position as children of darkness or children of light (12.35, 36).

None can take rank among the children of light by any right, power or merit of his own, but only by becoming (like John the Baptist) beacons who reflect a light of which they are not the source. But to those who so receive the Light when it comes, it (or He, for the Light is Jesus) gives *the right to become sons of God*.

Are we not all children of God? Yes, in one most true sense – by creation. 'It is He that hath made us and not we ourselves.' But the writers of the New Testament all observe a certain use of language which has deep significance. They often imply that God is the Father of all men; but they do not speak of all men as His children; that expression is reserved for those who, by the grace of God, are enabled in some measure to reproduce His character. So the Lord Himself commands us to imitate the universal and undiscriminating Love of God 'that ye may be sons of your Father which is in heaven' (St Matthew 5.4, 5). The phrase is used in the sense in which we sometimes say of a man 'he is the son of his father'; that is, in him we see his father again. In that sense there is only one 'Son of the Father'; but He makes it possible for us to share His Sonship; the Spirit whom He sends from the Father is 'the spirit of adoption whereby we cry Abba, Father' (Romans 8.15).

He gives the right to become sons of God to those who receive Him, that is to those who 'believe on His Name'. The Name is the manifested nature; to baptise into the Name of the Father, the Son, and the Holy Ghost is to plunge or bathe the person in the manifested love of God. To believe on, or put trust in, the love of God made manifest in Christ is the condition of becoming a son of God who reproduces the divine character. But we do not thereby acquire an equality with Christ. It remains true that only through Christ are we enabled to acquire a relationship to God which was, and is, Christ's apart from any mediation. (And even then how half-hearted is our faith! How defective our reflection of the divine love!)

Who was (or *were*) *born*. I have adopted above the text which Tertullian accepted; but I did so rather to challenge attention than because it is probably correct. The plural verb has far the greater weight of authority in the manuscripts. Yet the sense is the same. Nothing can explain the quite peculiar phrasing of this passage except the supposition that it refers to the Virgin Birth of our Lord. With the singular verb this is explicit; and the significance which it gives to that event is an insistence that the coming of our Lord into the world is not due to any human impulse or volition but is an act of God alone.

The reference in the language to the mode of our Lord's nativity secures that this meaning is still present even if the verb be plural – *who were born*. For the point is that the process whereby those who receive Him become sons of God – are re-born or re-generate as sons of God – is as much due to the sole activity of God as was the birth into the world of Him who alone is in His own right Son of God.

And now the great declaration is made. This Word, this Logos, which Greeks and Hebrews unite in recognising as the controlling power of the whole universe, is no longer unknown or dimly apprehended. The Light which in some measure lightens every man has shone in its full splendour.

14. *And the Word became flesh and tabernacled among us – (and we beheld his glory, glory as of an only begotten from a father) – full of grace and truth.*

The Word became flesh. The Word did not merely indwell a human being. Absolute identity is asserted. The Word is Jesus; Jesus is the Word. And it is said that the Word became flesh because 'flesh' is that part of human nature commonly associated with frailty and evil; commonly, but not necessarily. In Jesus the flesh is the completely responsive vehicle of the spirit. The whole of Him, flesh included, is the Word, the self-utterance, of God.

He tabernacled among us; He pitched His fleshly tent among us. The suggestion is of a brief sojourn, but all thought of a momentary apparition is excluded.

Full of grace and truth. He not only disclosed the divine reality, but therein also displayed its beauty. Truth is august, often austere, sometimes repellent. But here it is gracious and winning. John the Baptist, who is also in mind here (6 and 15), was full of truth, but there was not much grace about him!

We beheld his glory. Not all who set eyes on Him did that. 'We' does not mean all who ever met Him. Caiaphas and Herod and Pilate did not behold his glory. But His true disciples did. His glory was not something left behind to which one day He would return – as St Paul had sometimes suggested (Philippians 2.6–10; 2 Corinthians 8.9). Of course the Pauline doctrine is true. The Incarnation was an act of sacrifice and of humiliation – real however voluntary. But that is not the last word. For the sacrifice and the humiliation *are* the divine glory. If God is Love, His glory most of all shines forth in whatever most fully expresses love. The Cross of shame *is* the throne of glory. St John will take his own way of saying that with emphasis as the story goes forward. Now at the outset He makes the proclamation – *We beheld his glory, glory as of an only begotten from a father*. There are no definite articles; the statement is not a piece of technical Trinitarian theology, though it supplies the basis for such a theology. It is a record of experience. The glory which appeared seemed not to have its source in Him, but to stream through Him from beyond. To be with Him was – as it still is – to be with 'Him that sent Him'. He is the only Son (the word *monogenes* has no reference to the *process* of begetting and expresses uniqueness rather than mode of origin) who alone perfectly reproduces the Father's character. The glory is, in the phrase that He will use, *not mine but his that sent me*. The glory that the Word displays to us is the glory of God, whose is that Word. We are very close to the great utterance *He that hath seen me hath seen the Father* (14.9). Yet the reference is not yet quite explicit to the divine Father; the absence of the definite article excludes that. Only in verse 18 will that reference become quite explicit. Here all the emphasis is laid upon the fact apparent to the spiritual awareness of those who *beheld his glory* that this glory shone from a source beyond through the Figure with whom the disciples had converse.

That source beyond is the Eternal Father. Consequently, as we read the story, though it all happened long ago, we apprehend present fact. It is not only the record of a historical episode that we read; it is the self-expression of that God 'in whom we live and move and have our being'; so that whatever finds expression there is true now, and the living Jesus who is 'the same yesterday and today and for ever' still deals with our souls as He dealt with those who had fellowship with Him when He *tabernacled among us*. Our reading of the Gospel story can be and should be an act of personal communion with the living Lord.

ii The Woman at the Well: John 4.5–26

The course of the conversation is easily followed. The Lord is alone by the well and has no means of drawing water; so when the woman comes He asks her to draw and give Him to drink. She is surprised, for He is manifestly a Jew, and she is a Samaritan and a woman, both reasons why He should not address her. This gives Him the opportunity to go further; it is true that He is a Jew, but if she knew more, and perceived the opportunity offered to her by His presence, she would be asking Him for a greater boon – a truly living water. Of course she is puzzled; Jacob gave this well, and in the ordinary sense it contains living, that is, running, water; is He greater than Jacob, the father of all Israel? Yes; His gift at any rate is greater, for it is inexhaustible. Then, says the Woman, give it me, and save me all this trouble. He does not refuse, but bids her call her husband to share the gift. She is becoming mystified and impressed; and, no doubt fearing exposure of her manner of life, denies that she has a husband. The Lord reads her thought and says that this denial – intended as a lie in self-defence – is strictly true. She sees the sign of a prophet's insight and at once asks the prophet to decide the vexed question which kept Jews and Samaritans apart – Jerusalem or Mount Gerizim? He, as usual when confronted with a question which arises from the superficiality and unspiritual quality of men's thought, deals with the question by penetrating to the principle governing the sphere of life which it concerns. But this baffles her. The prophet's answer does not satisfy. She must wait for the Messiah, who, no doubt, will clear up this and all other difficulties. *I am he – I that am talking to thee.*

Having thus sketched the outline of the conversation let us first go through it in more detail, and then consider its symbolic significance. The Lord is travelling on foot, and is weary from His journey. He sits down just as He is near the spring which Jacob has made available by sinking his well. Anyone who is tired from walking is likely also to be thirsty. It is to satisfy a perfectly genuine need that He says to the woman who comes down from Samaria *Give me to drink*. None the less He is ignoring convention in making the request. It was a precept of the moralists of the time that 'a man should not salute a woman in a public place, not even his own wife'. There was a great contempt for women. One of the thanksgivings in the daily service of the Synagogue is 'Blessed art thou, O Lord . . . who hast not made me a woman'. The answer made by the women from their gallery or other separate place was 'Blessed art thou, O Lord, who hast fashioned me according to thy will'. If we now feel that the women had the best of the exchange, that is a Christian and not an ancient Jewish sentiment! The prejudice was very strong. But here is someone that ignores it, and ignores at the same time the equally strong and far more bitter prejudice of Jews

MEDITATING ON SCRIPTURE

against Samaritans. *How is it that thou, being a Jew, askest drink of me, who am a woman and a Samaritan?* (9). The answer begins that undercutting of the prejudices which is made complete in 21-24. The real marvel of this conversation is not that a Jewish Rabbi is conversing with a Samaritan woman, but that this woman is face to face with the Saviour of the world (4.2); *If thou hadst known the gift of God, and who it is that saith to thee 'Give me to drink', it would he thou that wouldst he asking him, and he would have given thee living water* (10). The last phrase does not of necessity mean any other water than such as was bubbling up in the spring at the base of the well. Yet (she thinks) He can hardly mean that; He seems to be pointing to some contrast; and anyhow He has no means of drawing water from the well. *Thou hast nothing to draw with and the well is deep; from whence then hast thou the living water?* (11). This spring was found by Jacob himself and given by him to his heirs and descendants, among whom (as the woman is, no doubt, glad of the chance to hint) Samaritans claim to rank no less than Jews. *Art thou greater than our father Jacob?* (12).

Already the conversation is turning, on the woman's side also, to the Person of her interlocutor. The Lord had given an impulse towards this (10), but waits to let that take fuller effect. At present He fastens on the difference between Jacob's gift and His own. The water in Jacob's well quenches thirst for the time; this other living water quenches for ever the thirst which it assuages, and is indeed an inward spring, bubbling up into eternal life. *Everyone that drinketh of this water shall thirst again, but whosoever drinketh of the water that I shall give him shall not thirst unto eternity; but the water that I shall give him shall become in him a spring of water, springing into eternal Life* (13, 14).

(*Water*. In 2.1-11 the water that is drawn at the command of Christ is wine for him who drinks it. Here is promise of an inward spring which is an elixir of life eternal for him who receives it. In 7.37-39 the water that Christ gives is a source of refreshment not only to him who receives it but to others, as the living water flows forth from him. For this living water is the Holy Spirit, who could only be given in fullness to men when Jesus was glorified. That was accomplished on the Cross, and from His crucified Body flowed Blood and Water – 19.34.)

The woman does not understand; how could she? The Lord is leading her on towards understanding by words to which she will attach some real meaning, but not the full meaning which is in His mind and which she may grasp later. At least she has reached the stage of asking for the offered boon, though mainly because it seems as if it will save trouble: *Give me this water, that I thirst not, neither come hither to draw* (15).

But the *gift of God* (10) cannot be received to be merely enjoyed. It must always be shared. Its very nature involves that; for it is Himself, His own Spirit, the Spirit of Love. To receive that does not mean to enjoy the knowledge that God loves us. It means that His active love is present in our hearts; and if so, it must go out to others. If we are not sharing with others the gift of God, that is proof that we have not received it. So the Lord tells this woman to call the person with whom she would naturally share first. *Call thy husband and come hither* (16). Unknown to herself, her conscience has been quickened. She shrinks from the exposure that may be before her: *I have no husband*. And that is true. By the standard of God's law, before Moses allowed exemptions for the hardness of men's hearts, the intercourse of marriage effects an irrefragable union; 'they are no more twain, but one flesh' (St Mark 10.5, 8). (How far St Paul regarded this principle as carrying us is clear from 1 Corinthians 6.16. Any pre-marital intercourse therefore makes true marriage with any other than the partner of that intercourse permanently impossible. This I have no doubt is the explanation of the 'exceptive clause' in St Matthew. At that point the Church, like Moses, has made allowance for the hardness of men's hearts. How far it should go is open to question. But there is no doubt about the principle upheld in the whole New Testament.)

This woman was probably within the requirements of the Mosaic law. But she has taken a liberal advantage of its exemptions from the truly divine law! By that only true standard the lie with which she hoped to save herself from exposure is itself true: *Thou saidst well, I have no husband; for five didst thou have as husbands, and he whom now thou hast is not thy husband; this thou hast said truly* (18) – more truly than she knew! But now the woman is sure that her interlocutor is a Prophet; He interprets the divine law in independence not only of the scribes, but of Moses himself; and He knows the secrets of her heart. So she forgets her request for the living water, and eagerly asks for a ruling from this seer of divine truth on the great question which separates Samaritans from Jews, and is at once the ground and the form of their mutual excommunication. *I perceive that thou art a prophet. Our fathers worshipped in this mountain; and ye say that in Jerusalem is the place where men must worship* (19, 20). But now the divine truth which inspired and justified that neglect of convention, which the whole conversation illustrates, can be stated. As so often with our Lord's replies to enquirers, it does not answer the question, but leads to ground where the question does not arise at all. It is often so. There is no Christian solution of the problems presented by human self-will; but there is a Christian cure for the self-will, and if that is effective, the problem is (not solved but) abolished. So when a man wanted the Lord to divide an inheritance, that is to arbitrate between two self-centred claims, He refuses to take that position. He will not settle the dispute; but He will tell them how to avoid having a dispute – 'Take heed and keep yourselves from all covetousness' (St Luke 12.13–16). For, of course, if there had been no covetousness, there would have been no dispute to settle.

So here, the dispute between Jews and Samaritans arose from an unworthy conception of God, and the fuller knowledge which the Lord brings will not solve the problem but abolish it: *the hour cometh, when neither in this mountain nor in Jerusalem shall ye worship the Father* (21). Yet the Jew has a certain priority; for the revelation recorded in the Scriptures of the Old Testament is more directly his by inheritance. The Samaritans had had a chequered religious history. Some see in the 'five husbands' a reference to the five gods whom the Samaritans had once served – cf. 2 Kings 17.29–31; later, when the priest sent by the King of Assyria arrived (*ibid.* 27, 28), there was a mixed cult – 'they feared the Lord and worshipped their own gods' (*ibid.* 33). The Samaritan tradition was far from pure: *Ye worship what ye know not* – a deity adopted, so to speak, because He was the deity of the place; *we worship what we know; for salvation is from the Jews* (22).

That last phrase is of supreme importance. The difference between East and West, which we so easily regard as geographical and racial, is really, as Mr. Edwyn Bevan has pointed out, a difference between those who have and those who have not come under the influence of the Bible. The world around the Mediterranean Sea – the spring of our modern 'western' Culture – was in many ways very like the Eastern countries of today. There was a lofty philosophy for those to whom it appealed; but they were few. There was great moral degradation, which the prevalent religions were powerless to remedy; some of them even intensified the degradation. There was one exception. Among the Jews was a living faith in a living God, to whom no honour could be paid without righteousness of life. The distinctive Jewish doctrine that God is a living God, a God of purpose and judgment, who is perfectly righteous, effected the union of religion and morality which was otherwise foreign to the prevalent cults. That is why the Old Testament revelation is the unique source of salvation. Salvation is from the Jews. It proceeds from them; but is not confined to them. For the God whom they know and worship is the universal Father.

The hour cometh and now is (because with the coming of Christ the full truth is declared and all exclusions are ended) *when the true worshippers shall worship the Father in spirit and truth; indeed the Father seeketh such for his worshippers. God is Spirit, and they that worship him must worship in spirit and truth* (23, 24). It is impossible to exhaust the wealth of this great declaration. God is Spirit. That is the most fundamental proposition in theology. God is not the totality of things – the All; nor is He an immanent principle to which all things conform; He is Spirit – active energy, alive and purposive, but free from the temporal and spatial limitations which are characteristic of matter. Consequently there is no need to seek Him in a local habitation. The kind of persons whom He *seeks for His worshippers* are those who will worship *in spirit and truth*. Both of these words combine two meanings. *In spirit* means (a) with that highest element in our nature which is the meeting-point of the divine and the human, and should be the controlling factor in the whole economy of our being; (b) in contrast with any literalistic legalism, it means a worship of heart and will, not tied to strict obedience to a code, but expressing a self-dedication more pervasive than the requirement of any code. *In truth* means (a) in sincerity – without hypocrisy or self-deception, but also (b) according to the real nature of God, so as to be free from all worship of God under a false image, which is idolatry. 'We are in him that is true, in his Son Jesus Christ. This is the true God and eternal life. Little children, keep yourselves from idols' (1 John 5.21).

But though what the Lord has said is so full of meaning, it has none for the woman. He may be a prophet; doubtless He is; but it is nothing new for the utterances of prophets to be obscure. Some day the Messiah will come and make all plain; we must wait for that. *I know that Messiah cometh; when he comes he will announce all things to us* (25). To that simple, waiting spirit the Lord discloses Himself as hitherto to no other. *I am he, I that am talking to thee* (26).

Stupendous affirmation! And with a strong suggestion, not for the woman, but for the reader, of something more stupendous still. The Greek idiom permits the omission of the pronoun 'he'; and it is omitted. So that the translation very literally is this – *I that am talking to thee, I AM.*

What St John records, apart from graphic details, is set before us in illustration of the way in which eternal life is actually offered in Jesus Christ, and therefore how we, believing, may find it (30, 31).

MEDITATING ON SCRIPTURE

Once more, then, we go back to the beginning of the conversation, and consider it as an example of the Lord's pastoral dealing – of His dealing with my soul. Here are the key-sayings, followed by a paraphrase of these:

1	*Christ*	Give me to drink
	The woman	How is it that thou askest of me?
2	*Christ*	If thou hadst known the gift of God –
	The woman	Give me this water
3	*Christ*	Call thy husband
	The woman	Thou art a prophet: solve our problems
4	*Christ*	Worship in spirit and in truth
	The woman	We must wait for Messiah to come
5	*Christ*	I am he.

In such a way the Lord leads us on to the knowledge which we chiefly need:

1	*The Lord*	Do me a service
	The soul	How is it that thou askest anything of me?
2	*The Lord*	If thou hadst known what gift from God is offered thee
	The soul	Give me this gift
3	*The Lord*	(a) With whom will you share it? (b) Lay bare your sin
	The soul	Solve my perplexity
4	*The Lord*	Worship in spirit and truth
	The soul	Ah! no solution yet. We must wait
5	*The Lord*	I AM

1 The way to call anyone into fellowship with us is, not to offer them service, which is liable to arouse the resistance of their pride, but to ask service from them. Of course the request must be prompted by a real need. The Lord was actually tired and thirsty when He said *Give me to drink*, and drew the woman into conversation by asking for her help. So social workers have found that they cannot bridge the gulf digged by education so long as they live in a style different from their neighbours and offer service. But all is changed when they adopt the manner of life familiar in the neighbourhood and share its needs. One has told of the difference for him when he left a well-appointed settlement in Bermondsey, where he needed nothing which his neighbours

could supply, and went to live in a workman's flat. The first evening he wanted a hammer to hang pictures, and went to borrow one from the people in the flat below. At once the relationship was different. There was something that they could do for him.

So the Almighty God seeks to win us to fellowship with Himself by putting some part of His purpose into our hands. 'The kingdom of heaven is as when a man, going into another country, called his own servants, and delivered unto them his goods' (St Matthew 25.14). That is the way in which God is King; and He takes that way because it is the way of fellowship. He who might be all-sufficient to Himself, entrusts His purpose to us. He makes Himself dependent upon us, as the Lord was dependent on the woman for the quenching of His thirst. He asks for our service.

But how can that be? *How is it that thou askest of me?* Thou canst do all things. I have nothing. I am not fit to offer the meanest service. Surely God will first require, and help me to form, a character worthy to serve Him, and then appoint me my task. No; in point of fact it is only through service that such a character could be formed. Canon Peter Green has often pointed out that Christ did not first make His disciples saints and then give them work to do; He gave them work to do, and as they did it other people (though not themselves) perceived that they were becoming saints. The service that He asks of me is a real service, not fictitious; yet it is for my sake, and out of love for me, that He so orders His world as to need my service. That is how it is that *He* asketh of *me*. Also because He loves us, He rejoices that we should be 'fellow-workers' with Him (1 Corinthians 3.9). If He were not Love He would have no need of us; it is His love that needs us. And behind His request is the love that prompts it – the love which He is ready to give me, the gift of God.

2 As I begin to understand this, I begin also to hear His voice saying that if I really appreciated what is offered in His request for service, the whole situation would be reversed, and the request would come from me – the utterance of my soul's thirst for its only satisfaction. And thereupon the plea rises in me – Give me this gift of God.

3 But then, like a lightning flash, comes the demand which means at once 'With whom will you share it?' and 'Lay bare your sin'. For I cannot receive the gift however truly it is offered if either I mean selfishly to keep it, or there is some sin to which, conscious of it and concealing it, I cling. But from that demand I shrink, and, recognising the voice of divine authority, quiet my conscience by recourse to intellectual riddles, which I ask that authority to resolve. How often does the weak will obscure

the clear call of conscience by resort to intellectual 'difficulties'! Some of these are real enough; but some are sheer self-protection against the exacting claim of the holy love of God.

4 Both for perplexity and for dulled conscience the remedy is the same; sincere and spiritual worship. For worship is the submission of all our nature to God. It is the quickening of conscience by His holiness; the nourishment of mind with His truth; the purifying of imagination by His beauty; the opening of the heart to His love; the surrender of will to His purpose – and all of this gathered up in adoration, the most selfless emotion of which our nature is capable and therefore the chief remedy for that self-centredness which is our original sin and the source of all actual sin. Yes – worship in spirit and truth is the way to the solution of perplexity and to the liberation from sin.

But to our superficial souls the divine answer seems to evade the problem precisely because it penetrates to the heart of it. We must wait till there is offered to us in fellowship and communion the eternal God Himself.

5 'I that am talking to thee, I AM.' That is the assurance that we need: that He with whom we know that we have dealings is none other than the eternal God. If my soul can hear that word, then it can rest. But it is not enough that I should believe on grounds satisfactory to myself. I need the divine assurance of the divine love. 'Say unto my soul "I am thy salvation"' (Psalm 35.3); 'He that believeth on the Son of God hath the witness in *Him*' (1 John 5.10). *I that am speaking to thee, I AM.*

iii The Prayer of the Son to the Father: John 17.1–5

Readings in St John's Gospel, pages 307–13

We now come to what is, perhaps, the most sacred passage even in the Four Gospels – the record of the Lord's prayer of self-dedication as it lived in the memory and imagination of His most intimate friend.

It consists of three main sections:

1. The Son and the Father (1–5)
2. The Son and the disciples (6–19)
3. The Son, the disciples and the world (20–26) . . .

Lifting up his eyes to heaven, he said 'Father': So it had been before the recalling of Lazarus from death to life (11.41). So it is now as He enters on His own passage from life to death. Always His trust is in the Father to whom His obedience is given. So it will be at the very close: 'Father into thy hands I commend my spirit' (St Luke 23.46).

Father, come is the hour; glorify thy Son. When the Greeks came He had greeted their approach with the words: *Come is the hour that the Son of Man may be glorified*, and went on at once to speak of the harvest that can only come through death (12.23, 24). When Judas had gone out into the night He said *Now was glorified the Son of Man.* Here is the third use of the solemn phrase: *Come is the hour; glorify thy Son*. It is the hour for the Son of Man to be lifted up (12.32, 34). His glory is about to reach its full splendour: for it is the glory or shining forth of love, and *greater love than this hath no man, that a man lay down his life on behalf of his friends* (15.13).

Glorify thy Son, that the Son may glorify thee. The glory of the Father and that of the Son are inseparable. The Father glorifies the Son by sustaining Him in His perfect obedience even unto death and the Son glorifies the Father by the perfection of the obedience which He offers. Because God is Love, the Cross is the glory, or, if we will, the 'effulgence of the glory' (Hebrew 1.3) alike of the Father and of the Son.

The Cross is the glory of God because self-sacrifice is the expression of love. That glory would be complete in itself even if it had no consequences. But in fact what is revealed in the Cross is not only the perfection of the divine love, but its triumph. For by its sacrifice the divine love wins those who can appreciate it out of their selfishness which is spiritual death into loving fellowship with itself which is true life: 'we know that we have passed out of death into Life, because we love the brethren' (1 John 3.14). But we do not effect that passage in any strength of our own; it is the gift of God through Christ: *as thou gavest to him to have authority over all flesh that all which thou hast given him – he may give to them eternal Life.*

To the Son is given authority to execute judgment because he is Son of Man (5.27). So far this might be displayed in condemnation or in pardon. But if the Father now perfectly glorifies the Son, and the Son perfectly glorifies the Father – if, in other words, that burning love which is the heart of the Godhead be displayed – then the authority of the Son will be exercised in the gift of eternal Life. For the Judge will be Himself the Saviour.

How far this salvation extends is left undefined. It reaches *all which thou hast given him*, for if any man responds to the love of God in

Christ he does so in virtue of the Father's act; He had said before, *No man can come to me except the Father which sent me draw him* (6.44); and those words were at once followed by the promise – *and I will raise him up at the last day*. So here the gift of the Son to those whom the Father has given to Him is *eternal life*. They are thought of as a single company, a single gift – *that which thou hast given him*. For in Him we are one; in so far as we are not one we are not yet in Him; and the prayer for the disciples which follows is primarily *that they may be one* (11). To every member of this fellowship, given by the Father to the Son, the Son will give eternal life, if so be that the Father glorify the Son and the Son the Father.

The condition is indispensable; but if it be fulfilled the consequence is inevitable. For *this is the eternal life, to know thee the only true God, and whom thou sendedst, Jesus Christ*. This knowledge does not earn eternal life; it is eternal life. Do we hesitate to accept that? Does it seem to us that just 'knowing' a theological truth cannot be an adequate occupation for eternity? Certainly it could not be. But the word for *know* here is not that which stands for a grasp of truth; it is that which stands for personal acquaintance. Even in human friendships there is the constant delight of new discoveries by each in the character of the other. Eternity cannot be too long for our finite spirits to advance in knowledge of the infinite God.

We constantly miss the spiritual value of the greatest religious phrases by failing to recall their true meaning. At one time I was much troubled that the climax of the *Veni Creator* should be

> Teach us to know the Father, Son,
> And Thee, of Both, to be but One.

It seemed to suggest that the ultimate purpose of the coming of the Holy Spirit was to persuade us of the truth of an orthodox formula. But that is mere thoughtlessness. If a man once knows the Spirit within him, the source of all his aspiration after holiness, as indeed the Spirit of Jesus Christ, and if he knows this Spirit of Jesus Christ within himself as none other than the Spirit of the Eternal and Almighty God, what more can he want? *This is the eternal life*.

This definition of eternal life can hardly be regarded as a part of the prayer addressed by our Lord to the Father. It is a comment inserted by the Evangelist. But his mind is so identified with its content – in this instance the prayer offered by the Lord – that he so phrases his comment as to make it, in grammatical construction, part of the prayer. It is a signal instance of the extent to which his mind and his theme have interpenetrated one another; this is the cause of modifications in the form of language used, but it is also the condition of the profound apprehension achieved and expressed.

I glorified thee on the earth by finishing the work which thou hast given me to do. His active obedience is the means by which He gives glory to God; so in Hebrews 'Lo, I am come to do thy will, O God' (Hebrews 10.7 quoting Psalm 40.7, 8). He has done all that can be done *on the earth*. He has loved *to the uttermost* (13.1) that life in this world permits. One ultimate perfection of love remains to be achieved, and He prays that now this may be His – the perfect expression of love in the perfection of self-sacrifice.

I glorified thee on the earth by finishing the work which thou hast given me to do. What work was that? The revelation of God and, therein, the establishment of His Kingdom; or, in other words, the living of a life of perfect love and thereby the winning of that new control in the hearts of men which is called 'holy spirit'. This He has done so far as it can be done at all on earth, that is, under the conditions of human life here. And therein He has glorified the Father. For all that we adore in Him is the Father's glory shining through Him – *glory as of an only-begotten from a Father* (1.14) – and His shewing forth of this is therefore a giving of glory to the Father.

We are all familiar with this double thought in other connexions; a boy is trained by his school to a life of discipline and public service; thereafter the school is proud of him and honours him; but what people admire in him is what his school has given to him, and he, by fidelity to what he has learnt, brings honour to his school. If we sometimes find this thought difficult when applied to the highest levels of spiritual attainment, that is only because of our disastrous tendency to sheer individualism in things of the spirit . . . it is never possible to divide up the credit for spiritual achievement and allot portions to different persons.

All that can be done *on earth* – under conditions of earthly life – has been done. But there remains what can be done through death, which is indeed *on earth* so far as it is the close of earthly life, but is already in heaven so far as it is the gateway to fulfilled fellowship with the Father. This it can be, without transition or mediation, only if he who dies is already 'made perfect in love' (1 John 4.18). That condition has once, and once only, been fulfilled. Because Jesus had *finished the work* of living the life of love, therefore for Him death is immediate passage to the eternal glory. *And now glorify thou me, Father, in thine own presence with the glory which I had before the world was, in thy presence.*

The love that was always perfect according to the existing reality – perfect in the manger, in the home, in the carpenter's shop, in the works of mercy, in the words of life – now reaches its culmination in the absolute self-abnegation of love undimmed – nay, victoriously intensified – by agony and death. This is the perfect fellowship with the Father manifested under the conditions of a sinful world. In one sense it is true to say that the death on the Cross was the gateway to that eternal fellowship and glory; but more profoundly it is true to say that the death on the Cross is itself the attainment of that fellowship and glory in absolute plenitude.

There is no contradiction between the thought that the Lord Jesus was always, from His Birth, perfectly united with the Father, and saying that He 'advanced in favour with God and men' (St Luke 2.52) or that He 'learned obedience by the things which he suffered' (Hebrews 5.8). If Herod had succeeded in killing Him in His infancy, there would have been an Incarnation, but no effective revelation of the divine love. He grew as boy and man; at every stage He was perfect in that stage; only by all the stages of a life matured to full manhood, and then cut short by the self-centredness of a world unable to bear the intolerable glory and judgment of love in its fullness – only so could the whole revelation be given, the whole power of divine love be exercised, the whole triumph of love over selfishness be won. The Cross is the focus of the eternal glory.

For this perfection of divine love, which had before the world was united the Father and the Son, is precisely what sent the Son into the world; *God so loved that he gave* (3.16). That love is now to pay the full price and win its longed-for result. It is not the Cross as an isolated episode which is thus the focus of the eternal glory; it is the Cross as the culmination of the life of love, as the achievement of the purpose of the Incarnation, as the projection of divine light across the spaces of the world's darkness. But in fact the Cross is all of these; therefore as He approaches the Cross, and with direct reference to the Cross, the Son prays to the Father, *Now – now glorify thou me, Father, in thine own presence, with the glory which I had, before the world was, in thy presence.*

The Aaronic High Priest entered into the Holiest Place (symbol of the immediate presence of God) to offer the blood of the victim (symbol of the consecrated life of Israel). Our High Priest enters the immediate presence of God in and by the very act of offering His own consecrated life; for to make that offering and to be in that presence are not two things, but one.

In that presence the Lord was before the world was; from that presence He has never moved; but, as is necessary in this world of time and change, has *on earth* (4) at once experienced and exhibited its meaning in progressive stages; now He will again be in that presence in the uttermost meaning of those words. And He wills that where He is, His disciples also may be with Him (24).

10

Guiding a Nation at War: Addresses and Letters

With the rise to power of Hitler and the Nazis in Germany the British Government under Neville Chamberlain at first followed the policy of appeasement. Temple, like most other church leaders, accepted this, though without the enthusiasm of Cosmo Gordon Lang the Archbishop of Canterbury. Also, like other church leaders, he had not really responded to the increasing persecution of the Jews in Germany in the 1930s. But, after the German invasion of Poland in September 1939 and the declaration of war between Britain and Germany, Temple suddenly and impressively rose to the challenge of the hour. One month after the declaration of war he was invited to give a broadcast to the nation on the BBC. He spoke about the spirit and aims of Britain in the war. He avoided the kind of jingoism that many churchmen had preached at the beginning of the First World War. With his natural and effortless delivery, he spoke with reason and feeling to that grim hour. He pointed out the contrast with the atmosphere in August and September 1914, at the outbreak of the First World War, when there had been some high spirits and exhilaration. This time there was less excitement but more resolution. The public mind now was 'completely void of excitement. There is a deep determination, accompanied by no sort of exhilaration, but by a profound sadness. Men are taking up a hateful duty; the very fact that they hate it throws into greater relief their conviction that it is a duty.' He described it as a duty first to Poland, but also a wider and greater duty 'to check aggression, and to bring to an end the perpetual insecurity and menace which hang over Europe, spoiling the life of millions, as a result of the Nazi tyranny in Germany'.

Temple then laid out the seven shameful events over the last eight years that showed the criminality of the Nazi regime, the last of which was the pogrom against the Jews on Kristallnacht. Temple argued (as Churchill was later to do) that the Government should make no terms with Hitler or his government, because they were simply not trustworthy. He also argued that whatever terms were made with a future German government these should include 'no kind of advantage for ourselves and no humiliation for the German people'. He finished by calling for a congress of nations to negotiate eventually a peace agreement (see Section i).

Temple's words crystallized what many were feeling and thinking at that moment: he seemed to capture the mood of many British people. The broadcast turned him into a national leader overnight. It was heard throughout the British dominions, including Canada and Australia, giving him an international standing. He seemed to become the voice of the Christian conscience at a time when Lang had lost credibility because of his handling of the abdication crisis. This was seen in a small way the following day after Temple took the chair at a National Society conference: Lord Sankey said, 'Before even the Minutes are read, I want in the name of all here – and I believe of all Englishmen – to thank our chairman for his broadcast last night' (Iremonger 1948, p. 541).

The broadcast also made it clear that there was now little doubt that after the retirement of Lang as Archbishop of Canterbury, Temple would replace him. This duly happened in April 1942. Churchill did not admire Temple's views on social reform, nor his lack of bellicosity. He also had no interest in Temple's theology nor in his leadership of the ecumenical movement. Nevertheless, he had no choice but to translate Temple from York to Canterbury (see Temple's letter in Postscript, pp. 248–9). No other bishop in the Church of England had his stature and authority.

Once installed as Archbishop of Canterbury, Temple continued to speak about the war and the Christian response to it. He argued against a pacifism which saw the taking of German lives as a simple breaking of the law of love. He argued that the question was not simply how Britain could show love to Germans. Britain also needed to show love to Frenchmen, Poles, Czechs and Germans, all at the same time. If it could be said that Britain was fighting to overthrow Nazi tyranny and secure for all Europeans a greater measure of freedom, then resistance to Germany by force was a way of loving Germans themselves as well as others: 'In the world which exists, it is not possible to take it as self-evident that the law of love forbids fighting. Some of us even hold that precisely that law commands fighting' ('A Conditional Justification of War', reprinted in Religious Experience, 1958, pp. 172–3; see further the letters in Section iv).

He linked his support for fighting with his theological and social thought and especially his key distinction (first described in his 1928 lectures, Christianity and the State: *see above pp. 87–8) between the 'power state' of the Nazis, which coerces its citizens to serve its own ends, and the 'welfare state', 'according to which state exists for the sake of its citizens, both collectively and individually' (see Section ii). The war was about fighting to secure the second of these and to defeat the first, for a democratic rather than a totalitarian future.*

As the war progressed it became more and more clear what the Nazis were doing to the Jewish populations of Easter Europe. As information came back from the Continent about the extent of Nazi plans, Temple called a meeting in the Albert Hall to speak about the crime. This took place on 29 October, when he shared the platform with other famous names. Temple's rousing speech sought to bring public opinion behind the call for action, and he also called on the Government to do everything possible to stop the outrage (see Section iii).

Then, towards the end of 1942, it was confirmed that there was a deliberate Nazi plan to exterminate the Jews of Europe, and that during that year most of Poland's 3 million Jews had already been wiped out. Temple wrote at once to The Times *expressing 'burning indignation at this atrocity, to which the records of barbarous ages scarcely supply a parallel' (5 December).*

It was then up to the Allies to attempt to rescue those Jews who were yet to be sent to the camps. Those in Bulgaria, Hungary and Romania would have been the easiest to save. Churchill would have liked to do something but his expressed wishes were disregarded. It seems that the Allied command thought that large numbers of Jewish refugees could only become a nuisance in whichever country they were given asylum (Hastings 1987, pp. 376–7).

Temple had at first tried to put pressure on the Government with private correspondence to the Foreign Secretary, the Colonial Secretary and the Prime Minister: what was the Government going to do about this outrage? In reply, ministers tried to divert Temple with their own questions: 'Had the Archbishop considered the possibility of an anti-Semitic outbreak in England which might follow on from some special favour being shown to Jews?' Or, 'Was there not the danger of giving Hitler an excuse for further barbarities if he could point to British acts of charity and tell his people that the Jews were now seen to be the friends of Britain and therefore the enemies of the Fatherland?' (Iremonger 1948, p. 565).

So, in the House of Lords, on 23 March 1943, Temple called for action. In a long and significant speech, one of his most important in that chamber, he moved a motion calling for 'immediate measures, on the largest and most generous scale compatible with the requirements of military operation and security, for providing help and temporary asylum to persons in danger of massacre who are able to leave enemy and enemy-occupied countries'. Temple quoted figures of the massacre and torture of the Jews 'before which the imagination recoils', and made several suggestions for government action, including the appointment of a senior official to oversee the measures. He concluded:

> *We know that what we can do is small compared with the magnitude of the problem, but we cannot rest so long as there is any sense among us that we are not doing all that might be done ... We at this moment have upon us a tremendous responsibility. We stand at the bar of history, of humanity, and of God (pp. 566–7). (For the full text, see Temple,* Nazi Massacre of the Jews and Others: Some Practical Proposals for Immediate Rescue.*)*

The Government's reply, as before, was that the best way of helping the Jews was winning the war, and all the attention of the Government should be on this rather than special relief efforts for those Jews imprisoned by Hitler. Temple's response to this narrow line of reasoning was not to slacken his efforts but to continue with writing letters and pressing for action. Whether or not his vociferous intervention would be effective at any given moment 'it ought to be said for the sake of the principles of justice itself, and I shall continue the advocacy which I have endeavoured to offer hitherto' (Iremonger 1948, p. 567).

The political importance of Temple's stand, in the midst of the Holocaust, should not be overemphasized. He was not effective in getting the British Government to do anything very significant about the concentration camps: even the railway lines to the camps were never bombed. But his was still a morally important attempt to provoke action, and on Temple's death was recognized as such by the World Jewish Congress. An official statement from that body said that he would be

> *particularly mourned by the Jewish people whose champion he was ... Profoundly conscious of the physical suffering of the Jews, and acutely sensitive to its spiritual significance, he was at all times ready to make every contribution to the alleviation of the great tragedy that had befallen a great people. (p. 567)*

GUIDING A NATION AT WAR

i The Spirit and Aims of Britain in the War

A BBC radio broadcast at the outbreak of the Second World War, 3 October 1939, reprinted in *Thoughts in War-Time*, 1940, pp. 54–5

Those who have vivid memories of August and September 1914 naturally compare with their recollections of that time the experiences through which we are passing now. There is less excitement, but there is even firmer resolution. Then modern war was a thing unknown. Few, certainly, entered upon it light-heartedly; yet there was a certain display of high spirits and exhilaration. There was very little bitterness or hatred, and there was a widespread sense of moral obligation, especially towards Belgium; but there was not, in my recollection, a sense of dedication. What had to be done appeared as a painful and vexatious interruption of a manner of life which it was hoped that we might resume before long. There was substantial unity among all sections of the community; but there were exceptions to this unity, and the exceptions were very vocal. Further, the great mass of public opinion, though clear that entry on the war was a moral duty and a political necessity, was none the less a little bewildered about it. For had not the crisis started with the murder of an Archduke who could not be a person of special interest to British citizens? The diplomatic history, when published, confirmed men's assurance that they must fight, but did not remove the feeling of bewilderment.

An Evident Duty

In 1939 there is no such feeling. The story is perfectly clear, and for months the public mind has been habituated to the thought that war might become an evident duty. Apart from those who hold that it can never be right to take up arms at all, there is no division of opinion. There are those who believe we ought to have risked war sooner in resistance to aggression; there is no one who believes that it can ever be right to engage in war and yet holds that we should have held back now. The unity of purpose in entry upon war is absolute.

Partly, perhaps, for this reason, it is completely void of excitement. There is a deep determination, accompanied by no sort of exhilaration, but by a profound sadness. Men are taking up a hateful duty; the very fact that they hate it throws into greater relief their conviction that it is a duty. It is a duty first to Poland; but that is rather the focus than the real essence of our obligation. It is in fact Poland; it might have been some other country: for our purpose is to check aggression and to bring to an end the perpetual insecurity and menace which hang over Europe, spoiling the life of millions, as a result of the Nazi tyranny in Germany.

A Dedicated Nation

We enter the war as a dedicated nation; and it is this fact which has called forth the response of the younger generation in so marvellous a manner. It is one of the most remarkable features of this crisis that it has found our young folk more ready to serve their country in arms in its service of a cause than ever they were, or could have been roused to be, for any imperial interest. No doubt there is in the background the reflection that, if the Nazi tyrants are again successful in aggression, our turn is not far off. But this is very much in the background. The prevailing conviction is that Nazi tyranny and aggression are destroying the traditional excellences of European civilisation and must be eliminated for the good of mankind. Over against the deified nation of the Nazis our people have taken their stand as a dedicated nation.

Such a stand might easily be self-righteous, but there is little trace of that. There is a widespread recognition that we carry a share of responsibility for the evil state of the world. Our people are confident, not in their own righteousness as individuals or as a nation, but in the justice of the cause to which they have now dedicated themselves.

In that spirit we enter the conflict, and it is worth while to give it expression in words, because we may need at many times in the ensuing months to recall our minds to the ideals which claim our devotion now. When the suffering of war becomes more acute, when perhaps air raids bring destruction and horror to our doors, it will be hard to maintain the lofty mood of sober resolution which is almost universal today. Temptation to bitterness of resentment and consequent ill-will and hatred will be very strong. If we yield to those temptations we shall betray the cause to which we are now dedicated. Let us then, now, before the strain is fiercest, register our high purpose and consider what is needed for its achievement.

It seems to me that the achievement of our purpose is possible only if two conditions are fulfilled. The first is that we should make no terms with Herr Hitler or his Government – not because it is undemocratic, which is Germany's concern and not ours, but because it is utterly untrustworthy. The second is that the terms which we make with an honourable German Government shall be arrived at in such a way as to show that we have sought no kind of advantage for ourselves and no humiliation for the German people.

The Men of Dates

First, we can make no terms with Herr Hitler or his colleagues. In my view, the events of the last few days make no difference to this decision. The Prime Minister has said that the word of Herr Hitler is not in our eyes worth the paper it is written on; he has broken too many promises ever to be trusted again. The series of broken pledges is vividly present to all our minds, from the militarisation of the Rhineland in breach of the Treaty of Locarno which he had himself reaffirmed, to the rape of Czecho-Slovakia and the device whereby he accused the Poles of rejecting the proposals which had never even been submitted to them. This is a series of outrages upon foreign States.

Even more fraught with shame and with unworthiness to speak for a great people like the German is the record of the scandalous action at home. It is a custom in France to use dates as the names of men and events. Danton was proud to be called the man of the 10th August – the date when the French Revolution entered on its final phase. Napoleon III is spoken of as the man of December; the reign of Louis Philippe is the July monarchy. We should similarly think of Hitler and his colleagues as the men of the 22nd August 1932; of the 27th February 1933; of the 30th June 1934; of the 25th July 1934; of the 3rd March 1938; of the 8th October 1938; of the 9th November 1938.

What do these dates stand for?

On the 22nd August 1932, that dreadful telegram known as the Beuthen telegram, was published which glorified six Nazis who trampled a helpless Communist to death in front of his mother. Those six men were on trial, and Hitler telegraphed to them: 'Your freedom is our honour.'

On 27th February 1933 the Reichstag building was set an fire. No one doubts who started that fire; but someone else was done to death as the culprit.

On the 30th June 1934, at least seven hundred Germans were shot in cold blood – some of them great patriots – one was a builder of the Reichswehr; some were comrades of Hitler from his earlier days.

On the 25th July 1934, Dollfuss was murdered. Can we acquit of guilt for this the men who set up a memorial in honour of the murderers?

On the 3rd March 1938, Pastor Niemöller was acquitted by the law courts, and at once imprisoned in a concentration camp. He is, so far as we know, still in a concentration camp.

On 8th October 1938, the palace of Cardinal Innitzer, who had welcomed Hitler at Vienna, was sacked.

On the 9th November 1938, the great pogrom against the Jews took place in Germany.

The best German citizens are deeply ashamed of all these things. Many of them, because they must endure at present that their country should be governed by the criminals, would be glad to forget those dates and what took place on them. But such deeds cannot be forgotten, and those who are guilty of them are unworthy to speak and act for a great people.

No Fresh Grievances

With the men whose names derive their meaning from those dates we must not make terms. But if the German people get other rulers in their place, what then? Then we have to show beyond all possible doubt that we aim at no advantage for ourselves, and no humiliation for Germany. To make that clear we have to take two steps.

First, we have to recognise certain facts, including mistakes and wrong on our own side. The Peace of Versailles was made by conquerors in the spirit resulting from a victorious war. Most of its clauses, taken separately, can be defended; some of them were admirable, including that which put Poland once again upon the map. But the total effect was such as inevitably to create the sense of genuine grievance. Moreover, the war-guilt clause, against which many of us have protested on the ground of Christian sentiment, could only have had value if it had been freely accepted.

Secondly, we have to recognise that the Allies and the League of Nations, which was in practice their organ, never utilised the machinery in the League Covenant for remedying by peaceful means any sense of grievance which had been created. Article 19 of the Covenant was never used. Moreover, the Disarmament Conference failed, with a resulting resentment in Germany, followed by a programme of intensive rearmament.

Our first step, then, towards the making of a just settlement must be a frank recognition of much wrong and failure on our side in the past and of certain facts which we have tended to ignore.

Agreed Terms of Peace

Many are pressing for a declaration of our terms of peace. They may be right, but I cannot support that demand. We do not know what the circumstances will be; it may not be in our power to satisfy the hopes that have been encouraged. In that case, only the bitterness of disillusionment would result. Nor can we profitably lay down principles, for most of the chief problems concern not the principles but their application. Certainly if there were no alternative to a statement of principles or practical aims, I should be silent on this whole subject. For I wish to speak as a representative of Christian opinion, and there is too much of a technical political character in this field for Christian opinion as such to be entitled to special attention.

But there is still another alternative, to which, as I think, a Christian outlook leads us, and which carries with it no such risk of disappointment or disillusionment as is inherent in a declaration of either guiding principles or detailed proposals. It is suggested by consideration of the most radical fault of the Treaty of Versailles – namely, that it was imposed and not negotiated. This may have been true of treaties which the Germans themselves have made; but, nevertheless, let us as Christians determine at all costs to avoid any repetition of a procedure by which it is hardly possible to create a general sense that justice has been done.

In other words, let us determine and declare that when the fighting stops, the terms of peace shall be drawn up in a true Congress of Nations, in which Germany – freed from the Nazi tyrants – shall take her place among the rest, but in which also the rights of Czechs and Poles shall have a first claim to consideration. If there are matters on which no agreement can be reached, let these be referred to a Court of Equity formed from neutral nations which are neither beneficiaries nor sufferers by the Peace of Versailles.

Justice or Arrogance?

Nothing, surely, can so clearly establish the disinterestedness of our aims as such a declaration. Nothing, surely, could give to the peoples of Poland, Czecho-Slovakia and Germany so clear an assurance that they will receive justice, so far as the tangle of facts bequeathed to us by history permits it and the wisdom of man can secure it. This frees us from the dreadful responsibility, and, indeed, the indefensible arrogance, of ourselves attempting to decide what is just and imposing it on others.

Before this Congress of Europe should be brought all outstanding grievances and problems containing the seeds of future wars – problems of frontiers, problems of colonies, problems of tariffs, problems of every sort – and we must ourselves be ready for sacrifices, provided the interests of minorities and of subject peoples are safeguarded. Such a Congress may take years to do its work; but some of the matters calling for adjustment are of old standing and have not yet led to grave trouble. Many of us hope that the Congress will pave the way for that Federal Union of Europe in which we see the only hope of a permanent settlement. But that is a large question, and certainly Europe cannot be federated until it is pacified.

Here, then, I suggest, is a programme which gives expression to the spirit and convictions with which our nation has taken up arms: no peace with Hitler or with those who have been his colleagues; but with the German people guided by a trustworthy Government a peace honourable to them as truly as to us, freely negotiated in a Congress of European nations.

ii   The Real Meaning of the War

William Temple Papers, vol. 67, p. 125: from a series of six articles, publication unverified, 1941

As I am allowed to contribute this series of articles, I should like to begin by stating again what this war is really about. It has often been done, but though the statements agree for the most part in substance everyone sees something from his own angle of approach and this may be just what someone else needs to fill in a gap in his apprehension or tip the balance of his judgment.

First let us rid our minds of some obsessions which very easily cloud our vision. When a great conflict of ideas is raging, it is no longer relevant to ask how far the human champions of either side are to blame for the state of affairs which led to the outbreak. There is one reading of the period 1918 to 1939 which attributes most of the blame to France and Great Britain, because (it is alleged) they treated Germany in a way bound to create resentment and at last an outbreak of fury and lust for domination. Personally I regard this reading as not entirely false, but as a gross exaggeration. I think the Prussian tradition was a much more potent factor than the economic clauses of the Treaty of

Versailles, or than the long exclusion of Germany from the League of Nations, or than the failure of the League of Nations to agree on measures of disarmament, or than all of these together. At the same time I agree that each and all of these contributed to catastrophe. My point now, however, is that all this for the moment is irrelevant. Two groups of nations are locked in a deadly struggle; those groups stand for different conceptions of the way in which human life should be ordered and conducted. The victory of either will give to the view of life which it represents a vast increase of influence in the next period of human history; the defeat of either will lead to the virtual eclipse of its view of life. This decision concerning the future is of importance so stupendous that in comparison all other considerations are negligible.

The issue at stake in the war is between two different conceptions of the nature of Man. Is every man and woman a child of God destined for eternal fellowship with Him? Or is the individual no more than a citizen of an earthly state, an episode in the ever-flowing stream of life? If the former is true, the State must recognise in every citizen something superior to itself; in other words we get the conception of the 'Welfare State', according to which the state exists for the sake of its citizens, both collectively and individually. But if the other doctrine of man is true, then each individual exists for the State, which is itself the object of his final allegiance and the prosperity of which is the measure of right and wrong – the conception of the 'Power-State'.

The Nazi philosophy takes this position and the conduct of the Nazi Government follows from it with perfect consistency. We put everything wrong if we suppose that Hitler and his colleagues are merely wicked but able men, who for the sake of their ambition do what in their hearts they know to be wrong. They believe with horrifying sincerity that they are right. They are not people who fail to practise what they preach, as all Christians do and always will; they preach what they practise; their right is our wrong.

This is what makes it important as few things in history have ever been important, that they should be defeated. But it is hardly less important that we, to whom Providence has entrusted the task of defeating them, should see clearly what the issue really is, and should know the grounds for our own faith and hope. For if we fail in this, we may ourselves betray our cause when we have won victory for it in conflict.

Of course it is evident that, if the formulation of the issue as I have given it is correct, then even more than the conception of Man, the doctrine of God is directly involved. For the claim that Man is a child of God is an assertion about God as much as about Man. If God is the

Creator and Father of all men, who loves each one; if Jesus Christ is the incarnate Word of God, and died to save each one; if there is available to men through Jesus Christ a power to live worthily as children of God (which power is the activity in us of the Holy Spirit), then the whole Nazi philosophy of government is false, and some other must be true. That other must be based on the recognition of personality in every man or woman as the seat of an ultimate value which may not be sacrificed to any end alien from itself. This will be a philosophy of Freedom; but not every conception or defence of Freedom meets the requirements, and it is supremely important that we who champion Freedom should be serving true Freedom in ways truly fitted to preserve and propagate it.

With that matter we shall be concerned in another article. From what has already been said two conclusions follow, one theoretical and one practical. The theoretical conclusion is that the most important political questions of our time are essentially theological questions. Our ordering of the life of the States and of the relations between them will very largely depend on our conceptions of God and of Man. Of course there will be many who support the Christian conception without themselves accepting the Christian doctrine from which it flows; they will support it because their particular sense of good and evil, of right and wrong, approves it; and we should whole-heartedly welcome their support. But that kind of personal preference will have no strength for resisting the pressures expressed in the totalitarian philosophy and embodied in the totalitarian States. For that, a philosophy as coherent as the Nazi philosophy is needed.

So the practical conclusion is that Christians have today a terrifying load of responsibility to carry – the responsibility of becoming fully conscious of the tradition entrusted to us, and of securing its effective influence in the direction of the present phase of history.

Justice and Faith

The difference between the democratic and the totalitarian view of life is clearest when we consider their different conceptions of Justice. It is notoriously difficult to define Justice; but it is easy to recognise some definitions of it which are offered as a complete repudiation of its very essence as our civilisation has valued it. Such a definition is that attributed by Plato to the sophist Thrasymachus, which declares that Justice is the interest of the stronger. But this is the definition accepted by the Nazis for the regulation of the relations between States. They think it inherently right that the stronger State should dominate weaker States. That they would think so might have been inferred from their legal code, according to which Justice is that treatment of the citizen which most conduces to the interest of the State or, to put it more shortly and in a form nearer to Plato's – Justice is the interest of the State. But if so, then of course successful robbery by the State is justified – the seizure of Prague for example. All Hitler's attacks without warning upon his neighbours are implicit in the system of secret police and concentration camps. Let us always remember that Dr Niemöller was acquitted by the Court of Law, and was then immediately re-arrested by the secret police and shut up, not this time in a prison but in a concentration camp.

Our slowness in Great Britain and America to understand what was happening in the world and our failure to take vigorous action when it could have been done at comparatively small cost was due to an incapacity to believe that such a perversion of civilisation was possible. It is true that Hitler had said these monstrous things; but we said they were the ravings of a man irritated by his imprisonment, and that when actually responsible for his nation's welfare he would not act on his proclaimed principles. Even when he began to do so, we still expected him to sober down. When after treacherously murdering his most intimate friend and a large number of his colleagues on June 30, 1934, he announced that in that moment he was in his own person the Supreme Court of Judicature, few people in other countries were ready to declare that a reign of barbarism had been instituted. I am more concerned for the moment with our blindness than with Hitler's wickedness. We all recognise his wickedness, unless we become ashamed of our own blindness, we may easily relapse into it. We were partly infected, not with the evil symptoms of the disease but with the disease itself. We thought Hitler deplorable rather than damnable; and that is our own condemnation.

Let us try to recover an appreciation of the grounds on which we are, not so much able as, obliged to use such words about what has lately been happening in Germany. What is the sanctity attaching to Justice as between man and man, nation and nation, State and citizen? A totalitarian regime may establish and uphold real justice as between man and man; it may come nearer to this than some liberal or democratic State; and then multitudes of people who have no occasion for collision with the State, are prepared to praise that State for its achievement. But they rest on a rotation foundation. Unless the State recognises the claim of Justice as between itself and its subjects, it will only uphold Justice as between these subjects so long as its own interest is furthered by doing so. The vital question is whether the State (the Sovereign) recognises itself as subject to the demands of Justice and thereby acknowledges something superior to itself.

This is why the permanent struggle of the Christian Church must be against Caesar-worship, as it was in the first age of persecution, as it is depicted in the Book of Revelation, as it is presented to us in Germany today. For if the State is supreme, then it is not required to deal justly, but only to serve its own interests; and if it does not uphold Justice, the foundation of human society is destroyed.

Yet plainly the State is supreme unless there is a God to whom it owes allegiance. None but God can in fact claim to stand above the State. Only faith in God can preserve us from totalitarianism and the repudiation of Justice inherent in it.

We may look at the same truth from the side of the individual. How can he possibly have a claim against the State? If he is the creature of a moment, one of some millions of contemporaries in the flow of successive generations, this is impossible. He can have that claim only if he is a child of God, a citizen of an eternal Kingdom.

Justice and Freedom alike depend politically upon the complete distinction between the Executive and the Judicature – upon the denial of Hitler's claim after the thirteenth of June. Unless a citizen may appeal from the executive officers of the State to its judicial officers, and unless the latter give their decision independently in accordance with duly promulgated law, there is no freedom and there will soon be little Justice. But the Executive in a modern State is immensely powerful. It will not submit its actions to Courts of Law unless it has . . . a reverence for something greater than the State and acknowledge in every citizen a kinship with that Higher Power.

We are horrified when we see Nazi Germany outrage Justice, Freedom and Truth; but we shall not save them by defeating Germany alone; we can save them only by a faith in God which controls our political philosophy as well as our political action.

Here is a manifest function for the Christian Church. It has the responsibility of recalling men to the fundamental principles of their own secular civilisation. It has other tasks beyond this, in one sense higher than this. For where the principles of Justice, Freedom and Truth are admitted, there is still the Gospel call to be sounded forth, the call of the love of God to the capacity for love implanted in man's heart by God. But the Law comes before the Gospel, and the Gospel fulfils or completes, it does not destroy the Law. So today, though there are other and higher tasks beyond, the most indispensable task of the

Church is to recall men to acknowledgment of the Sovereignty of God, over all States and persons, as well imperial as private, throughout His universe supreme.

iii   Nazi Massacres of the Jews

Albert Hall address, 29 October 1942, in the William Temple Papers, vol. 67

We are witnessing such an eruption of evil as the world has not seen for centuries. What is happening in Europe is so horrible that the imagination refuses to picture it. Our people as a whole remain very largely unaware of it. And even when we are aware, it is difficult to feel the horror which is appropriate to the facts. Our sensitiveness is dulled. There is a terrible line in Mark Anthony's speech over the dead body of Julius Caesar in Shakespeare's play – 'All pity choked with custom of fell deeds.' We are in danger of sinking to that condition.

Events which would have aroused consternation in the first decade of this century now pass almost unnoticed. The sufferings of the years of war – 1914–1918 – and of much of the period between the two wars led to a hardening of hearts. The drain upon sympathy began to be unbearable. We are in danger of becoming morally numb.

For this reason alone it would be right that we should meet, as we are met today, to face the fact of monstrous evil and realise its meaning. The purpose is not to stir up hatred or the spirit of vengeance. Nothing can be gained by that. It only means that we begin to be infected with the evil which we denounce. But the purpose is to keep our moral perception clear, to utter the judgment of civilised men upon a reversion to barbarism, and to pledge ourselves once more to the effort and the sacrifice by which deliverance must be wrought.

In all the countries occupied by Germany there has been exhibited a ruthless belief in terror as the chief instrument of Government. The destruction of whole villages with the extermination of their inhabitants as reprisal for the death of one or two Germans illustrates the mentality with which we are confronted. We recall today the sufferings of Poles and Czechs, of Greeks and Yugo-Slavs, of Norwegians, Dutch and Belgians; we salute the noble courage with which those sufferings are endured; and we look forward to the day of liberation for those peoples. We salute at the same time the heroic Russian people in their agonising yet indomitable resistance. All of these are present in our minds. But there is one people which has no national home, which lives among other peoples as in some sense their guests, ready to be most loyal citizens to whatever extent the opportunity is opened to them, but true with a constancy that claims our admiration to their own great culture and tradition. Upon this people – the Jews – the fury of the Nazi evil has concentrated its destructive energy. It is hard to resist the conclusion that there is a settled purpose to exterminate the Jewish people if it can be done.

What else is the explanation of recent occurrences in France? At first it seemed possible to explain the German demand for the surrender of Jewish refugees in Unoccupied France as due to a need for additional labour-power; for at first only men of working age were demanded. But now this seems to have been an instance of the Nazi technique, whereby smaller demands are presented first, the granting of which makes harder the refusal of later demands. For later women were claimed, with the option of leaving their children, not expecting ever to see them again, but hoping they might live to see the better day. But now the children also are being deported, from two years old and upwards. There is something familiar about that; but when Herod earlier massacred the Innocents of Bethlehem it was on those of two years or less that destruction fell; and that is a smaller number.

It may be that those who have labour power to give are being called upon to give it. But there is every reason to fear that a large proportion of those deported are destined for the ghastly ghetto in Eastern Galicia, where thousands of Jews have already perished. Of that horror I shall not speak further. We have others here better acquainted with the hideous facts. But I am grateful for this opportunity to share in today's effort to express our horror at what has been and is being done, our deep sympathy with the sufferers, our claim that our own Government should do whatever is possible for their relief, and our steadfast resolution to do all and bear all that may be necessary to end this affliction.

iv Some Letters about the War

Forgiving the Germans?

A correspondent has asked if it was really possible to love or forgive a nation like the Germans who had committed terrible atrocities.

Lambeth Palace, S.E. 1.
27th June, 1942.

My dear —,
This letter from — appears to me to rest on a complete misunderstanding both of the New Testament and of Christian Theology. I suppose a good deal turns on what people mean by the word 'Love', and I have myself carefully avoided urging that we should love the Germans because the word is so readily misunderstood. Of course love means desiring and promoting the welfare of its object, and if so there can be no doubt that Our Lord loved the people He drove out of the Temple and the Pharisees. Similarly forgiveness means a readiness to receive people back into fellowship. But it does not take effect until on their side they have changed their outlook. Of course the trouble with anyone like myself is that however carefully one expounds these things the Press omits three-quarters of what one says. I do not think that anyone has denounced German policy or German atrocities more strongly than I have, but there is an immense difference between the severity undeniably called for and ill will in the sense of desiring evil to befall people. The last paragraph of —'s letter requiring some sort of balance of suffering as distinct from punishment of those most directly responsible is of course flatly anti-Christian. The whole doctrine of the Atonement turns on the precise denial of this.
Yours sincerely,
William Cantuar:

Rebuilding Canterbury after bombing by the Luftwaffe

To the Editor of *The Times*
July 2, 1942.

Dear Sir,
On June 24 there was held in Canterbury Cathedral a service 'for the renewed dedication of our city to the service of God and of thankfulness for the spirit of its people in the recent time of trouble'. Those who were present found in it an abiding inspiration for the future. The Cathedral has suffered damage, though not beyond repair; but with the sunlight streaming through its glass-less windows it was more beautiful than ever. We feel that there is here a parable of what the war may mean. We speak of Canterbury, which is itself a national treasure,

indeed a treasure to all men; but we think of the nation and indeed of the civilised world.

Here is a wonderful opportunity to rebuild a city with the Cathedral set in it as a jewel, so that all may share the joy of its beauty. Much is lost in the city of which the charm cannot be recovered; but also some of what is lost was poor or bad. It is quite possible that the result of all our suffering should be gain. But if this is to happen at least two conditions must be met: the first is that the plans should be designed with the advice of an artist or artists of real vision; the second is that each and all should be ready, as we believe they are and know that many are, to subordinate their private interests, even at the cost of real sacrifice, to the good of the whole. If these two conditions are fulfilled the city may be more worthy than ever of its place in English history and in the affection of the English-speaking peoples, and set to the whole nation an example of what true public spirit can achieve.

William Cantuar:
Lang of Lambeth, Abp.
C. Lefevre, Mayor of Canterbury.
Hewlett Johnson, Dean of Canterbury.

The bombing of the dams

Lambeth Palace, SE. 1.
May 21, 1943.

Personal

Dear Mrs. —,
I have duly received the letter from yourself and Miss —. I have on previous occasions, for example in connection with the raids on Lübeck and Rostock, protested against gloating over the sufferings of Germans, in the press and otherwise. I have not myself come across it in connection with the bombing of the great dams. That there should be satisfaction in the achievement of such an enterprise is inevitable; the thing itself is, in my judgment, a legitimate act of war, and I have not, in listening to the news, detected any gloating in the B.B.C. of late. To state the fact that we are now dropping more bombs on Germany than they did on us is itself perfectly reasonable, if it is a fact, and once more if we are right to be fighting at all there is

no harm in deriving satisfaction from it. Nothing is so wrong as to fight ineffectively; but to maintain the right spirit while we fight is extremely difficult, and spokesmen of the Church must do their best to choose the right occasions for any sort of protest: that is, occasions when it may be hoped that the protest will receive some attention and produce some effect.

Yours sincerely,
William Cantuar:

Forms of prayer in wartime

To the Archbishop of York (Cyril Garbett)
Lambeth Palace, S.E. 1.
February, 1944.

My dear Cyril,
I am afraid I distress you by the fact that the forms of prayer which I draw up do not contain direct prayers for victory. I have always felt that it is wiser to avoid this, and have publicly stated that it ought to be avoided. I am of course prepared to say, with the form in the Book of 1928, 'Grant us victory, if it be Thy Will'; but I am sure that clause ought to be added in such a case, even though it governs all our praying at all times.

But I have tried always to draw up prayers which do not range us over against any of our fellow-Christians in Germany or elsewhere, because it seems to me that the primary concern in prayer – and I mean 'primary' quite seriously – must be the approach to the Father of all men, with recognition that all His other children have the same right of approach, and that if we pray as our Lord taught us, we are never praying against each other, because we are always praying not that what we want shall be done, but that what God wants shall be done, and that we may be used for doing it. I regard this as really fundamental, and while it may lead one to be perhaps excessively sensitive about some kind of petition, I believe that sensitiveness is a pretty sound guide.

I am very much encouraged by knowing that on this point I am in agreement with Abraham Lincoln, who seems to me to have led his people in war more Christianly than pretty well anybody in history.

I was horrified when, in the exhortation inserted in one of the official forms, the words occurred: 'Do not hesitate to pray for victory'; that came out with a note to say that it was issued under the authority of the Archbishops of Canterbury and York, Cosmo having in fact telegraphed to say that there wasn't time to let me see the form and he was assuming my agreement!

But apart from that there has not, I think, been a direct and unqualified prayer for victory officially issued, and I do not see how I can be associated with the issue of one. I think the maintenance of the spiritual fellowship of all Christians is for the Church a concern that takes precedence even of the military defeat of Nazi-ism.

I thought perhaps I had better try to open my mind to you about all this.
Yours affectionately,
William Cantuar:

The bombing of German cities: From the Introduction to Stephen Hobhouse, *Christ and Our Enemies*, London: SPCK, 1944; in the William Temple Papers, vol. 67, p. 166

March 25, 1944: What 'love' requires of us now is a matter of disagreement – as Mr Hobhouse shews by his comments on a sentence from a sermon of mine which he quotes [a radio sermon preached on 26 December 1943: 'At this time we almost daily hear and read of the devastation caused by our bombers. We are bound to take satisfaction in their achievements . . . But oh! The misery and horror of it all! – a bitter fruit of wickedness, of the refusal of the world to acknowledge its rightful King.' Hobhouse 'profoundly disagreed' with the taking of satisfaction in the bombers' achievements]; but by 'love' we must be guided, he and I agree. It must of course be 'love' for all concerned – Poles, Czechs, Norwegians, Dutch, Belgians, French, and so forth – not only for Germans. I call attention to this point, because it enables me, without distorting the balance of my thought, to call attention also to another . . . To me it seemed at an earlier stage of the war that the peace terms must for a limited period include a penal element, if justice were to be done. But the intensification of the bombing of German cities seems to me to have altered that. Those of us who believe that this intense bombing is justified as a military measure, aiming at the checking of Germany's power to produce war material, must also recognise that it constitutes a penalty for German aggression so great that no other can be called for . . . Punishment has come to them by the operation of that 'wrath' to which St Paul tells us to 'give place': we are to let that 'wrath' or attachment of calamity to selfishness, which is characteristic of the world as God has made it, have its way; we are *not* called to be the conscious and deliberate executants of God's justice. Dr [Reinhold] Niebuhr has urged the same consideration in a recent article. Anyhow, whatever may be appropriate as a policy for the prevention of future aggression and the establishment of security in Europe, or as an execution of justice in relation to some individuals, any thoughts of 'punishing Germany', more than the course of the war is punishing her, must henceforth be excluded from the minds of those who are under obligation to find and to follow the way of Christ.

'Thou shalt not kill'

Lambeth Palace, London S.E. 1.
31st July 1944.

Dear Mrs. —,
There is no record that our Lord ever said 'Thou shalt not kill'. The Mosaic sixth commandment is more accurately represented by the Prayer Book than by the Bible version, for the Word in the Hebrew does not refer to killing of any kind but definitely to 'Murder', that is to say to killing for personal advantage or the satisfaction of personal passion. There is a great deal in the Gospels that is very terrible, as well as all that is said there about love and peace, and we have no right to take one part without the other.

I am quite sure that it is our duty at present to fight the war through and win it, and if we are to fight then of course we must do so effectively; but it is quite possible to fight without malice, indeed the malice is much more likely to be found among folk at home than in the Fighting Forces.

When one remembers what the Nazi Government has been like one also knows that to defeat Germany, infected as it is by the Nazi doctrine, can be an expression of real charity towards the Germans.
Yours sincerely,
William Cantuar:

Suggestions for a victory service

To the Bishop of Southwell
Lambeth Palace, London S.E. 1
12th July 1944

My dear Bishop.
... I imagine that my own dream for that Service is impracticable. I am told that it would puzzle people who cannot wholeheartedly entertain two different emotions at the same time, but I should dearly like it to start with a penitential introduction. I should like that at the central National Service after the King and Queen were seated the Choir should enter singing the Miserere in procession, omitting the last two verses, and that this should then be followed by an Exhortation in which it was explained that at all times when our hearts are lifted up we should none the less approach God in penitence for our share in the whole sin of the world out of which come the calamities which afflict mankind, and that it should be as penitents that we offer our thanksgiving and our dedication which must always be the final expression of thanksgiving. As I have said, those to whom I have mentioned this think that it would too much puzzle the kind of folk who come to church on these occasions and on no others and that they would be irritated and even indignant. I expect that is true. At the same time I do want to put the idea forward for consideration. In its favour I may say that two years ago the Prime Minister asked me about using the word 'humiliation' in connection with National Days of Prayer. He was strongly in favour of it though he found that his colleagues differed from him. I told him that I did not want that word used until after we had won, but I should like it then. He was silent for a little while and then said 'Yes, I understand that'. Do not let yourself or your group be the least influenced in your consideration of this proposal by the source from which it comes, but if you consider it at all consider it quite objectively as one suggestion that has been offered for consideration, and if you yourself regard it as quite impossible do not even trouble your group with it.
Yours affectionately,
William Cantuar:

11

Looking Forward to a New Society: Addresses and Writings

Reinhold Niebuhr, the great American Lutheran theologian who knew and worked with Temple in the 1930s, shows why Temple's writings on social issues are of particular importance:

> The primary significance of his life lay in his ability to carry the radical social implications of the Christian faith into higher ecclesiastical office than any other churchman. The real fact is that Dr Temple was able to relate the ultimate insights of religion about the human situation to the immediate necessities of political justice and the proximate possibilities of a just social order more vitally and creatively than any other modern Christian leader. (Niebuhr 1944, pp. 584–5)

Niebuhr also described Temple as combining a poise of spirit with a logical force and an ethical passion (1944, p. 586).

These qualities are especially apparent in Temple's wartime writings about social questions, above all his Penguin Special of 1942, Christianity and Social Order. *This became a bestseller and has subsequently been reprinted on several occasions. It remains one of his most enduring publications and has provided the inspiration for subsequent studies of social questions from a Christian perspective (e.g. Atherton, Baker and Reader 2011). It represents a high point in his influence, as Niebuhr suggests, and so provides a suitably climactic subject for this final chapter.*

The book emerged out of Temple's concern about what should happen after the Second World War. What kind of society was going to be rebuilt? How were the resources of the nation going to be distributed? What about income and education? What about the living conditions in which people would grow and live? It was well known that at the end of the First World War the opportunity for social reconstruction had been hopelessly squandered. What was going to happen this time? Temple knew that leadership must be provided, and he believed the Church should provide a prophetic kind of leadership on behalf of the poor as well as the rich. How, though, was he going to rise to this challenge?

While still at York he began by planning the Malvern Conference with P. T. R. Kirk, the director of the Industrial Christian Fellowship. An impressive group of speakers was brought to Malvern for three days in January 1941, including John Middleton Murry, T. S. Eliot, Dorothy Sayers, Sir Richard Acland MP, the philosopher Donald MacKinnon and the social theologian V. A. Demant. In the audience there were about 200 clergy and laity.

The conference was poorly managed and the final resolution was vague, but overall it made a strong impact: 'As far as the Church of England was concerned, Malvern undoubtedly expressed a resurgence of the more radical Anglican attitudes to unemployment and poverty which had dropped into the background after 1926' (Kent 1992, p. 161). And, as Kent shows, for Temple it was the start of a movement for social reform. This is seen in a letter to Kirk in the month after the conference where he speaks of 'the movement' and the need to keep a broad range of support behind it, including Anglo-Catholics and Evangelicals and those in the centre as well as on the left of politics (p. 163).

The increasing strength of the movement is seen the following summer when Kirk informed Temple that the Industrial Christian Fellowship had printed and distributed 200,000 copies of a brief summary of the conclusions of the conference. Temple went on to write a 16-page summary of the conference, which sold 30,000 copies, and in that same summer planned further meetings in London with a small hand-picked group to discuss practical objectives for reform, the objectives that became 'A Suggested Programme' in Christianity and Social Order *(see below, Sections ii and iii). That book was itself written in the summer and autumn of 1941, and drew crucially on the Christian social principles he had identified in the 1920s and had refined between then and now. They were a succinct distillation of his understanding of God's will for the future development of society, and they were open to being applied to a range of social questions (see Section i).*

The first he described as liberty, or the principle of respect for personality in all people. He did not follow J. S. Mill in believing that freedom was the simple absence of coercion. He believed that freedom depended on society and all its communities and associations, including that of the state, fulfilling a positive role, especially through education, in equipping a person for a purposeful and creative life in which they would play their part in moving society forward. In Christianity and the State *(1928), as we have seen, he developed the contrast between a notion of a 'power state', where citizens serve the interests of the state, and the kind of state that serves the welfare of its people, the 'welfare state'. Here he argued that the state's role was to positively foster the freedom of its citizens. He was clear that the state had only a conditional authority and jurisdiction to do certain things: it could never be an ultimate object of political loyalty. (See further* Citizen and Churchman, *1941, p. 35, the unpublished article 'The Real Meaning of the War' (see pp. 198–9 above), and Rowan Williams on this use, in* Williams 2009.)

The second social principle spelled out the social dimension of this freedom:

> No man is fitted for an isolated life; every one has needs which he cannot supply for himself; but he needs not only what his neighbours contribute to the equipment of his life but their actual selves as the complement of his own. Man is naturally and incurably social.

This principle of social fellowship is expressed through family life, school, college, trade union, professional association, city, county, nation, church.

The third social principle was also an extrapolation from what had already been said: 'The combination of Freedom and Fellowship as principles of social life issues in the obligation of Service.' Temple was thinking here of both individuals and groups, that they were to seek not their own welfare first but the general welfare of all people.

These three principles, of freedom, fellowship and service, were then applied to contemporary English society. Temple found the state completely failing to fulfil its responsibilities. He noted that the war had removed some of the unemployment so prevalent before the war but there was still much that was wrong: 'the problems were urgent enough before the war; the war has vastly increased their urgency.' In a clearly written and cogent chapter entitled 'The Task Before Us', he deduced, from the social principles, some important and radical conclusions about the future order of society. There were six points concerned with housing, education, levels of income, representation, leisure and freedom of worship and expression. These points are examples of 'middle axioms', practical social objectives that show how abstract theory impinges on social problems and issues. He did not generally use the term itself and it was only after the war that it became widely known and used. But in this chapter he provided a notable example of the method it represented. He showed how it was possible to make telling connections between Christian theology and social and economic problems, through the drawing up of these objectives, which all kinds of different groups could implement in their own fields.

In an appendix, 'A Suggested Programme' (reprinted here in Sections ii and iii), Temple took one further and very important step. He drew on current academic expertise, through consultations with the economist John Maynard Keynes, the social scientist William Beveridge, the historian R. H. Tawney and the Labour politician Stafford Cripps, who later became Chancellor of the Exchequer in the post-war Labour Government. Temple was clearly determined to draw up a practicable programme, with radical proposals for eradicating poverty and unemployment, but one which would be supported by a broad range of opinion. Beveridge was especially important in helping Temple to form proposals. He was the author of the historic report of 1942, Social Insurance and Allied Services, *also known as the Beveridge Report, which became the foundation of the post-war legislation that established the welfare state under the Labour Government. Temple in turn supported the report when it was published (see Temple's letter below, pp. 240–1). Tawney and Keynes read Temple's manuscript of the whole book and, according to the Preface, made many suggestions. But, more importantly, his proposals followed naturally from the principles and 'middle axioms' he had described earlier in the book. In this appendix the explanatory notes show how they could be put into practice. It was all quite tentative and exploratory and Temple was not sure whether to include it, but Keynes was adamant that he should: he thought it the most useful part of the book.*

Temple, then, was clearly determined that the opportunity of the moment should not be lost. He was going to make a deliberate attempt, through consulting, discussing, editing, writing, corresponding and speaking up and down the country, to influence national political life, and all of this on top of his existing duties as an archbishop.

And it began to work. Not only was the Malvern material being bought and read but Christianity and Social Order *went on to sell 139,000 copies. His social thought was clearly being absorbed by a wider public than the restricted church circles that had previously read his books. There is evidence that his book was read by members of the armed forces overseas and passed between them. And when, in the same year that it was published, Temple planned some mass meetings to raise the profile of his agenda, he had no trouble in attracting Cripps and Acland, as well as other church leaders, to share his platform. The meetings, organized by Kirk and the Industrial Christian Fellowship, took place at the Albert Hall (September 1942), in Birmingham (November 1942), Leicester (February 1943), Edinburgh (June 1943), and ended with a youth rally back in London (October 1943), all under the title 'The Church Looks Forward'. They created excitement, and anticipation that when the war ended there would be significant social reform and progress. Temple himself ran into controversy over some proposals he made to limit the power of banks to issue credit (see further Spencer, 2001, pp. 101–3), but in general his influence was felt very widely. David Jenkins, who later as Bishop of Durham was himself no stranger to controversy, has already been quoted on this at the start of this book (see pp. xix–xx).*

The movement which had begun at Malvern, then, and which led through Christianity and Social Order *to 'The Church Looks Forward', clearly touched and inspired a great many people, from a variety of standpoints, to support what was proposed by Temple. As a result of this, as already mentioned, he has been described as one of the architects of the welfare state created by the post-war Labour Government. There were other powerful forces behind these developments, but Temple and those who supported him showed that the Church was both a herald and an instrument of their realization. (See Field's, 2010, assessment above, p. xix; for the broader impact of Temple and his colleagues upon national political life, see Grimley 2004.)*

Finally, it is necessary to mention his impact upon education, represented by the address in Section iv. This issue had been close to his heart since WEA days. During the middle years of the war, R. A. Butler, who was president of the Board of Education, set about drawing up proposals for a new national framework for schools, to come into effect at the end of the war. Up to this point schooling had been divided between church schools, whether Church of England, Nonconformist or Roman Catholic, and schools funded by the state. In the inter-war years the funding of state schools had overtaken that of the church schools, and many church schools had fallen into a poor state of health, not only in the quality of the teaching but in the state of the buildings. The Church of England alone had 400 school buildings on the Board's blacklist. Up to now, however, the churches had sought to keep a distance from the state in order to preserve the religious character of the education they were providing, and they had kept their distance from each other in order to preserve their denominational identity. It was now clear that they seriously lacked the resources to bring their own schools up to national standards. What was to be done?

Butler published his proposals on educational reconstruction in July 1943; he published a bill to go to Parliament in the following December. He proposed, significantly, raising the school leaving age to 15, and to maintain the dual system, but with the state and the churches aligning the services they provided. This meant that both the churches and the state would provide education for whoever lived near their schools, and the church schools would be brought into a national framework. The churches would also have to make sure their schools achieved certain minimum standards. This would be expensive, but Butler also proposed that the state would fund 50 per cent of the cost of modernizing and maintaining the church schools. Furthermore, he proposed that it now be compulsory for state schools to provide for an act of worship in the school each day, and that religious instruction be included within the state curriculum (though parents could withdraw their children from this if they wanted). The bill therefore represented a certain amount of give and take for both the churches and the state. It would require some new funding from the churches for their schools, but it would also bring significant extra funding from the state.

When the bill was published there was concern from the Nonconformists that in some areas their children would have to attend a Church of England school. Also, from some non-church teachers in the state system, there was consternation that they would have to lead prayers. The last bill to propose education reform, the Birrell Bill of 1906, had been wrecked by quarrelling between the churches. Would this happen now?

Temple wholeheartedly supported the idea of a co-ordinated dual system. He saw that the churches were simply not able to maintain their schools on their own and they must start to work with the state as partners. He believed that Butler was offering a positive and generous way forward for church schools and, equally importantly, he believed that the general raising of the school leaving age to 15 was an important step forward for English society as a whole.

Temple spoke for the bill to church and non-church audiences up and down the country advocating its proposals (see Section iv). R. H. Tawney movingly describes another of these addresses:

> The last public gathering at which I heard Temple speak was a conference of representatives of Labour and educational organisations, with Sir Walter Citrine in the chair, to demand the passage of the Bill

at any early date. He was greatly overburdened at the time and, as usual, arrived late. He spoke simply, avoiding technical details, and making no attempt to give the impression of special knowledge. The effect of his speech on the audience was due to his transparent sincerity and to the fervour of moral conviction with which he spoke: it was, I think, profound. (Iremonger 1948, p. 575)

Temple's final advocacy for the bill was in the House of Lords. Another member of the House reported that his speeches for the bill 'were notably successful and he spoke with great authority' (p. 577). When the bill returned to the House of Commons there was none of the bitterness between denominational traditions that had wrecked the Birrell Bill. In the end, the main parts of the bill were all passed, including the requirement to have a daily act of corporate worship in state schools.

Temple's final act of political intervention, then, was notably successful. The Education Act of 1944 belonged to Butler, but Temple's support at his right hand was crucially important in ensuring that its proposals became law, and it was fitting, perhaps, that Temple's career should conclude on the issue with which it had begun: education.

i Christian Social Principles

'Christian Social Principles (B) Derivative', from *Christianity and Social Order*, [1942] 1950, Chapter Five, pp. 59–65

Freedom

The primary principle of Christian Ethics and Christian Politics must be respect for every person simply as a person. If each man and woman is a child of God, whom God loves and for whom Christ died, then there is in each a worth absolutely independent of all usefulness to society. The person is primary, not the society; the State exists for the citizen, not the citizen for the State. The first aim of social progress must be to give the fullest possible scope for the exercise of all powers and qualities which are distinctly personal; and of these the most fundamental is deliberate choice.

Consequently society must be so arranged as to give to every citizen the maximum opportunity for making deliberate choices and the best possible training for the use of that opportunity. In other words, one of our first considerations will be the widest possible extension of personal responsibility; it is the responsible exercise of deliberate choice which most fully expresses personality and best deserves the great name of freedom.

Freedom is the goal of politics. To establish and secure true freedom is the primary object of all right political action. For it is in and through his freedom that a man makes fully real his personality – the quality of one made in the image of God.

Freedom is a great word, and like other great words is often superficially understood. It has been said that to those who have enough of this world's goods the claim to freedom means 'Leave us alone', while to those who have not enough it means 'Give us a chance'. This important difference of interpretation rests on a single understanding of freedom as absence of compulsion or restraint. But if that is all the word means, freedom and futility are likely to be so frequently combined as to seem inseparable. For nothing is so futile as the unhampered satisfaction of sporadic impulses; that is the sort of existence which leads through boredom to suicide. Freedom so far as it is a treasure must be freedom for something as well as freedom from something. It must be the actual ability to form and carry out a purpose. This implies discipline – at first external discipline to check the wayward impulses before there is a real purpose in life to control them, and afterwards a self-discipline directed to the fulfilment of the purpose of life when formed. Freedom, in short, is self-control, self-determination, self-direction. To train citizens in the capacity for freedom and to give them scope for free action is the supreme end of all true politics.

But man is a self-centred creature. He can be trusted to abuse his freedom. Even so far as he wins self-control, he will control himself in his own interest: not entirely; he is not merely bad; but he is not altogether good, and any fraction of self-centredness will involve the consequence that his purpose conflicts to some extent with that of his neighbour. So there must be the restraint of law, as long as men have any selfishness left in them. Law exists to preserve and extend real freedom. First, it exists to prevent the selfishness of A from destroying the freedom of B. If I am left untouched when I knock my neighbours on the head, their freedom to go about their duties and their pleasures may be greatly diminished. But the law which restrains any occasional homicidal impulse that I may have, by threatening penalties sufficiently disagreeable to make the indulgence of it seem to be not good enough, also protects my purpose of good fellowship against being violated by that same impulse. In such a case the restraint of the law increases the true freedom of all concerned.

(This book is about Social Order and not about conversion or the power of the grace of God. But for the avoidance of confusion I must here remark that no Christian supposes that anyone can reach perfect freedom except through perfect faith – that is, a complete personal response to the love of God. Only the love of God working upon his conscience, heart and will can set him free from the self-centredness which otherwise will vitiate both his own life and his contribution to the life of society. This is never completely accomplished, in all probability, for anyone at all in this life, certainly not for many; therefore we cannot hope to see the Kingdom of God established in its perfection in this mortal life. That belongs to eternity; but if it is our eternal goal, We have to do all we can to make of history a movement in that direction.

Before passing on it is worth while to notice how absolute was Christ's respect for the freedom of personal choice. He would neither bribe nor coerce men to become followers. Judas must be allowed to betray Him if he is so determined. Not even to save a man from that will the Lord override his freedom. For on freedom all spiritual life utterly depends. It is astonishing and terrifying that the Church has so often failed to understand this. Blindness to it is, as some of us think, the conspicuous defect of Rome to this day, leading to a never repudiated belief in persecution and to a spontaneous sympathy with authoritarian regimes. But to use, in the name of Christ, any other means of persuasion than spiritual appeal and rational coherence is to betray His first principle of action.)

Social Fellowship

No man is fitted for an isolated life; every one has needs which he cannot supply for himself; but he needs not only what his neighbours contribute to the equipment of his life but their actual selves as the complement of his own. Man is naturally and incurably social.

Recent political theories have given ostensible emphasis to this truth and have then, as a rule, gone far to ignore it. Certainly our social organisation largely ignores it. For this social nature of man is fundamental to his being. I am not first someone on my own account who happens to be the child of my parents, a citizen of Great Britain, and so forth. If you take all these social relationships away, there is nothing left. A man is talking nonsense if he says: 'Well, if I had been the son of someone else . . . etc.' He *is* his parents' son; what he is supposing is not that he should be someone else's son, but that he should not exist and someone else should exist instead. By our mutual influence we actually constitute one another as what we are. (Note: Of course each must be something on his own account to start the whole process of mutual determination. The vice of Determinism is that it ignores this platitude. It says truly, that in a complex ABC A is A because of B and C. B is B because of A and C, C is C because of A and B. But if that is all that can be said we have the spectacle of nothing at all differentiating itself into this variegated universe by the inter-action of its non-existent parts. Which is absurd. Q.E.D. But though something must be there before mutual determination begins, it remains true that what actually exists is in its essence a product of this process of determination. Each child that is born brings something quite new into the world; God there creates a new thing, the parents acting for the Creator and therefore being said to 'procreate'. The child is not a mere resultant of his parents' family history. But neither is he anything at all apart from it.) This mutual influence finds its first field of activity in the family; it finds other fields later in school, college, Trade Union, professional association, city, county, nation, Church.

Now actual liberty is the freedom which men enjoy in these various social units. But most political theories confine attention to the individual and the State as organ of the national community; they tend to ignore the intermediate groupings. But that makes any understanding of actual liberty impossible; for it exists for the most part in and through those intermediate groups – the family, the Church or congregation, the guild, the Trade Union, the school, the university, the Mutual Improvement Society. (Only in the nineteenth century could English people devise such a title as the last or consent to belong to a society so named; but the thing which that name quite accurately describes is very common and very beneficial.)

It is the common failing of revolutionary politics to ignore or attempt to destroy these lesser associations. They are nearly always the product of historical growth and do not quite fit any theoretical pattern. So the revolutionary, who is of necessity a theorist, is impatient of them. It was largely for this reason that the great French Revolution, which took as its watchword Liberty, Equality and Fraternity, degenerated into a struggle between Liberty and Equality wherein Fraternity was smothered and Liberty was judicially murdered. For the isolated citizen cannot effectively be free over against the State except at the cost of anarchy.

Liberty is actual in the various cultural and commercial and local associations that men form. In each of these a man can feel that he counts for something and that others depend on him as he on them. The State which would serve and guard Liberty will foster all such groupings, giving them freedom to guide their own activities provided these fall within the general order of the communal life and do not injure the freedom of other similar associations. Thus the State becomes the Community of Communities – or rather the administrative organ of that Community – and there is much to be said for the contention that its representative institutions should be so designed as to represent the various groupings of men rather than (or as well as) individuals. To some extent our Parliamentary system does this, with its differentiation of boroughs and shires, and probably Parliament should not go further in this direction. But there is much to be said for the establishment of subordinate functional Councils with powers of action in their several provinces subject to Parliamentary veto – a real Board of Education, for example; an up-to-date Board of Trade which would actually meet! – and above all an Industrial Council with effective powers. To this last we shall return.

In any case the Christian conception of men as members in the family of God forbids the notion that Freedom may be used for self-interest. It is justified only when it expresses itself through fellowship; and a free society must be so organised as to make this effectual; in other words it must be rich in sectional groupings or fellowship within the harmony of the whole.

It is impossible to lay excessive emphasis on this point. Pope Leo XIII gave great prominence to it in the Encyclical *Rerum Novarum*; its prominence there was pointed out with strong approval by Pope Pius XI in *Quadragesimo Anno*; and the profound importance of it has lately been pointed out again by the distinguished French thinker, Jacques Maritain. In his recent book, *Scholasticism and Politics*, he draws a valuable distinction between Personality and Individuality; of course every person is an individual; but his individuality is what marks him off from others; it is a principle of division; whereas personality is social, and only in his relationships can a man be a person. Indeed, for the completeness of personality, there is needed the relationship to both God and neighbours. The richer his personal relationships, the more fully personal he will be.

This point has great political importance; for these relationships exist in the whole network of communities, associations and fellowships. It is in these that the real wealth of human life consists. If then it is the function of the State to promote human well-being, it must foster these many groupings of its citizens.

But modern democracy, though more in its continental than in its British forms, was cradled in 'rationalism' with its concepts of the particular and the universal; it was from Rousseau onwards calamitously insensitive to spiritual and cultural affinities. So it has been impatient of these intermediate groupings, and has moved towards 'individualism' or 'collectivism', as if there were no third alternative. But it seems scarcely too much to say that neither individualism nor collectivism is compatible with a truly Christian understanding of man or of life.

In the course of the French Revolution we watch a struggle between a rationalistic and individualist Liberty on the one side and a mechanical and therefore materialist Equality on the other. (The third member of the trio – Fraternity – was not engaged in this conflict, and found its chief expression in the unity so useful for fighting those who were not of the brotherhood.) In the end both Liberty and Equality were suppressed by the triumphant Absolutism of Napoleon.

The English history of Freedom is different from this continental movement towards Liberty such as we have described. Freedom here – as in Holland – has its origin chiefly in the claim of Dissenters from the Established Church to worship God as their consciences might direct. It was rooted in faith. Hence the great Dutch social philosophy has more than any other laid stress upon the State as the Community of communities. (Althasius, the inspirer of Gierke, is the great name here. His dates are 1557–1638, so that he was a contemporary of the more famous Grotius (1583–1643) who used the same idea in his effort to supply a firm foundation for International Law. See my *Christianity and the State* (1928).)

A democracy which is to be Christian must be a democracy of persons, not only of individuals. It must not only tolerate but encourage minor communities as at once the expression and the arena of personal freedom; and its structure must be such as to serve this end. That is the partial justification of Fascism which has made its triumphs possible. It sins far more deeply against true freedom than it supports it; yet in the materialist and mechanical quality of the democratic movement from Rousseau to Karl Marx and his communist disciples, it had real justification for reacting against them.

It is impossible to say how much we owe in our own country to the schooling in democratic habits provided, first by the old Trade Guilds, then, when the fellowship of trade had been broken up by the release of individualist acquisitiveness, by the Trade Unions, and ever since the seventeenth century by the dissenting congregations. Many of our most effective Labour leaders learned their art of public speech as local preachers; and the self-government of the local Chapel has been a fruitful school of democratic procedure. Our 'Left Wing' has by no means always maintained this close association of democratic principle with conscientious worship of God! But the historical root is there. And the British tradition of freedom has probably more of the element which consists of the claim to obey God rather than men and less of the element of mere self-assertiveness than has the democratic tradition in most other countries. The element of self-assertiveness is morally bad and politically disastrous; a freedom based upon it is only an opportunity for selfishness and will decline through anarchy to disruption of the State; the claim to obey God rather than men is a source both of moral strength, for it inspires devotion to duty, and of political stability, for such freedom may only be used in the service of the whole fellowship.

Service

The combination of Freedom and Fellowship as principles of social life issues in the obligation of Service. No one doubts this in so far as it concerns the individual. Whatever our practice may be, we all give lip-service to this principle.

Its application to the individual is pretty clear. It affects him in two main ways – as regards work and leisure. In England we have depended a great deal on voluntary service given in leisure hours. We want a great deal more of it; and we have a right to expect more than we get from the Christian Churches. Yet it is certain that a very large proportion of the day-to-day drudgery of social service is done by Christian men and women in the inspiration of their Christian faith. We want more of them; but the greater part of what is done at all is done by Christian folk.

What is less often recognised in practice is the obligation to make of the occupation, by which a man or woman earns a living, a sphere of service. This may be done in two ways. Some young people have the opportunity to choose the kind of work by which they will earn their living. To make that choice on selfish grounds is probably the greatest single sin that any young person can commit; for it is the deliberate withdrawal from allegiance to God of the greatest part of time and strength. This does not mean that no attention is to be paid to inclinations. Inclination is often a true guide to vocation; for we like doing what we can do well, and we shall give our best service by giving scope to our own aptitudes and talents. But a young man who is led by his inclination to take up teaching or business or whatever it may be, must none the less make his choice because in that field he can give his own best service. This will enormously affect the spirit in which he does his work and his dealings with the other people engaged in it or with whom it brings him into contact. Let no one say that this has no application to modern business; there are many men engaged in business today, and leaders of industry on the largest scale, who entered on their work in this spirit of service and have maintained that spirit in the conduct of their business.

But there are many for whom there seems to be little choice; life offers one opening and no more; or they have to take what the Labour Exchange can suggest. For them it is harder to find in daily work a true vocation; but it is not impossible. Circumstances as well as inclination may be the channel through which God's call comes to a man. And His call is sometimes to self-sacrifice as well as to self-fulfilment. (No doubt self-sacrifice is in the end the truest self-fulfilment, as Christianity alone of religions or ethical systems teaches. And this explains how it may happen that the God of love calls men to self-sacrifice.) It is possible to accept the one job available, however distasteful and dreary, as God's call to me; and then I shall enter on it in the spirit of service.

Of course, this does not justify an order of society which offers to many men only such forms of livelihood as require a miracle of grace to appear as forms of true vocation. But we must recognise that the source of my vocation is in God and not in me. It is His call to me. And when it is said that we need to create or restore a sense of vocation in relation to all the activities of men, it does not mean chiefly that every individual should be able to find there his self-expression or self-fulfilment otherwise than by self-sacrifice. But it does mean, first that he should do his work, interesting or dreary, 'as unto the Lord', and secondly that the alternatives presented be such as shall not make this insuperably difficult apart from a true miracle of grace.

It is not only individuals who must, if Christianity is the truth, guide their policy or career by the principles of service; all groupings of men must do the same. The rule here should be that we use our wider loyalties to check the narrower. A man is a member of his family, of his nation, and of mankind. It is very seldom that anyone can render a service directly to mankind as a whole. We serve mankind by serving those parts of it with which we are closely connected. And our narrower loyalties are likely to be more intense than the wider, and therefore call out more devotion and more strenuous effort. But we can and should check these keener, narrower loyalties by recognising the prior claim of the wider. So a man rightly does his best for the welfare of his own family, but must never serve his family in ways that injure the nation. A man rightly does his best for his country, but must never serve his country in ways that injure mankind.

Of course, this apparent collision of claims will not arise so far as he accepts in its completeness the Christian standard of values; for in that scale of values service itself, even at cost of real sacrifice, is highest. But no man can in fact apply this exacting code, and it is of the utmost importance that we recognise this in ability and the reasons for it.

A man cannot regulate his service of his family and of his country by the Christian scale of values in its purity, first because he does not effectively accept it for himself, and secondly because his family and country do not accept it. Nothing is so offensive as a man who applies a higher standard to other people than to himself. If a man says to his children: 'I might have given you an expensive education, but decided that it would be better for you to go to the freely provided State school because my Christian principles teach me that wealth ought not to confer privilege', he must show in his whole life that he sets no store by the advantages which money can buy; otherwise he will only be stingy and his account of his conduct will be hypocrisy, or (as we call it nowadays) 'rationalisation'. Now no one does accept the Christian standard for himself; that Jesus of Nazareth did so is precisely what constitutes the gulf between Him and all other men. Only a perfect Christian can follow the purely Christian way of life; and so far as an imperfect Christian – i.e. any Christian who actually exists – forces himself to a line of conduct which his own character does not support, it will have bad effects on both him and his neighbours: on him, because it will be an assertion of self-will and must root him more firmly than ever in his own self as centre of his life, that is in his Original Sin; and on others, because he will appear as a Pharisee and a prig, and will alienate people from the standard by which he is self-righteously guiding this part of his conduct.

(I am finding it very hard to write this book about Christianity and the Social Order without bringing in everything else. Here I will content myself with one recollection. When a man asked St Augustine, 'What must I do to be saved?' he answered, 'Love God and do what you like' – because, of course, if he loved God he would like and could do the right thing, and if he did not love God he could not do it however much he tried.)

But it is not only his own defect of Christianity that a man must consider. He must not force its standard on others who are as yet unwilling or unable to receive it; for it is of the essence of spiritual faith that it be freely accepted. If a man applies in the training of his children standards not generally accepted in their circle, and fails to bring the children themselves to accept them, the result is likely to be an alienation of the children, both from their father and from his standards.

That is one obvious illustration of the difficulty presented by the claim that Christian standards should regulate our conduct. Of course they should, but they must first regulate our souls; and even then they are to be followed in that way – and in that way only – which will, in fact, secure a result truly expressive of them.

We see then why a man cannot without more ado take as his guide for the treatment of his fellows the Christian standard that service to the point of self-sacrifice is our truest welfare. Let him live by that as far as he can; and let him invite others to join him in that enterprise; but let him not force that standard on his fellows, and least of all on those dependent on him. They will always have the opportunity to act on it if they are so minded.

The general rule in such matters must be very general indeed, and gives little help beyond an indication of the direction in which we must move. A man must chiefly serve his own most immediate community, accepting as the standard of its welfare that which its members are ready to accept (though trying, it may be, to lead them nearer to a fully Christian view), but always checking this narrower service by the wider claims, so that in serving the smaller community he never injures the larger.

But as a member of each small group – with a voice in determining its conduct and policy – e.g. as a Christian Trade Unionist or Managing Director, or as the Governor of a School – he will do all he can to secure that his own group accepts for itself the principle of service and sets its course in the way that will benefit not only its own members in their own self-interest, but also the larger community in which this group is a part.

Freedom, Fellowship, Service – these are the three principles of a Christian social order, derived from the still more fundamental Christian postulates that Man is a child of God and is destined for a life of eternal fellowship with Him.

ii Practical Social Objectives

From the Appendix, 'A Suggested Programme', *Christianity and Social Order*, [1942] 1950, pp. 101–10

I believe that every Christian ought to endorse the substance of what I have so far said, though, no doubt, many of the details are disputable. I think it most improbable that every Christian should endorse what I now go on to say. But it seems right to indicate how I personally think we should do well to begin. Very likely better ways than these can be found for the realisation of our six-fold aim; very likely one or another of my proposals is definitely ill-founded and would, in fact, frustrate its own object. I offer them as suggestions for criticism rather than for adoption, and beg that readers will consider them in that spirit.

Before going on to my own suggestions it may clear the air if I say why I do not simply advocate Socialism or Communal Ownership. Socialism is a vague term, and in one sense we are committed to Socialism already. No one doubts that in the post-War world our economic life must be 'planned' in a way and to an extent that Mr. Gladstone (for example) would have regarded, and condemned, as socialistic. The question is how the planning authority is to be constituted and through what channels it is to operate. We can so plan for efficiency as to destroy freedom; Fascism does this. Or we can so plan for freedom that we lack efficiency. Our aim must be to plan efficiently for the maximum of freedom. Security is necessary to real freedom; legal freedom with economic insecurity may be personal bondage. So much restriction of legal freedom as is necessary to a reasonable measure of security leads to an increase in personal freedom. To put it shortly, we have talked in a doctrinaire fashion about socialism and individualism long enough; it is time to try to get the best out of both. The question now is not – Shall we be Socialists or shall we be individualists? But – How Socialist and how individualist shall we be?

Of course, Communal Ownership cuts the knot – that is the knot in which we are tied up now; but it would tie us up in a great many others, or in one enormous other! Sir Richard Acland argues that so long as there are opportunities for acquisition and for advancement by means of it, so long will economic motives govern society and shape character. But these are only forms of self-interest, and until the vast majority of us are almost perfect saints, self-interest will play a large part in governing society and shaping character. Moreover, not all forms of self-interest are bad. A man is right to demand for himself and his children what is needed for the fullness of personal life, though it may be noble that when he has it he should sacrifice it. Our need is to find channels for right self-interest which do not encourage exaggeration of it as our present order does. Communal ownership would entirely close one channel to it and open others – especially the road to the bureaucratic aristocracy which is an evident feature of the Russian system. The art of Government is not to devise what would be the best system for saints to work, but to secure that the lower motives actually found among men prompt that conduct which the higher motives demand. The law which associates imprisonment with theft leads a dishonest or defectively honest man to act honestly. We must seek to provide such outlets for self-interest while it remains – i.e. 'till Kingdom come' whether here or hereafter – as well as harness it to the cause of justice and fellowship. It is with such a general principle to guide us that we shall consider possible means of advancing our six-fold objective.

1 'Every child should find itself a member of a family housed with decency and dignity so that it may grow up as a member of that basic community in a happy fellowship unspoilt by underfeeding or overcrowding, by dirty and drab surroundings, or by mechanical monotony of environment.'

Great strides were made before the war to deal with housing. But we need still more provision of decent flats or houses near the places where men work and at rents within their compass. There should be a Regional Commissioner of Housing (whether the same person as the Regional Commissioner for other purposes or not) with power to say what land shall be used for this purpose. If well-established vested interests are disturbed there should be compensation; but in no case should speculation in land values or vested interests be allowed to interfere with the use of the land to the best public advantage. If anyone has bought land in devastated areas in the hope of making money out of it, he should in any case be prevented from doing this, and ought in justice to lose the capital so selfishly invested. It is to be hoped that the steps taken by the Government in this matter will prove effective. If they do, it will be a welcome novelty! Our handling of problems connected with land has hitherto been very feeble.

When the proper sites are settled, it is likely that State subsidies will be needed in order to secure that the accommodation provided is both good and cheap. These ought to be readily voted; but care should be taken that only those who may be supposed genuinely to need this help should receive it. Municipal authorities have found that this can be successfully achieved. But this subsidising of rents would be a temporary measure, ceasing when our other measures are operative.

It is improbable that wages will commonly be such as to enable the wage-earner in most grades of labour to bring up a large family in proper decency and comfort. Family allowances – perhaps in the form of food and clothes coupons having the value of money – should be paid by the State to the mother for every child after the first two; the wages earned should be raised to and maintained at a level sufficient for a family of four – father, mother and two children.

While more hygienic traditions about feeding are being developed, it is desirable that free distribution of milk at schools should be universally established, and one good meal should be provided daily at all schools, with a scientifically balanced diet.

2 'Every child should have the opportunity of an education till years of maturity, so planned as to allow for his peculiar aptitudes and make possible their full development. This education should throughout be inspired by faith in God and find its focus in worship.'

We now have universal education until the age of fourteen, and improvements are being made, especially in rural districts, to bring this into closer accord with local interests and needs. This should be pressed forward in every possible way. But the 'under 14' problem is generally well understood and is being handled.

If variety before this age is important, it is vital afterwards. Our principle should be that enunciated as a goal by Mr. Fisher when introducing the Education Act of 1918: 'Every citizen until the age of eighteen should be regarded as primarily a subject of education, not primarily a factor in industry.' The word 'primarily' is important, because it leaves room for the development of part-time education including in some instances an industrial apprenticeship under the authority and supervision of the Education Authority.

3 'Every citizen should be secure in possession of such income as will enable him to maintain a home and bring up children in such conditions as are described in paragraph 1 above.'

The present threat of unemployment to the maintenance of home and family must be ended. It has been mitigated by recent legislation, but it must be completely brought to an end.

Yet it is most uneconomical to maintain men in idleness and the fact of being useless and unwanted is morally the most destructive element in unemployment as we know it. The State should maintain a certain number of works beneficial to the community, from which private enterprise should be excluded, which it would expand or contract according to the general demand for labour at any time. Such works would include prevention of coast-erosion, afforestation, new roads and the like. There is much to be learnt from the Scandinavian countries in this field. But such provision could not cover the ground, and training centres for unemployed men must also be established on a large scale.

4 'Every citizen should have a voice in the conduct of the business or industry which is carried on by means of his labour, and the satisfaction of knowing that his labour is directed to the well-being of the community.'

The lack of any participation by labour in the conduct of the actual work of production is a manifest sign of the broken fellowship of our economic life. The ideal arrangement would be a revival of something like the medieval guilds on the basis of national charters. An alluring illustration of this was afforded by the Zeiss glass-works at Jena before 1914; I do not know what became of this admirable scheme, and I hope it is flourishing still. But the guilds were sometimes bitter in their rivalry with one another and selfish in their exploitation of public need. Some of our later proposals will include steps towards a Guild Constitution, but it seems probable that the share of Labour in control should be secured by other means. Already, at least in wartime, the great Trade Unions are consulted freely by the Government and have thus acquired a recognised status. Our previous proposals involve 'Planning' on a considerable scale. We now urge that Planning should be the responsibility of a specially created Planning Authority, fashioned on the model of the National Joint Industrial Council, but expanded so as to be generally representative of Industry. This should regulate the Articles of Association of Limited Liability Companies, and should be instructed to secure that Labour is effectively represented on their directorates. Thus the wage-earners in any given concern would be represented, if not directly, then through the great Labour organisations. It is likely that for some time to come such representation would be the most effective. There should also be provision for the nomination by the State of one or more directors to represent the public interest, that is to say the interest of the 'consumer' which should always be paramount. Where the product is of the kind known as consumers' goods, the principle of Consumer's Co-operation may well be followed.

5 'Every citizen should have sufficient daily leisure, with two days of rest in seven, and if an employee, an annual holiday with pay, to enable him to enjoy a full personal life with such interests and activities as his tasks and talents may direct.'

We have been moving steadily towards a five-day week in industry, and experts are of opinion that to adopt it would increase rather than diminish output, by saving industrial fatigue and with it much wastage of material. Its human advantages are evident. In large cities it may be late in the afternoon before a man gets home from his work for his 'half day' of leisure. In some industries it would be necessary to 'stagger' the days, so that some staff should always be available to keep the plant running. But in most, the whole business could close down for Saturday and Sunday, as some already do. Incidentally, there would be a better chance of restoring to Sunday its character as a day of worship and rest if there is full opportunity on Saturday for exercise, fresh air and amusement.

The principle of holidays with pay has importance in three ways. First, it recognises the status of the worker in the industry and is a repudiation of the notion that he is an external factor hired for the hours when his labour is needed and no more; secondly, it recognises that the process of recreation is essential to the quality of his work and therefore to the welfare of the industry; thirdly, it gives better opportunity for that freedom of enjoyment which is necessary to fullness of personal and of family life.

6 'Every citizen should have assured liberty in the forms of freedom of worship, of speech, of assembly, and of association for special purposes.'

These provisions are of high importance, but do not call for any present action, though perpetual vigilance is needed to safeguard them. In taking care to preserve these forms of liberty the State must, of course, prevent such abuse of liberty by one person or group as imperils it for others.

We now come to the question how we should set about securing these various objects. It is as well, therefore, to recall some of the considerations set forth earlier.

Actual Freedom is realised in fellowships of such a kind and size that the individual can take a living share in their activities. Personality is made real in and through such fellowships, and we need what Maritain has called Democracy of the Person and not only Democracy of the Individual. This has led some Christian social reformers to favour the ideal of the 'Corporative State'. But this swings the pendulum too far. No citizen expresses through his activity in various fellowships the whole of his significance. It is true that to be a Person is more than to be an Individual; but it is necessary to be an Individual; and indeed the fundamental doctrine that each man is a child of God, capable through Christ, the true Son of God, of rising to the height of that status, implies that every man is always more than can be expressed in all his social relationships taken together. The scheme of the Corporative State is therefore as unsatisfactory as either Individualism or Communism. Yet it contains some truth, as do the other two also.

Consequently we should leave untouched the House of Commons as representative of all citizens in their individuality: one man or woman, one vote. But we should not ask this supreme authority to handle directly all the departments of national life. Rather we should initiate a combination of Functional and Regional Devolution.

Few people now doubt the necessity for a development of regional administration. We need means of coordinating the activities of County and Borough authorities. And to regional authorities larger powers of administration could be entrusted than to local authorities dealing with smaller areas.

But along with this I suggest that we need Functional Devolution, of which the essential principle is that we set whole departments of national life to order their own affairs – a way of extending effective democracy and checking the tendency of a mass[corporate]-age to bureaucracy. In particular, we should apply this principle to Education and to Industry.

Thus I would urge the establishment of a real Board of Education, consisting of representatives of the main types of educational institutions and of the public; it would in fact need to contain representatives of the various grades of teachers, or teaching institutions, of local education authorities, of the governing bodies of independent schools; the representatives of the public might be elected by the House of Commons from among its own members, being parents of children actually at school. This representative Board of Education should have power to legislate in educational matters subject to Parliamentary veto.

Similarly I would urge the establishment of a statutory National Industrial Council, so constituted as to represent all the main factors in the industrial process – labour, management and dividend-earning investment – and also the consumer, that is to say the general public. This Council also should have power to legislate in its own sphere subject to Parliamentary veto.

iii Industry, Trade, Finance and Land

From the Appendix, 'A Suggested Programme', *Christianity and Social Order*, [1942] 1950, pp. 110–22

We have already indicated the lines on which it is to be hoped that the educational system should set about its own reform. Can we suggest similar lines to be followed by the industrial system when it is free to organise itself? Here I come to territory where my judgment is of even less value than in what precedes; but I will indicate the direction in which my mind moves.

The early Christian Socialists – Ludlow, F. D. Maurice, Kingsley, etc. – strongly urged, when 'limited liability' was first devised, that this should always be accompanied by conditions securing the public interest against exploitation. I cannot doubt that they were right or that we ought now to remedy the omission. What is required here is an amendment of the Companies Acts imposing certain conditions wherever limitation of liability is granted. What should these conditions be?

It is not desirable altogether to eliminate the 'profit-motive'. Room must be made for a reasonable satisfaction of self-interest. But it should be subordinated to the service-motive, so that the initiation or expansion of a business shall be governed more by public needs than by private advantage when these two diverge. Above all we should seek to end the right to bequeath from generation to generation a power to levy private taxes on industry in the form of dividends, thus placing on industry a burden disproportionate to the benefit received and maintaining a distinct 'shareholding' class in the community. With these objects I suggest for consideration the following.

(a) Whenever limitation of liability is granted a maximum rate of dividends should be fixed. To secure this the Articles of Association should provide for the allocation of surplus profits to such purposes as (i) a wage-equalisation fund, for the maintenance of wages in bad times, even though working-hours may be reduced; (ii) a dividend equalisation fund; (iii) a fund for extension, as distinct from renewal, of fixed capital, and so forth. The list of objects need not, of course, be identical in every case.

(b) Though it is true, as Lord Stamp observed, that the State already checks unlimited inheritance by Death Duties, this does not go to the root of the matter. He himself favoured the so-called 'Rignano principle' by which those duties would be light at the first transfer, heavy at the second, and annihilating at the third. I should myself prefer the principle of 'withering capital' in accordance with which, so soon as the interest paid on any investment is equal to the sum invested, the principal should be reduced by a specified amount each year until the claim of the investor to interest or dividends was extinguished. The rate of annual reduction would be fixed specially for each enterprise in accordance with the relevant factors involved.

Subject to these or similar conditions, and to the restrictions involved in planning for the basic needs of the less fortunate members of society, there should be room for private enterprise and initiative with the free play of choice and interest which these facilitate.

It is computed that three-quarters of the businesses which are started go into liquidation within three years. Frankly, it would seem to be a gain all round, that there should be less inducement to start these precarious businesses, of which the extinction must cause inconvenience and may cause real distress. It is important, moreover, to remember that the majority of firms are small . . .

There is a sentimental value in these little firms. But they are a hindrance to progress in the science and art of management, and are the scene of most of the remaining bad conditions of employment. Under our proposals men will be less likely to 'start a little business' because it is more 'respectable' than to become a wage-earner; so much the better. The man of real enterprise and vision will stake his career on his capacity and will win through. But it is, of course, very important to leave room for such enterprise on the part of men with initiative and 'drive'. Also the units of organisation should be kept down to a size making oversight possible to men with less than Napoleonic gifts, and also increasing the opportunities for men of capacity.

Those who accept the existing system naturally ask what compensation on the side of losses will be given to set off restrictions on the side of gains. But our whole contention is that the existing system is unjust; it is heavily weighted in favour of capital. And it is to be remembered that under the present system the wage-earners bear the losses to a great, often a quite unjustly great, extent; for the bankruptcy of a firm means unemployment for its employees. A plan for reducing wages in bad times would not be intolerable if the wage-earners were effectively represented on the Board of Directors, provided an adequate basic rate were maintained. Whatever the system, those who have a surplus to invest, and invest it, must bear the main risk of loss.

If all of these suggestions were carried out it would probably be more convenient that some department of the Public Trustee's Office should normally own any business with more than a specified capital value as holding trustee, its administration being in the hands of a Board of Directors, representing, directly or indirectly, Capital, Management and Labour, in accordance with the scheme set out in the Articles of Association and authorised by the Industrial Council or other Planning Authority.

(c) It must be recognised that the economic problems of the nation are bound up with international trade. It is in this sphere that unregulated competition produces its worst effects. If we are to establish effectively minimum standards of life and work, we must be prepared for a bold policy of international action. The International Labour Office has done most valuable work which can be greatly extended. Backward nations can be helped with expert advice. But our chief need is to recognise that the world, and in particular Europe, is economically one and that the policies of economic nationalism recently pursued by almost every State have been disastrous to all. It is quite unreasonable and contrary to Natural Order to make political and economic frontiers identical. By recent analogies, if Wales had Home Rule, England and Wales would begin to 'protect' themselves against each other. We must learn to treat questions of commercial policy, as also migration and the means of communication, as matters of general, not particular, concern, to be decided not by national governments but by an international authority.

As a step towards an equalisation of the treatment accorded by nations to their neighbours, and pending the submission of these questions to international control, it might be well for all nations to adopt, as an *interim* measure, a tariff policy based on the principle that in the case of such goods as can be efficiently produced in any country, a tariff be imposed on imports calculated to raise the price of the imported article to that of fully efficient producers of the home-product – but no further. It is hoped that this would prevent undercutting, and also tend to raise the standard of life in countries where labour is cheap by removing some of the advantage gained by exploitation of that cheap labour. It would certainly involve a drastic lowering of existing tariffs in many countries.

A specially evil feature of the recent economic nationalism has been the search by many nations, including our own, for a 'favourable trade balance'. (Why so called it is hard to see; for the phrase means giving something for nothing, not getting something for nothing. It is possible only by the export of capital, i.e., involving the other nation in debt.) I know, of course, that an influential school of Political Economists defends this. But we have here a case of the proper subordination of Political Economy to ethical standards. However 'profitable' this policy may be, it remains wrong. It is an attempt to gain advantage at a loss to others; that is one mark of what St Paul calls 'the mind of the flesh'. Commerce should be and can be a source of gain to all concerned in its transaction. In order that commerce may follow its own 'natural law' in this respect it is suggested that international commerce should be to the maximum extent a negotiated volume of trade, so planned as to utilise to the utmost the productive capacity of all parties to the transaction. Gold might play a part here as a means of adjusting balances when each transaction is complete. Steps could be taken in this direction before international control is established; that such control would aim at a similar result is hardly open to question.

There remain two fundamental factors in the situation about which something must be said – Money and Land.

(d) The private minting of money has long ceased and we have reached a stage where the private manufacture of credit is become an anachronism. Money has three functions: (i) it came into existence as a means to the facilitation of exchange, but it was able to perform this function because – (ii) it is a storehouse of value. Money facilitates exchange because the value transferred in any transaction can be stored up in it for use at another time; otherwise barter would be equally convenient. But so soon as money is owned, it has another function as (iii) a claim to goods and services. It is for this function that it is chiefly wanted by ordinary folk, and it is this function which makes interest on an ordinary loan reasonable. If I postpone making effective my claim to goods and services so as to enable someone else to utilise my store of value in the meantime, it is quite reasonable that he should pay me for this service.

But actual money covers very little of the commercial field today. Far the greater part of our business is carried on by means of credit.

We all have reason to be grateful for the public spirit and integrity with which our banking system has been administered. There would not be a proverbial phrase 'as safe as the Bank of England' if its management had not been so conspicuously sound. But the system whereby a bank of any sort charges interest on credit created by the making of a book entry and issued for the benefit of the public is evidently open to question. Moreover, the interest of the financial houses and of the producing firms may conflict; and it is wrong in principle that finances should control production.

For with all its three functions, money is primarily an intermediary. This strongly suggests that it should not be possible to 'make a living' (let alone a fortune) out of its manipulation. If one citizen lends his money to another citizen or to the State he is entitled to some recognition in the shape of interest, at least up to an agreed total, because he is transferring a real claim. But when money, or an effective substitute for money, is created and lent by a book entry, as may be the case in the issue of credit, it seems that no more charge is ethically defensible than what will cover the cost of administration, perhaps a half or two-thirds per cent. But no private person or group would find here any incentive to embark on it; nor should this power to issue what is in effect money be in private hands.

There seems, in fact, to be as strong a case for converting the Bank of England and the Joint Stock Banks into publicly administered institutions as there is for the State's monopoly of minting money; whether these should be owned and worked by the State or should be Public Utility Corporations is open to question. My own preference is for the latter wherever the method can be followed.

(e) The fundamental source of all wealth is Land. All wealth is a product of human labour expended upon God's gifts; and those gifts are bestowed in the land, what it contains and what it nourishes. Most truly the 'Malvern Conference' [1941, chaired by Temple] declared that 'we must recover reverence for the earth and its resources, treating it no longer as a reservoir of potential wealth to be exploited, but as a storehouse of divine bounty on which we utterly depend'. The land legislation of the Old Testament rests on the principle that the land in a special sense belongs to God. This principle appears in our own Common Law in the doctrine that only the King has full Dominion over land; only its use is granted to landlords.

There is good reason to insist more strongly on this principle. In the case of urban sites it will lead towards public ownership, for there is little service, if any, that the owner of urban sites can render which cannot as well or better be rendered by the public-authority. There is no reason why we should pay certain citizens large sums of money for merely owning the land on which our cities are built. Of course there should be compensation for expropriation, or else a time-limit so long as to meet the claims of reasonable expectation; but the case for public ownership is at this point very strong.

In the case of rural land the balance of public advantage tips the other way. Certainly the existing rights of landlords are excessive if social function is taken as the justifying correlative of rights of ownership; and we are here dealing with a commodity on which the whole public welfare depends.

The primary necessities of life, bountifully supplied by nature, are Air, Sunshine, Land and Water. No one claims to own the first two, or to exclude others from them except on condition of paying a fee.

The old principle that justifiable property is a right of administration and not a right to exclusive use should certainly be applied to the other two.

Land is not a mere 'material resource'. The phrase 'mother earth' stands for a deep truth about the relationship between man and nature; and this is most fully developed where a man owns land which he works himself and works land which he owns. But he must own it in the sense mentioned – not as a possessor of so much material resources, but as steward and trustee for the community. Land not beneficially used should involve liability to fine, or, in extreme cases, to forfeiture. But if the necessary safeguards are established, the best results are to be expected from an encouragement of Occupying Ownership. The landlord–tenant system need not be abolished, but it is likely in any case to decay, and the Occupying Owner should so far as possible take its place. If Nationalisation of the Land is adopted on other grounds, the tenants of the State-landlord should be given such security of tenure as will make them feel the responsibility and enjoy the independence commonly attached to ownership.

But in no case should land be regarded as a purely personal possession. How often we hear of an estate being 'mortgaged up to the hilt' because some heir to the property was a wastrel! It should be made illegal for an owner as distinct from a purchaser to mortgage land or to burden it with debt except by licence from the Minister of Agriculture, who would only grant this either to meet a temporary depression for which the owner was not responsible, or for some socially valuable development of the land. Overburdened estates should be compulsorily liquidated.

Occupiers who are not owners must have security of tenure at fair rents, with right to make improvements and with compensation on leaving. All occupiers must also have full control over game.

But a great deal of what is amiss alike in rural and urban areas could be remedied by the taxation of the value of sites as distinct from the buildings erected upon them. In this field, that inversion of the natural order, which is characteristic of our whole modern life, is especially important. If house property is improved (a social service) the rates are raised and the improvement is penalised; if it is allowed to deteriorate (a social injury) the rateable value is reduced and the offending landlord is relieved. Taxation of the value of sites, as distinct from the buildings erected on them, would encourage the full utilisation of the land. There is no need for an expensive valuation. The owner should be called upon to value the land himself, the State having power to purchase it at the figure named or to levy a tax upon it, as may seem more expedient in each case. Land values, therefore, should be taxed and rated; houses might well be de-rated. Charges levied on land are quickly distributed over all which the use of the land facilitates. Death duties on land, where the principle of inheritance can have a high social value, should be modified, perhaps by a provision that payment be made by transfer of part of the estate to the Crown on the death of an owner with a right in the heir entitling him to buy back that part by a system of hire-purchase.

If all of these proposals were adopted, a great transformation of our social and economic structure would result. Yet this would involve no breach of continuity. It would be transformation by adaptation, not by destruction. Moreover, this method of approach to the whole problem has the advantage that the various suggestions can be adopted separately and in varying degrees of completeness. No violent revolution is involved; no rigid system would be imposed.

There is urgent need for thought about these matters now. We cannot return to the pre-war situation. If when peace is restored all the existing controls were removed, that would not put us back where we were; too much has already happened. When peace returns action will be inevitable. We are fighting for democracy; but that crucial action will be democratic only if public opinion is alert and informed. To these suggestions I add three notes.

1 I have offered the suggestions contained in this Appendix in answer to the frequent challenge, What would you *do*? I deny the distinction here implied between talking and doing. By talking we gradually form public opinion, and public opinion, if it is strong enough, gets things done. Yet it seems fair to ask the proclaimer of principles if he has any proposals for bringing life into conformity to them. So I offer my suggestions as an object of criticism or as a quarry from which a better builder may take a few stones to use for a house better than I can design. I have no special competence to speak of these practical steps towards a more Christian social order. It is highly probable that they are far from the best that can be devised. Very well; in criticising these someone may find a better way; and at last someone may even find the right way.

2 Let no one quote this as my conception of the political programme which Christians ought to support. There neither is nor can be any such programme. I do offer it as a Christian social programme, in the sense of being one which seeks to embody Christian principles; but there is

no suggestion that if you are a Christian you ought to think these steps wise or expedient.

3 Above all I would insist as I close that these political proposals must not be substituted for the truths of the Gospel as the mark of the real Christian. If we have to choose between making men Christian and making the social order more Christian, we must choose the former. But there is no such antithesis. Certainly there can be no Christian society unless there is a large body of convinced and devoted Christian people to establish it and to keep it true to its own principles. They can and should co-operate with all who share their political hope and judgment at any time. But they must maintain their independence so that they may judge whatever exists or whatever is proposed with so much as their faith has won for them of the Mind of Christ.

Postscript: The Beveridge Report

To Major Guy Kindersley, stockbroker and former Member of Parliament, who appealed to Temple not to support the Beveridge Report because it imperilled the liberty of the citizen through creating an 'omni-competent state'.

Personal
Lambeth Palace, London, S.E. 1.
July 2, 1943.

Dear Major Kindersley,
I am very grateful to you for writing as you did . . .
   It is certainly true that there are dangers in any such scheme as that of Beveridge, and it is right that they should be pointed out and guarded against effectively. None the less I think the dangers on the other side are much greater: the development of education carries with it the development of critical faculty, and consequently the raising of many questions about the justice of any prevailing social order. No one, I imagine, would propose to go behind the provision for the unemployed made since the last war. But the result is that we may now have within the same family some whose necessities, due to no fault of their own, are met by the Public Assistance Board, and others by various agencies representing a levy in large measure upon more fortunate members of the

community. All of this promotes jealousy and discontent and the gain of simplifying the whole scheme will be enormous.

As regards the psychological change in the attitude to Parliament of which you speak, I should suppose that that had already taken place. It is one of the main points of course in Professor E. H. Carr's recent book that this change has come and cannot now be reversed.

I believe myself that the Beveridge plan at any rate can be so administered as to increase actual liberty, for it seems to me that the primary necessity for effective liberty is security as regards the basic consumer goods: a liberty in which one of the alternatives theoretically open is existence below the level of civilised life is not a real liberty. I believe that by a deliberate ordering of the economic basis of life we can greatly increase personal freedom. But I cordially agree with you that this must be prominently in mind and that all this planning, which I regard as quite inevitable but also, as an alternative to the condition we have been in for the last thirty years, desirable, will result in servitude unless it is quite consciously what [Karl] Mannheim describes as 'planning for freedom'; and I believe that this country, which has a peculiar genius for working out in practice the correlation of principles that seem to be logically opposed to each other, may be able to shew the world what is not so much a middle path between communism and individualism as a genuine expression of the sound principles lying behind each.

Of course I do not expect you to accept this view, but as you wrote so kindly, I should like you to understand how my own mind is working in this matter. And there are certain Christian principles alongside of liberty – notably fellowship – which find peculiarly vivid expression in the Beveridge plan.

Yours sincerely,
William Cantuar:

iv True Education

Part of 'Our Trust and Our Task', the presidential address delivered at the annual meeting of the National Society, 3 June 1942, in *The Church Looks Forward,* **1944, pp. 46–53**

Now, first of all, I believe we are all agreed that the experiences through which the world has passed have impressed upon us more forcibly than ever before that all true education must be religious in its basis and texture. The question at issue in this war is fundamentally a religious question. It is the question whether the form of civilisation which has grown up out of the Christian doctrine about God and man is to have a wider scope in the affairs of men in the coming time, or whether, on the contrary, it is to be the subject of very grave restrictions, and an added influence given to an outlook upon life which denies those fundamental doctrines of our religion and which virtually puts the State of every nation, or, at any rate, of one nation, in the place of Almighty God. If we try to penetrate into the fundamental difference between the outlook of those peoples who now dominate Europe and the outlook that has been traditional among ourselves, and which is still the prevailing outlook of our people, we find it really does go back to those principles upon which you can affirm the dignity of human personality as we have known it, to the doctrine that man is a child of God, and that in his relationship to God he has a status independent of, and prior to, his membership of any earthly community. The freedom for which we are fighting is a freedom which has come down from those who believed that they ought to obey God rather than man, a freedom which is religious at its roots. This has very often been forgotten by the later exponents of the doctrine of liberty, but it is fundamental to any kind of liberty which is not to be the source of mere self-seeking in the individual and of chaos in society.

So more than ever the responsibility rests upon us to insist, not only that there shall be religious instruction as part of the whole curriculum in our schools, but that education is only adequate and worthy when it is itself religious. For the fact is that education must be in its effect, whatever the motive of those who organise and impart it, either religious or atheistic. There is no possibility of neutrality. To be neutral concerning God is the same thing as to ignore and deny Him. This is one of those questions to which the answer 'No' is automatically given unless you deliberately give the answer 'Yes'; to give no answer is to answer 'No'. If the children are brought up to have an understanding of life in which, in fact, there is no reference to God, you cannot correct the effect of that by speaking about God for a certain period of the day. Therefore our ideal for the children of our country is the ideal of a truly religious education.

Let us put the matter from another standpoint. It is the purpose of education to fit children for their life in the world so that they may conduct it in appropriate relation to their environment. There are three levels of environment. There is, undoubtedly, the sub-human environment: the world of physical nature. There is also the human world, the world of human relationships, and all that is included in the dealings of one man with another. No one disputes the fact that these two environments condition our life at every point, and no education can be adequate or worthy which does not fit people for dealing with both. But is there also a super-human environment? If there is, then it is certainly the most important of the three. If there is, then the relationship of the child to that which is above him, to God Himself, will determine in very large measure the mode of his activity in relation to the other two. To leave out this, or to treat it as optional, as a matter of private opinion, or something which is dependent upon individual temperament, is entirely to ignore the reality of the whole situation in which our work is to be conducted.

I am speaking of it in this way because I am persuaded that the primary need of our country is to recover a real philosophy of education. I asked a leading headmaster a little time ago what result would be obtained if you were to line up the members of the Incorporated Association of Headmasters, and moving along the line seek an answer to the question, 'What are you aiming at with your boys? What do you want to produce?' And he said, 'There is only one thing upon which any large number could possibly agree, and that would be the largest number of certificates and the highest possible number of credits.' That is a rather satirical exaggeration. None the less I venture to suggest that a great deal of our difficulty in moving forward at the present time is that there is no general conception of what education really is. As Dr. [J. H.] Oldham has put it: We have learnt that the purpose of education is not the matter taught, but the person who has to learn it. We are concerned with teaching persons rather than subject matter, but we have at the same time apparently ruled out of court all enquiry concerning the nature and destiny of personality. We are concerned in training people: we never ask what kind of thing people ought to be. That is a hopeless position. Dr. Arnold knew perfectly well what he was aiming at: and we have learned a great deal in many departments of education in the hundred years since he died. (We celebrate the centenary of his death on Saturday week.) We have learned a great deal about the technique of education. We have learned so much, indeed, of the technique of it, that we are in danger of forgetting the purpose of it. Though we should certainly not be able to obtain general agreement on his aims concerning education, it is, surely, of the utmost consequence that we should recover, and, if possible, secure general assent – it would hardly be universal – for a fundamental conception with regard to the real purpose of education. These are questions that should arise from time to time out of our changing circumstances, and which should find their appropriate answers.

Now there is hope that something of this kind is possible today, mainly for two reasons. There is, undoubtedly, a growing public concern, both about education and about the religious quality of education. Certainly there is about education as a whole. Large sections of the nation are becoming deeply concerned who, until lately, have paid very little attention to it. That is partly due to motives more commercial than strictly educational; but it is a fact of which some advantage can be taken. Along with that is a very widespread sense of need, and the consciousness of a gap which needs to be filled, and which we know can only be filled by religious faith. It is not true to say that there is as yet any great measure of agreement that it is that which alone can fill the gap, but there is a growing consciousness of that empty space which must be filled if we are to have a sense of direction, and of power to follow it.

In the past the main instrument of the Church in upholding its principles has been the Church School. At first there was no other instrument for the purpose at all. Let us remember always, partly in order that we may claim for the Church the credit due to it, and partly also as a guide to our own thinking, that in the period in which the Church began establishing Schools, the State was not doing it. Other religious bodies were also taking an active part. But education was provided entirely through voluntary agencies, and until 1870 the activity of the State in that field was very small. The tentative quality of its approach is always vivid to my mind because of my father's experience. He was appointed Principal of the first Training College there ever was. It was at Kneller Hall, now a place for training bandmasters. The teachers whom my father was to train were going to teach in the new institutions erected under the new Poor Law of 1834. But when he had trained the teachers there were no schools for them to teach in; and that Training College came to an end because the teachers when trained could not exercise their profession. The approach of the State to the matter has been rather hesitant and tentative! In 1870 however, it took it up in good earnest, and from that time onward the part played by the State in the field of education has been steadily developing. Nor is there any possibility that it can be hindered, and I do not suppose that any of us wish to hinder it. What we are concerned about is that we should continue to uphold in any system now mainly administered by the State, those principles, those elements of supreme value, which were characteristic of the Church Schools, and were the chief aim for which they were planned.

In that early period when the Church was itself the founder of the Schools, there were various tendencies that, to some extent, have created a prejudice against us. There was, for example, the very natural tendency for the incumbent to regard the schoolmaster as part of his parochial staff, and to hold that he was there apparently to carry on one particular department of the Church's work. That is what he was there for. The Church had founded the School; it maintained it; it found the stipend of the teacher; and, of course, the teacher was, therefore, part of the staff of the parish. That is a state of things that cannot continue, when the State itself has become the main source of the educational supply, and there is a great teaching profession spread far beyond the Church Schools. But there are some areas which have never been adjusted to the new situation; thus there has grown up an unhappy prejudice in the minds of the teachers leading them to suppose that their position in Church Schools is one of less dignity than in other schools. Now that is quite disastrous. I know everyone in this hall will agree with me when I say we must take the utmost pains to secure that there is no ground for that suspicion; that the status of a teacher in the Church School is every bit as dignified and independent as in any other school; though, of course, he is appointed to carry out certain specified aims which are therefore part of his duty.

Along with the increase in the activity of the State has gone the growth of professional feeling among teachers. This, again, is not only all to the good, but is something quite indispensable to education. It is of the most vital importance that the whole body of the teachers should feel themselves to be a responsible and honourable part of the public service, and we must not desire, upon our part, anything that can hinder the growth of such a sense among them; for in all walks of life professional honour is a main safeguard against tendencies of any kind to slackness or neglect.

Further, there has been a very great development in the growth of the efficiency of educational administration. With the growth of variety of the type of schools, which we all recognise to be necessary, especially in the later stages, the central administration becomes more and more important. Dr. [Albert] Mansbridge this morning was urging upon us that a very much larger part, at any rate of later education, ought to be through manual activity. There are a great many children whose brains are better developed by setting their fingers to work than by calling upon them to read books. The number of children who can absorb freely out of the printed page is really limited. The very same ideas, to a large extent, can be imparted by setting children to do things, and when what they attempt to do goes wrong, to find out the reason why. The best way for very many boys, at any rate, to learn mathematics is for them to do constructive work: the necessary training must then be given in order that they may be able to carry through the work entrusted to them. But, amid all this variety, if boys and girls are to have the opportunity of obtaining the sort of education that will really fit them for their work in life, then there must be great development of central organisation and planning. So you get built up the whole civil service of education which has conferred such great benefits upon the nation, and which inevitably regards the field from the point of view of administrative efficiency.

Well, it is in that situation that we find our tradition in many ways challenged from without; and if we are to meet that challenge we must do it much more thoroughly than merely by saying 'We believe in the dual system', or 'We believe in Church Schools'. We must say what it is about the dual system that we believe in and why the thing we believe in can be secured by the dual system and in no other way. We must say what it is about Church Schools that we believe in, and to what extent it is true that that can be secured by Church Schools and in no other way.

I would very daringly suggest that one value of the dual system is its duality. I wish to suggest that there is a very great advantage in the educational field in maintaining real variety of type, with a considerable measure of individual liberty and autonomy. Many of the non-provided schools represent that element in our system at the present time, and we want to find a way of retaining, quite apart from all religious interest in the matter – of retaining, and, if it may be, of extending this element of freedom and autonomy in the individual schools. I do not think our administration desires mechanical uniformity; but there is an inherent and inevitable tendency in any bureaucratic control towards mechanical uniformity; with the best will in the world the administration cannot prevent it increasing. In face of what has been happening in Europe, the importance of regaining the real independence of the several schools ought, surely, to be obvious to all of us. If we wish to avoid totalitarianism, there is a merit in the very duality of the dual system. I should not in the least mind it becoming a triplicity; but I should regret it becoming a mere unity. There is no doubt, for example, that the Church Schools are able, as a general rule, to give more sense of corporate unity to the school, to create a stronger sense of corporate life, to bring into the Schools elements of special and outstanding interest, often of a quite inspiring type, which is far more difficult for schools administered under public authority. The managers appeal to friends who may come in on special occasions in the life of the School, lending a touch of special individuality to it in a way that would hardly be possible otherwise. Moreover, when the children reach the age for leaving school, they do not feel that they have gone out of that building for ever, for the building goes on, and is used for many functions in which they take a part. There is a bridge between the school and the wider life outside, which is very hard to produce where there is no society besides the State to which the school belongs.

Those are general educational considerations, not, I suppose, of the first importance, but, I believe, of very real importance, if we are to avoid the mechanising of the whole scheme.

Postscript:
Some Personal Letters in Wartime

Appointment to Canterbury

To his older brother, Colonel F. C. Temple, from Bishopthorpe, York, 27 January 1942, after the current Archbishop of Canterbury, Cosmo Gordon Lang, had announced his retirement.

My dear Old 'un

I shall be surprised if just at this moment the 'powers' select me for Canterbury. Some of my recent utterances have not been liked in political circles, and it would be thought by some that to choose me now is to endorse them. I don't deny I should like to be asked! But if I were, I should have to go; and I do not think I should like the job there as much as the job here. Anyhow – it's as it will be.

 Confidentially – yes Cosmo does want me to follow him and has told me so quite plainly.
 . . .

Your loving,
W. E. [i.e. William Ebor, his signature as Archbishop of York]

20th Feb 1942.
My dear Old 'un,

I have received a letter from the P.M. [Winston Churchill] as follows:

'I write to inform you that I propose to recommend to The King that you should be translated to the Archbishopric of Canterbury. Few in the long succession since St Augustine can have received the summons to Canterbury at a time when the burden of the Primacy was heavier. I trust I may have your consent to this course which I commend with a deep sense of responsibility.'

So of course I had to say Yes. One is pleased to be selected, but I shall not enjoy the work nearly so much as this.

I hope I shall have notice when the news is to be published so that I can let this reach you before that happens.

Your loving,

W. E.

Printed note sent to many friends after the announcement

So many letters have reached us that is impossible to express our thanks to those who have written except in this way. It is unnecessary to say that the kindness of our friends is a very great help and encouragement as we look forward to new and largely unknown work. These are fearful times in which to take up so great a responsibility. May God give us His guidance and strength to meet it.

The departure from our many friends in Yorkshire and from the beauty both of Bishopthorpe and of so many parts of the Diocese will be a terrible sorrow. We have become so attached to the Diocese of York and to the Northern Province as to feel that we belong to them and cannot be separated from them without very great pain. That is the price to be paid for the blessings of friendships like those which we have made here. But though we shall not meet our friends so often, the friendships themselves will not be broken.

At whatever home we are able to establish either in what remains undamaged of Lambeth or in Canterbury there will always be a warm welcome for the friends we are leaving in the North as well as for those whom we hope to make as we take up work in the South. Please do not forget this or hesitate to act upon it.

Many of the letters which have come refer to the anxieties which are unavoidable when we think about the future of our country and of the world. The difficulties and opportunities will both be very great. The only hope of meeting these in such a way as to bring the world nearer to what we know must be God's purpose for it is to be found in a strong faith in God and His upholding power.

Life after death

Written to a business man who had consulted the Archbishop on the 'appearance' of his wife after her death.

Old Palace, Canterbury.
Nov: 7th, 1942.

Dear Mr. —,
I am deeply touched that you should consult me about this experience. I wish I felt more competent to help. I have always thought it a mistake to go into questions connected with spiritualism unless one could do it thoroughly; and for that I have had no time. But of course I have been interested and have reached some conclusions, which have, I regret to know, very inadequate bases. However, here they are:

(1) I draw a sharp distinction between any experience which, like yours, is unsought, and anything resulting from resort to a medium or deliberate waiting for messages – e.g. by automatic writing; the latter so obviously makes opportunities for the sub-conscious mind to act;

(2) So far as I have considered psychical phenomena, I know nothing that would persuade me to accept so great a conclusion as survival of death if I did not believe it on other grounds; but as I do believe it on other grounds I am strongly inclined to interpret some of the phenomena as actual communication;

(3) The evidence for appearances at the moment of death, or in a dream state at later times, of those who were very closely bound by love to the person concerned is stronger than for any other such communication.

With that background of thought I am led by the description of your own experience to believe that it was a perfectly real communion between you and your wife, in which she took the first step by coming to you. It cannot be more than a 'probable' judgment; but the probability seems to me to lie on that side rather than on the side of hallucination. I think therefore that you should think it both possible and even probable that the experience was due to an external cause and that God did thus permit your wife to make known to you her love and (so far as that might be called for) her forgiveness.

But all this rests on (1) faith in God and His care for us, (2) consequent faith in our survival of death and continued fellowship. And this order of priority is very important both for the logic of the belief reached and for the spiritual outlook of anyone who holds it. I was glad to see your phrase about God's permission to your wife to help you, because that shews that the right order of priority is in your mind.

Yours sincerely,
William Cantuar:

POSTSCRIPT

What would Christ do?

Lambeth Palace, S.E.1.
27th March, 1944.

My dear —,
I am away from home so your letter was a little delayed . . .
. . . the question – what Christ himself would do if he was alive – puts it all wrong. He came into the world to do a particular thing – it is not the job of anybody else at all. He came into the world, putting it quite shortly, to redeem it, which none of the rest of us can begin to do. For this purpose he kept himself detached from all ordinary local or sectional obligations. He was unmarried; from the time his ministry began he had no trade or profession; while it is true one cannot picture him as a soldier, it is also true that one cannot picture him as a lawyer or as a professional member of an orchestra.

What is certain is that he did not require the Centurion whom he praised so highly to leave the army, and there are many of his sayings which imply that it may be right to use armed force when the circumstances require that from people who have not got some responsibility incompatible with it.

If he had been teaching pacifism in his ministry why were there two swords in the possession of his Apostles right at the end of his ministry?
Yours very truly,
William Cantuar

A letter of sympathy in bereavement

Lambeth Palace, London, S.E. 1.
April 24, 1944.

Dear Mrs. —,
I cannot say how deeply I sympathise with you in your sorrow and the shock that it has brought to your faith. I trust that as time heals the surface of the wound, which of course it does, though never perhaps its depth, you will see things in a rather different proportion and be able once more to trust in God.

If we are Christians, we cannot possibly suppose that we have a right to expect God to save either us or those we love from death. If He, as St Paul puts it, 'spared not His own Son', it is quite clear that the way of suffering may be the way by which we are to fulfil His purpose. When Our Lord says that God cares even for the sparrows, He does not for a moment conceal or ignore the fact that they do fall to the ground and die; what He says is that when this happens, it is within the loving care of the Father of all creatures. And Christ, by His Resurrection, has made clear to us that death after all is not the end, nor of necessity any great evil; it is the one thing in life that some time or other we all have to face; it is therefore part of God's ordering of the world for us, and we must trust to Him not so much to save us from it but to uphold us through it and beyond it.

I hope that as you think of these things you may begin once again to feel that your only son is still in God's keeping as truly as when he was here, and that you too are in His keeping and can look forward to the happiness of renewed fellowship in God's closer presence in the world beyond.

Yours sincerely,
William Cantuar:

To his brother

Lambeth Palace.
June 21, 1944.

My dear Old 'un,
Yes, I expect to be here for breakfast on June 30th and we shall look forward to seeing you. I must start for Worcester pretty soon afterwards: in fact I may have to leave the door at 9.0; then we shall breakfast at 8.30, I expect. I must catch the 9.45 at Paddington. I have a luncheon and an afternoon meeting in Worcester. Next day I go on to Shrewsbury for Harry Hardy's last speech day there and a sermon next morning.

These flying bombs are rather horrid. They have ceased to shoot at them in the London area because they do so much damage when they are hit. So one hears them zooming along in complete silence; then the zoom ceases, and a little later there is a bang. I do not think they are doing any damage that can affect the war; but they cause a lot of havoc . . .

Canterbury so far has been safe from them; they leave it on their right, so to speak, on their way to London.

Your loving,
W. C.

POSTSCRIPT

To his brother

As from Lambeth Palace.
Aug: 20, 1944.

My dear Old 'un,
Just after I last wrote we got away to the Quantocks. They are as lovely as ever. And we have had three weeks of amazing good weather – really too hot for the most enjoyable walking. Now it has broken, at any rate for the moment. The farmers who have not quite finished carrying are, of course, anxious; most of the harvest round us is in and looks very good.

The post has been more troublesome than it usually is at this time of year, so I have cut down unofficial letters, including those to you. But I have nothing to say these days. We have no 'news' in holidays.

What a bore your car trouble must have been. I hope it is all over now.

We go back on Aug. 31 and hope our troops will occupy the Flying Bomb sites soon after that.
Your loving,
W. C.

To his wife

Lambeth Palace, London S.E. 1.
September 4th 1944.

. . . The knee has steadily improved all day; there is not much amiss with it now. I am again level with letters, so I can go off tomorrow with no arrears, as I can certainly do tomorrow's post in the morning. That is capital . . . I don't expect to be able to write again till Friday, when we hope to arrive for tea . . .

To his brother

Old Palace, Canterbury.
Sept. 21, 1944.

My dear Old 'un,
Please forgive a dictated letter: that attack of gout which Alice found me recovering from returned before it was quite gone in prodigious

violence, and I have now got acute gout in both knees, which, as you can imagine, is quite immobilising.

I just wanted to send this as an explanation of why I have not written. Of course it may clear quite quickly as it sometimes does – but at present I am able to make no plans.
Your loving,
(for William Cantuar:)

To the Archbishop of York

Lambeth Palace, London, S.E. 1.
September 22, 1944.

My dear Cyril,
I am still completely in bed and it seems inconceivable that I should get to London at any time during next week: this thing has been a definite illness, and when I can get up I think I shall go away for a few days and recover a little strength. I have been on my back for more than a fortnight and it is bound to leave one pretty feeble . . .

To the King's Private Secretary

Rowena Hotel, Westgate-on-Sea
October 24, 1944.

My dear Tommy,
I do not think I ought to be off duty, apart from correspondence, so long as this without letting you know the situation so that, if you think appropriate, you may tell His Majesty at once, or may be able to give any appropriate information if suggestions or comments made seem to call for it.

I was laid up early in September with a violent attack of gout, and I have never been able to throw it off at all completely. This is apparently because it is kept alive by an infection that has got into my system and must be cleared up first. That of course is being tackled, but they tell me it is likely to take a long while. Meanwhile I have naturally become pretty weak and in fact cannot stand without support. That can all be put right fairly quickly when once the infection, with the gouty consequences of it, is removed.

POSTSCRIPT

I am of course able to attend to the most urgent matters of business so far as they can be dealt with by correspondence, and I hope that no great damage is resulting from my inactivity – no doubt there are those who would say that great gain might be anticipated from it!
Yours ever,
William Cantuar:

He died two days later.

A blessing of William Temple's

May the love of the Lord Jesus draw you to himself;
May the power of the Lord Jesus strengthen you in his service;
May the joy of the Lord Jesus fill your souls.
May the blessing of God almighty,
the Father, the Son and the Holy Ghost,
be among you and remain with you always.

Bibliography

Books by William Temple (in chronological order)

The Faith and Modern Thought. Lectures. London: Macmillan, 1910.
The Nature of Personality. Lectures. London: Macmillan, 1911.
The Kingdom of God. Lectures. London: Macmillan, 1912.
Repton School Sermons: Studies in the Religion of the Incarnation. London: Macmillan, 1913.
Studies in the Spirit and Truth of Christianity. Sermons. London: Macmillan, 1914.
Church and Nation. Lectures. London: Macmillan, 1915.
Plato and Christianity. Lectures. London: Macmillan, 1916.
Mens Creatrix: An Essay. London: Macmillan, 1917.
The Challenge to the Church. Mission account. London, 1917.
Issues of Faith. Lectures. London: Macmillan, 1917.
Fellowship with God. Sermons. London: Macmillan, 1920.
The Universality of Christ. Lectures. London: SCM Press, 1921. Reprinted in *About Christ*, London: SCM Press, 1962.
Life of Bishop Percival, London: Macmillan, 1921.
Christus Veritas: An Essay. London: Macmillan, 1924.
Christ in His Church. Diocesan charge. London: Macmillan, 1925.
Christ's Revelation of God. Lectures. London: SCM Press, 1925. Reprinted in *About Christ*, London: SCM Press, 1962.
Personal Religion and the Life of Fellowship. London: Longmans Green, 1926.
Essays in Christian Politics and Kindred Subjects. London: Longmans Green, 1927.
Christianity and the State. Lectures. London: Macmillan, 1928.
Christian Faith and Life. Oxford Mission addresses. London: SCM Press, 1931. Reissued 1963. Page references to this edition. New edition, ed. Susan Howatch, London: Mowbray, 1994.
Thoughts on Some Problems of the Day. Diocesan charge. London: Macmillan, 1931.
Nature, Man and God. Gifford Lectures. London: Macmillan, 1934.
Basic Convictions. Addresses. London: Harper & Bros, 1936.
Christianity in Thought and Practice. Lectures. London: SCM Press, 1936.
The Church and its Teaching Today. Lectures. New York: Macmillan, 1936.
The Preacher's Theme Today. Lectures. London: SPCK, 1936.

Readings in St John's Gospel. 2 vols. London: Macmillan, 1939–40. Complete edition, 1945 (page references to this edition). Paperback edition, 1961.
Thoughts in War-Time. Sermons and addresses. London: Macmillan, 1940.
The Hope of a New World. Sermons and addresses. London: SCM Press, 1940.
Citizen and Churchman. London: Eyre & Spottiswoode, 1941.
Christianity and Social Order. Harmondsworth: Penguin Special, 1942. New edition, London: SCM Press, 1950 (page references to this edition). New edition, London: Shepheard-Walwyn and SPCK, 1976, with Foreword by the Rt. Hon. Edward Heath and Introduction by Professor R. H. Preston.
The Church Looks Forward. Sermons and addresses. London: Macmillan, 1944.
Religious Experience and Other Essays and Addresses. Posthumous collection, London: James Clarke, 1958.
Some Lambeth Letters, ed. F. S. Temple, Oxford: Oxford University Press, 1963.

Other writings by William Temple (select list, in chronological order)

The Education of Citizens. Address. London, 1905.
'The Church', 'The Divinity of Christ' and 'Epilogue', in *Foundations: A Statement of Christian Belief in Terms of Modern Thought by Seven Oxford Men.* London: Macmillan, 1912.
Competition: A Study in Human Motive. London: Macmillan, 1917. Written by a committee including Temple.
'The Christian Social Movement in the Nineteenth Century', *Christian Social Reformers of the Nineteenth Century,* ed. Hugh Martin, London: SCM Press, 1927.
'Revelation', in *Revelation,* ed. John Baillie and Hugh Martin, London: Faber & Faber, 1937.
'Chairman's Introduction', in *Doctrine in the Church of England: The Report of the Commission on Christian Doctrine Appointed by the Archbishops of Canterbury and York in 1922.* London: SPCK, 1938.
'Christian Faith and the Common Life', in *Christian Faith and the Common Life,* vol. IV of the Oxford Conference, 1937, On Church, Community and State. London: Allen & Unwin, 1938.
'Introduction', *Men Without Work: A Report Made to the Pilgrim Trust.* Cambridge: Cambridge University Press, 1938.
'The Chairman's Opening Address' and 'A Review of the Conference', in *Malvern, 1941. The Life of the Church and the Order of Society, Being the Proceedings of the Archbishop of York's Conference.* London: Longmans Green, 1941.
'Prologue', 'Pacifists and Non-Pacifists', with C. E. Raven, 'Christmas Broadcast to Germany', *Is Christ Divided?,* ed. William Temple, Harmondsworth: Penguin, 1943.
Nazi Massacre of the Jews and Others: Some Practical Proposals for Immediate Rescue, The Archbishop of Canterbury and Lord Rochester, London: Victor Gollancz, 1943.

Other letters and papers

The William Temple Papers at Lambeth Palace Library, in multiple volumes, contains his official correspondence as Archbishop of Canterbury as well as many letters from his earlier life. They also contain copies of many of his newspaper and magazine articles, and pamphlets, and some unpublished writings.

MS 1765 at Lambeth are the letters he wrote to his brother throughout his life, about 700 in all. There are also editorials and articles in *The Challenge*, *The Pilgrim*, *The Highway* and *The Listener*.

Books on William Temple (select list)

Carmichael, John D. and Goodwin, Harold S., *William Temple's Political Legacy*, London: A. R. Mowbray, 1963.
Dackson, Wendy, *The Ecclesiology of Archbishop William Temple*, Lewiston, New York: Edwin Mellen Press, 2004.
Fletcher, Joseph, *William Temple: Twentieth-Century Christian*, New York: Seabury, 1963.
Iremonger, F. A., *William Temple, Archbishop of Canterbury: His Life and Letters*, London: Oxford University Press, 1948.
Kent, John, *William Temple: Church, State and Society in Britain 1880–1950*, Cambridge: Cambridge University Press, 1992.
Padgett, Jack F., *The Christian Philosophy of William Temple*, The Hague: Martinus Nijhoff, 1974.
Spencer, Stephen, *William Temple: A Calling to Prophecy*, London: SPCK, 2001.
Suggate, Alan D., *William Temple and Christian Social Ethics Today*, Edinburgh: T. & T. Clark, 1987.
Thomas, Owen C., *William Temple's Philosophy of Religion*, London: SPCK, 1961.

Other books and articles

Atherton, John, Baker, Christopher and Reader, John, *Christianity and the New Social Order*, London: SPCK, 2011.
Begbie, Harold, 1920, 'Religion and Politics: A Talk with Canon Temple', *Daily Telegraph*, 6 April 1920.
Bell, G. K., 'Memoir', in *William Temple and His Message*, ed. A. E. Baker, Harmondsworth: Penguin, 1946.
Brown, Malcolm, 'Politics as the Church's Business: William Temple's *Christianity and Social Order* Revisited', *Journal of Anglican Studies*, vol. 5 (2), 2007.
Bruce, Malcolm, *The Coming of the Welfare State*, London: Batsford, 1961.
Dackson, Wendy, 'Archbishop William Temple and Public Theology in a Post-Christian Context', *Journal of Anglican Studies*, vol. 4 (2), 2006.

BIBLIOGRAPHY

Emmet, Dorothy, 'The Philosopher', in F. A. Iremonger, *William Temple, Archbishop of Canterbury: His Life and Letters,* London: Oxford University Press, 1948.

Field, Frank, 'The Temple Family', *Saints and Heroes: Inspiring Politics,* London: SPCK, 2010.

Forbes, Duncan, *The Liberal Anglican Idea of History,* Cambridge: Cambridge University Press, 1952.

Grimley, Matthew, *Citizenship, Community and the Church of England: Liberal Anglican Theories of the State Between the Wars,* Oxford: Oxford University Press, 2004.

Hastings, Adrian, *A History of English Christianity 1920–1985,* London: Collins, Fount Paperbacks, 1987.

Hastings, Adrian, 'William Temple', in Adrian Hastings, *The Shaping of Prophecy,* London: Geoffrey Chapman, 1995.

Hastings, Adrian, 'William Temple', in *The Oxford Dictionary of National Biography,* Oxford: Oxford University Press, 2004.

Hinchliff, Peter, *God and History: Aspects of British Theology 1875–1914,* Oxford: Clarendon Press, 1992.

Hinchliff, Peter, *Frederick Temple, Archbishop of Canterbury, A Life,* Oxford: Clarendon Press, 1998.

Jenkins, David, 'Christianity, Social Order and the Story of the World', *Theology* (September), London: SPCK, 1981.

Lowry, Charles, 'William Temple after Forty Years', *Theology* (January), London: SPCK, 1985.

Macquarrie, John, 'William Temple: Philosopher, Theologian, Churchman', *The Experiment of Life: Science and Religion,* ed. F. Kenneth Hare, Toronto: University of Toronto Press, 1983.

Niebuhr, Reinhold, 'Dr. William Temple and His Britain', *The Nation,* New York, 11 November 1944.

Norman, E. R., *Church and Society in England, 1770–1970: A Historical Study,* Oxford: Clarendon Press, 1976.

Oliver, John, *The Church and Social Order: Social Thought in the Church of England 1918–1939,* London: A. R. Mowbray, 1968.

Peacocke, A. R., 'The New Biology and *Nature, Man and God*', in *The Experiment of Life: Science and Religion,* ed. F. Kenneth Hare, Toronto: University of Toronto Press, 1983.

Preston, Ronald H., 'Thirty-Five Years Later: 1941–1976: William Temple's *Christianity and Social Order*', in *Explorations in Theology 9,* London: SCM Press, 1981.

Preston, Ronald H., 'Middle Axioms in Christian Social Ethics', in *Explorations in Theology 9,* London: SCM Press, 1981.

Preston, Ronald H., 'William Temple as a Social Theologian', *Theology* (September), London: SPCK, 1981.

Ramsey, A. M., *From Gore to Temple: The Development of Anglican Theology between Lux Mundi and the Second World War,* London: Longmans, 1960.

Rogerson, J. W., 'William Temple as Philosopher and Theologian', *Theology* (September), London: SPCK, 1981.

Spencer, Stephen, 'William Temple's *Christianity and Social Order* after Fifty Years', *Theology* (January/February), London: SPCK, 1992.

Spencer, Stephen, 'History and Society in William Temple's Thought', *Studies in Christian Ethics*, vol. 5, no. 2, Edinburgh: T. & T. Clark, 1992.
Spencer, Stephen (ed.), 'William Temple', a themed edition of the journal *Crucible* with articles by John Atherton, Frank Field, Jane Shaw, Rupert Hoare and Chris Baker, *Crucible*, January–March 2003.
Suggate, Alan D., 'William Temple and the Challenge of Reinhold Niebuhr', *Theology* (November), London: SPCK, 1981.
Tawney, R. H., 'William Temple: An Appreciation', *The Highway*, January 1945.
Vidler, A. R., 'The Limitations of William Temple', *Theology* (January), London: SPCK, 1976.
Visser 't Hooft, Willem Adolf, 'The Genesis of the World Council of Churches', in *A History of the Ecumenical Movement 1517–1948*, ed. Ruth Rouse and Stephen Neill, second edn, Philadelphia: Westminster Press, 1968.
Williams, G. A., *Viewed from the Water Tank: A History of the Diocese of Blackburn*, Preston: Palatine Books, 1993.
Williams, Rowan, 'Anglican Approaches to St John's Gospel', *Anglican Identities*, London: Darton, Longman & Todd, 2004.
Williams, Rowan, *Christian Imagination in Poetry and Polity: Some Anglican Voices from Temple to Herbert*, Oxford: SLG Press, 2004.
Williams, Rowan, 'From Welfare State to Welfare Society: The Contribution of Faith to Happiness and Well-Being in a Plural Civil Society', *Crucible*, January–March 2009.

Index of Names and Subjects

Anson, Francis (wife) xiv
Arnold, Thomas 243
Ascension, the 48–52

Bell, Bishop George xx, 141, 147
Beveridge, William xvii, 214, 240–1
Butler, R. A. xviii, 215–17
British Council of Churches 141, 162–3
Browning, Robert 11

Canterbury xiv, xvii, 190, 205–6, 248–9
Christ xii–xiii, 7–12, 15, 16, 17–18, 20, 23, 28–36, 38, 43, 44–5, 46, 48–9, 51, 53, 54, 55–6, 59, 60–2, 64, 65, 96–9, 99–102, 103, 104–5, 109–11, 118–19, 121, 122, 126, 127, 147–50, 154, 158–60, 161, 163, 165–88, 200, 217, 219, 225, 240, 251, 252
Church, the 16, 17–18, 42, 46, 47, 48, 93, 103–4, 104–7, 138–64, 202–3
Church schools 244–7
Churchill, Winston 190, 191, 210, 248
Conscientious objection 90
COPEC (Conference on Politics, Economics and Citizenship, 1924) xvi

Cripps, Stafford 214
Cross and Resurrection 33, 34, 35–6, 51, 52, 53, 54, 55–62, 67, 70, 99, 101, 103, 175, 184, 187, 200, 205, 217

Davidson, Archbishop Randall xiv, 1
Democracy 14, 88, 221–2, 230, 231–2, 239
Discipleship 44–5, 47, 65, 101–2, 106–7, 107–11, 119, 188, 240

Eastern Orthodox Churches 139, 143, 152
Ecumenism xviii, 138–64, 190
Edinburgh Conference 1910 139
Edinburgh Faith and order Conference 1937 139–40, 141, 154–60, 161
Education 43–4, 45, 212–13, 215–17, 229, 232, 241–7
Emmet, Dorothy 20, 115
Episcopacy 142–54
Evil 5, 20–1, 36, 55, 117–18

Fellowship 81, 82, 105, 213, 219–23, 241
Field, Frank xix, 215
Finance 232–7
First World War 19, 20, 71, 87, 89, 189, 197, 198–9

261

Forgiveness 8–9, 55–62, 102, 205, 210
Freedom/Liberty 64, 71–80, 82, 113, 114, 200, 202, 212–13, 217–19, 219–23, 227, 231–2, 241, 242
French Revolution 78, 195, 220, 222

Germany xvi–xvii, 87–8, 160–1, 189–210
God 2–7, 12, 13, 12–15, 18, 22–3, 30–1, 35–6, 38–43, 46, 50–2, 54–5, 56–8, 58–62, 62–5, 66–70, 94–9, 116–22, 124–7, 134–6, 137, 158–9, 161, 167–8, 173–4, 180–3, 183–8, 199–200, 242, 250, 251–2
Green, T. H. 19, 71

Hastings, Adrian 94, 140, 141
Hegel 112–13
History 32–3, 38–9, 48, 54, 64, 68, 104, 107, 113, 114, 122–30, 167, 170–1, 189–90, 220
Holidays 230–1
Holland, Henry Scott 82, 83
Holy Communion 9, 42–3, 48, 60, 99–102, 104–5, 151, 152, 157
Housing 228–9

Industrial Christian Fellowship 212, 215
Industry 230, 232–7
International relations 84–91, 235–6
Israel 28–9, 30, 40, 48, 49–51, 65, 118, 119, 170, 172, 176, 179, 187

Jenkins, Bishop David xix–xx, 215
Jewish massacres by the Nazis xviii, 189–92, 203–4

John's Gospel 10–12, 15, 20, 31–2, 33, 34, 41, 43, 45, 49, 56, 60, 63, 100–1, 142, 165–188
Justice 86, 200–203, 208–9

Kent, John 212
Keynes, John Maynard xvii–xviii, 214
Kingdom of God xiii, 28–9, 30, 35, 81, 89–90, 100–1, 103, 105–6, 111, 135, 219

Lambeth Conference 1930 142–154
Lang, Archbishop Cosmo Gordon xvii, 189, 190, 208, 248
Labour Movement and Party xviii, 76, 78–9, 80–83, 214, 216–7
Land 237–9
League of Nations, The 87, 88, 89, 90, 196, 199
Liberalism, Theological xiv
Life after death 250, 251–2
Life and Liberty Movement xiv, 37
Locke, John 25
Love 9, 12–16, 17, 26–7, 29–30, 34, 35, 41–2, 49, 51–2, 54, 56, 60, 63, 65, 66–70, 80, 7, 100, 103, 108, 132, 136, 158, 175, 186–7, 205, 208–9, 219, 224, 225

Malvern Conference 212, 214, 237
Manchester Diocese xv, 53
Mansbridge, Albert xiv, 245
Marriage 178
Maurice, F. D. 82, 233
Marx, Karl 112, 113, 114, 222
Middle axioms 213–4
Mill, J. S. 72, 83, 212

Niebuhr, Reinhold 140, 209, 211
Niemoller, Martin 196, 201

INDEX OF NAMES AND SUBJECTS

Oldham, J. H. 140, 243
Ordination 145-8
Oxford University xiii-xiv, 1, 19, 53, Chap. 6

Pacifism 251
Paton, William 140, 163-4
Paul 10, 13, 18, 29, 59, 61, 104
Peacocke, A. R. 15
Personality 24-7, 71-5, 104, 115, 116-8, 217-8, 221
Plato 14, 73, 124, 172, 200-1
Prayer 10, 46-7, 62, 94-99, 207-8, 210, 255
Protestant Churches of the Reformation 138-9, 143, 145-9, 150, 151, 162, 163-4
Purpose, principle of 4-7, 103, 105, 117

Revelation 114, 116-122
Rogerson, J. W. 21
Roman Catholic Church 143, 152, 153, 158
Rousseau, Jean Jacques 88, 222

Sacraments 114, 116, 130-7, 144-152, 154
Science 4-7, 14, 19, 120
Second World War xvii-xviii, 189-210, 252, 253
Service 107-11, 223-6
Social conditions xv

Socialism 78, 227-8, 234
Society 26-7, 54, 82, 133-4, 211-247
Spirit, Holy 8, 10, 12, 14-17, 18, 34, 43-6, 49, 65, 66-70, 104, 117, 126-7, 135, 137, 154-5, 159, 166, 180, 185, 186, 200
State, the 71-80, 83-91, 199-200, 202, 216, 217-8, 220-223, 226-232, 238-9, 242, 244
Student Christian Movement 1, 92, 139

Tawney, R. H. xi, xiii, 214, 216-7
Temple, Archbishop Frederick xiii
Trinity, the 66-70

Unemployment 229-30

Value 25-6, 53-4, 69, 115-6, 128-9

Wages 229-30, 233
Welfare State, the xvi, 83-4, 87-8, 191, 199-200, 213, 215
Westminster Abbey xiii, xiv, 37-52
Whitehead, A. N. 113
Worker's Educational Association (WEA) xiv, 80, 215
World Council of Churches 141, 160-1, 162, 163

York xvi, 112, 138, 142, 165, 212, 249

www.ingramcontent.com/pod-product-compliance
Lightning Source LLC
Chambersburg PA
CBHW071335080526
44587CB00017B/2848